Dalit Exclusion and Subordination

Dalit Exclusion and Subordination

Rabindra Kumar

RAWAT PUBLICATIONS
Jaipur • New Delhi • Bangalore • Hyderabad • Guwahati

ISBN 978-81-316-0560-8

Published by
Prem Rawat for **Rawat Publications**
Satyam Apts, Sector 3, Jawahar Nagar, Jaipur 302 004 (India)
Phone: 0141 265 1748 / 7006 Fax: 0141 265 1748
E-mail: info@rawatbooks.com
Website: www.rawatbooks.com

New Delhi Office
4858/24, Ansari Road, Daryaganj, New Delhi 110 002
Phone: 011 2326 3290

Also at *Bangalore, Hyderabad* and *Guwahati*

Typeset by Rawat Computers, Jaipur
Printed at Chaman Enterprises, New Delhi

Dedicated
to
My Parents

Contents

Acknowledgements

Some of the essays assembled in this volume were presented at national level seminars, while some were published in journals and books between 2002 and 2010. The essays on Dalits are based largely on my doctoral research, teaching experiences and research, between 2003 and 2008, at the National Institute of Social Work and Social Sciences (NISWASS) in Bhubaneswar, Orissa. I am grateful to Dr R.K. Nayak, founder of NISWASS, who provided me this opportunity to serve at his institute in various capacities. I take this opportunity to thank all those people who helped me at various levels and made this work possible: Dr S.C. Kumar, ex-principal, NISWASS; Prof. A.B. Singh, ex-principal, NISWASS; Prof. H.S. Verma, ex-member of State Planning Commission, Government of Uttar Pradesh, and ex-principal, NISWASS; and Dr Y. Chinna Rao, Associate Professor, Jawaharlal Nehru University (JNU), New Delhi.

I owe a lot to my teachers, Prof. Ehsanul Haq, Prof. Nandu Ram and Prof. S.K. Thorat of JNU. Prof. Ehsanul Haq, who was my research supervisor at the JNU guided me through the process of my transition, made it possible for me to recover a sense of identity at the academic level.

I am thankful to my colleagues, Prof. Debal K. Singha Roy, Prof. Tribhuwan Kapur, Dr Nita Mathur, Dr Archana Singh, Dr B. Kiranmayi, Dr R. Vashum (Department of Sociology) and Dr B.S. Prakash (Economics Faculty), for their encouragement. I am also thankful to my research scholar Mr Karunakar Singh who has helped me in checking the proofs of this manuscript.

I am most indebted to my parents, Chetharu Paswan and Asarfi Devi, who taught me life's most valuable lessons and shaped my ethos. I draw my strength from their unrestricted love, unconditional support and relentless encouragement. I am also grateful to my brother, Harendra Paswan, and bhabhi, Meena Bharti, my sister, Manju, and brother-in-law, Dr Vijay Kumar, who have been constant sources of inspiration to me. I am also indebted to my father-in-law, R.D. Paswan, mother-in-law, Shanti Devi, and brothers-in-law, Dipak and Shakti Paswan, who have been sources of constant inspiration and are always ready to help my family and me. I am grateful to my wife, Anita, and daughters, Selena and Shayna, who have been loving and understanding, sacrificing their own pleasures so that I could work, and encouraging me vigorously at all times. I consider myself fortunate to have enjoyed such loving family support.

I am also thankful to my office staff, Yashwant Raj, Shailendra Kumar Singh and Sonia Pal, who have shown a good deal of dedication towards the completion of this work. I am obliged also to Pranit Rawat of Rawat Publications for the publication of this book.

Rabindra Kumar

1

Introduction

Hindu society is not a homogenous whole, but is vertically divided into four varnas – the Brahmins, the Kshatriyas, the Vaishyas and the Shudras. Varna refers broadly to the ascribed status of different castes or jatis in the social order that distinguishes each group in terms of their social hierarchy, which is fixed at birth. Under the varna system, several jatis with similar ascribed ritual status are clustered together and hierarchically graded and grouped as one. Thus, Hindu society is not the same as an individual Brahmin, Kshatriya, Vaishya or Shudra. It includes all of them and many more sub-castes or *up-jatis* under each of the main varna. It is an all-inclusive frame.

The doctrine of divine theory prescribes that the different varnas were created from different parts of the divine body. The Brahmin is said to have been born from the head or mouth of the creator, the Kshatriya from the arms, the Vaishya from the thighs, and the Shudra from the feet of the divine creator. Accordingly, each of these castes is assigned with traditional functions, from which its members cannot escape, come what may. Acquiring and disseminating knowledge and performing sacrifices and rituals, the functions of the Brahmin, enjoy the highest position in the social order. Next in the ranking ladder are the work of administration/government and fighting for the nation/kingdom or defending the country, which are assigned to the Kshatriya. The Vaishya comes third in the social ranking based on the work assigned to him – trade and commerce and agriculture. Finally comes the Shudra, whose birthright is to serve the first three castes, which involves engaging in craft and labour.

The caste system has been so powerful that people have come to believe that it must be divine will that they remain separate and distinct. It is this belief that has created among individual Hindus an instinct to be different from each other. At any point of time, Brahmins and Kshatriyas represent a particular caste, but the term, Vaishya, is associated with some particular caste groups with some qualifying adjectives. As a matter of fact, none of the four varnas now represent anything but groups of castes.

The Hindu social order is a ladder of castes placed one above the other, together representing an ascending scale of respect and a descending scale of contempt. As opposed to the principles of liberty, equality and fraternity, according to Dr Ambedkar, the Hindu social order is based on the principle of graded inequality, fixation of people with their occupation and with their respective castes.

The Hindu dharma is based on the theory of karma, three *gunas* or qualities and the transmigration of the soul. All these three theories are applied to justify the social order. Karma (action) causes the various conditions of men – the highest, the middle and the lowest. Due to the consequences of the many sinful acts committed by body, voice and mind, a person will become a bird, a beast or a low caste person, respectively, in his next birth. There are three *gunas* (qualities) that predominate the body distinguished by quality. The study of Vedas, austerity and knowledge and purity, etc., are marks of the quality of activity whereas cruelty, covetousness, evil of life, etc., are marks of dark quality.

However, there is one more social category, which is beyond the four varnas – the Panchama or outcastes or untouchables. The untouchables occupy the extreme lowest position in the social hierarchy of Hindu society. Who are they and how did they become untouchables? Why they are treated as slaves, looked down upon as sub-human in society? There are several theories about how this social category came to be looked upon as untouchables:

- Some of them were of tribal origin. This theory is supported by Oppert, Fick, Bose, Sharma and also by Dr B.R. Ambedkar, who called them 'broken men'.
- They originated from family and village slaves. This is based on the fact that within a family, there were domestic slaves who did all the menial or unclean jobs, although they lived within the household. To begin with, in spite of the 'impure' nature of their work, the family slaves were not considered untouchables, though they were not allowed to cook food for the family.

- According to Brahminic literature, the untouchables were born of miscegenation among the four varnas. The Sanskrit term for such children being Varna-Sankar, or born out of a mix of the four varnas. Children born of hypergamous marriages (known as *pratiloma*) were worse than those born of hypogamous marriages (known as *anuloma*); *pratiloma* children were considered untouchables.

All the above three hypotheses are based on the physical origin of the untouchables. None of them alone can explain the origin of untouchability satisfactorily or provide a valid reason why these three groups of people became untouchables. Some of the reasons that are offered are:

- The untouchables are ritually impure because they carry out unclean activities as their profession or vice versa. But, did they choose their loathsome occupation voluntarily? And why are those engaged in occupations such as basket-making, weaving and finishing and village security guards also considered untouchables? These hypotheses need a closer scrutiny because the purity-pollution factor may well be the effect and not the cause of untouchability.
- It is proposed by some that untouchability is essentially of urban origin as the kind of services rendered by the untouchables is required only in towns and cities. This, however, does not explain their presence in villages.

Thus, the existing analyses of the origins of the untouchables are not sufficient. Ambedkar has taken a more pragmatic view of these questions.

Ambedkar started with the specific term, 'Antyavasayin' (living at the end), because this term happened to be connected quite often only with the untouchables. His argument was that it was not true that the untouchables had once lived within the village. No mention of their exclusion from the village is to be seen anywhere, nor could it have been feasible to evict forcibly such a vast community and settle it outside the village boundaries.

Ambedkar was of the opinion that the bulk of the untouchables were from conquered tribes, who, separated from their own tribes, had nowhere to go and occupied a place outside the village boundaries. Ambedkar called these people 'broken men'.

The ranks of the village outskirt dwellers further swelled, Ambedkar continues, when the Buddhists joined them. When Buddhism fell into decline, Brahminism regained lost ground and the Brahmins became powerful once again. As a retaliatory measure, the Buddhists were treated with contempt and allowed to live on sufferance. But, not all of them were reduced to this plight. Men from every walk of life had embraced Buddhism and those belonging to the higher castes and/or having wealth remained unaffected. But others, probably those without any influence, were forced by the Brahmins to live outside the village. Still, none of them were untouchables as yet.

Then, Ambedkar comes to the crucial point – the reasons for untouchability. In this context, he first discusses the existing reasons for untouchability. There were two reasons offered for the rise of untouchability at that time – racial and occupational. Ambedkar rejected the racial theory, which was propounded by Riseley, with the help of physical anthropology. He proved that so far as physical characteristics were concerned, there was hardly any difference between the Brahmins and the untouchables. Next, he examined the occupational aspects of untouchability because of the oft-repeated purity-pollution theory held by many, and concluded, by quoting from the *Narada Smrti*, that even when household slaves were engaged in sweeping the streets and gateways and cleaning the privies, they were not treated as untouchables.

According to Ambedkar, religion played an important role in this respect. From about the 4th century AD, Brahminical orthodoxy took a firm hold in society and killing of cows became a punishable offence. Before that, whether during the rule of Asoka or in the law book of Manu, cow slaughter was not considered a serious offence.

Gradually, however, excessive veneration of cows and cow worship were advocated, possibly as a reaction to Buddhism, and the Brahmins, therefore, promulgated several laws against cow slaughter. Since they did not believe in half-way measures, the Brahmins then went a step further and banned the eating of beef, although they had eaten it previously. Cows were now held sacred and eating beef was considered profane. Consequently, those who ate beef came to be regarded with contempt in society. Ambedkar thought that hatred for Buddhism, coupled with contempt for those who ate beef, were the main reasons why certain people came to be considered untouchables.

One may question why the untouchables did not accept the ban on cow slaughter or stop eating beef. In Ambedkar's opinion, since the untouchables did not kill cows for eating themselves, but only ate the meat of already dead cows, whether killed by others or those that had died naturally, the ban was not applicable to them. The untouchables tried to emulate caste Hindu manners and customs, some of them even converted to other religions, such as Islam, Christianity, Sikhism and Buddhism, thinking erroneously that such a move would raise their social status. But, none of their efforts made any difference to their status. Untouchability is deep-rooted in our society. While it has come to be more of a mindset in urban areas, it is more tangible and visible in rural areas, where physical touch is still prohibited. Untouchability has passed from generation to generation through socialization processes and the untouchables have continued to suffer innumerable forms of discrimination, exploitation and even socio-economic disability.

In recent years, the term, 'Dalit', has come to be used for untouchable castes (scheduled castes, or SCs) all over the country.

This book is a collection of ten papers published in various journals, presented as seminar papers and a few of them have been written recently specifically for this book.

In Chapter 2, 'Evolution of the Concept of Dalit', I try to trace the history of the Dalits from the ancient through medieval to modern times in Indian literary and historical literature. I find that the terms, 'Dalits' and 'untouchables', are interchangeable and that their usage is limited only to denote the SCs.

In the chapters on the profile of the Dalits and the provisions the Constitution of India has made for them, I attempt to show the distribution of the Dalit population in the country, measure the schemes being run by the government, and their impact on the targeted people. Ambedkar, who was the chief architect of our Constitution, considered it necessary to make special provisions for enabling Dalits to join the mainstream by providing them with an equitable share in governance and public wealth through a policy of reservation in the elected bodies, public services and educational institutions to protect them from social and economic exploitation and enhanced financial allocation for expediting their socio-economic development.

The chapter, 'Systematic Exclusion of Dalits', deals with the worst kind of disadvantages that the Dalits suffer as a group in our society. They are a stigmatized people and are thus excluded from the mainstream and suffer from numerous kinds of discimination, which are regulated through religious beliefs and practices. In other words, they experience a systematic exclusion which is inbuilt in our hierarchical social system, which excludes the Dalits from interaction and access to social resources through social arrangements, customs and a normative social value system.

In the chapter, 'The Mahadalits of Bihar: Myth and Reality', I trace some of the features common among the Dalits, such as untouchability, low economic status, social segregation, lack of political power, low literacy levels and poor social mobility. All these together reinforce their wretched condition. Despite this, some states are dividing the SCs into A, B, C and D, or Dalits and Mahadalits. But, Bihar has not adopted any criteria to divide the SCs. The state government has arbitrarily included and excluded some castes in the Mahadalits. While the myth of this division is to distribute the fruits of development among the SCs, the reality is to perpetuate inequality, hatred and prejudice among them and to re-establish the *Manuvadi* principles and rule over them.

The chapter, 'Atrocities on the Scheduled Castes: Structural Dysfunction', shows that atrocities on Dalits have become almost a regular feature today. Every day, newspapers and other media report inhuman activities such as beating, torture, arson, usurpation, molestation, rape, killing and so on of Dalits by caste Hindus. Such occurrences not only portray the pitiable state of the Dalits, but also raise several questions. Why are the Dalits being murdered, killed, burnt, massacred, lynched, discriminated and assaulted in public places and in full view of the public? Why should a caste Hindu feel resentment if a Dalit enters a profession, obtains a position of authority, buys land, enters commerce, becomes economically independent and occupies a position in the higher echelons of society? Why should all caste Hindus, whether officials or non-officials, make common cause to suppress the Dalits? Does all of the above emanate directly from the Hindu social order, which empowers them to do so? It is found that the discrimination and atrocities practised against the Dalits are merely the reflections of that deep and strong Hindu sentiment, which is carried over in law and administration and which justifies the making of distinctions between Hindus and Dalits to the disadvantages of the Dalits. These discriminations have their roots in the fear of the Hindus that in a free field, the Dalits may rise above their prescribed status in life and become a menace to the Hindu social order, the cardinal principle of which is the maintenance of Hindu superiority and Hindu domination over the untouchables. So long as the Hindu social order exists, discrimination against the Dalits will continue in various forms and degree.

In the chapter, 'Issues and Challenges Facing SC Women', I examine the issues of Dalit women's identity and their plight in our social context. Dalit women are triply oppressed because of their caste, class and gender and, therefore, should not be equated with upper caste women in terms of their role and identity.

The chapter, 'Naxalism or Survival for Existence', tries to establish that Naxalism, the symptom of entrenched discrimination and failure of the state to reach the fruits of development to those who need it the most, cannot be resolved by strong-handed police or military action. The Centre and state governments must channel their budget more meaningfully and honestly to the development programmes for the poor and initiate more radical land reform measures, bringing about attitudinal changes among the upper castes, bureaucrats, as well as humanize the police forces in the Naxal infested areas. If all this is done, Naxalism will gradually vanish. Naxalism is not just an economic or law and order problem, it is a mix of sociocultural issues and, more importantly, one that has been created by the Brahminical social order, which is supported and dominated by the bureaucracy and policymakers of the nation.

In the chapter, 'Resistance Movements in Orissa and Bihar', I try to show that India is a semi-feudal (*ardh-samanti*) country, dominated by Brahminism and Brahminical culture. Similarly, Bihar and Orissa represent an extreme case of multi-standard dominance by upper castes such as Brahmins, Bhumihars, Rajputs and Kayasths (in Bihar) and Brahmins, Karans and Khandayats in Orissa. Although these are small groups numerically, they have always been dominant in ritual status, land rights, social hierarchy and control of economic resources. They have been controlling Indian society for at least ten centuries now.

In the course of time, the Oriya Dalits tried to reform the caste system and solve the problem of untouchability, even as they remained within the fold of Hinduism. On the other hand, in Bihar, they are trying to create an alternative sociocultural structure by aligning themselves with or forming radical movements. Besides, Dalit organizations and their leaders have also developed a consciousness among the oppressed classes about socio-economic structures and cultural realities in the given milieu.

In the last chapter, 'The Relevance of Ambedkar in Social Reconstruction', I try to prove that the thoughts of Ambedkar are more relevant today than ever before. The recent developments in the socio-economic and political arenas of our country pose a serious threat to the judicial, socio-economic and political liberties of some sections of society, especially the scheduled castes (SCs), scheduled tribes (STs) and other marginalized groups. Ambedkar's writings and speeches offer solutions to the problems faced by the marginalized groups as a whole.

His concept of an ideal society is most suited to the needs of modern society. The efforts to achieve 'liberty, equality and fraternity', which Ambedkar took as his goal of social action, and by which he evaluated the socialist and other economic systems of his day, also help us analyse the burning economic issues of the contemporary polity. From his examination of 'riddles' to his essays on 'revolution and counter-revolution' in society to his efforts to analyse the foundations of caste and unsociability to his conversion to Buddhism, Ambedkar attempted to lay the basis for the cultural reconstruction of the nation. In brief, he played an incomparable role in the history of India, in improving not only the conditions of the marginalized sections, but also of all sections of society, and thereby helped in implementing the ideal of social justice. Not just that, he ensured that these ideals and liberties were guaranteed in various constitutional provisions and legal enactments. He fought to establish an egalitarian society on the principles of liberty, equality and fraternity.

References

Ambedkar, B.R. 1990. *Writings and Speeches,* Vols. 3, 5, 7. Education Department: Government of Maharashtra.

Dube, S.C. 2000. *Indian Society*. New Delhi: National Book Trust.

Gupta, Dipankar (ed.). 1991. *Social Stratification*. Kolkata: Oxford University Press.

Mukherjee, Prabhati. 1988. *Beyond the Four Varnas*. Delhi: Motilal Banarasi Dass.

Ram, Nandu. 1995. *Beyond Ambedkar*. New Delhi: Har Anand Publications.

2

Evolution of the Concept of Dalit

Time and again, we come across terms such as 'untouchable classes', 'depressed classes', 'Harijans', 'scheduled castes' and, more recently, 'Dalits'. Often, laymen and intellectuals think that the untouchables are part of the *chaturvarna* system or part of the Shudra caste. This is one reason that the Dalits are exploited on a regular basis by Shudra politicians. The main objective of this chapter is to show how the different groups of untouchables evolved and developed over time. These different groups include Chandalas, Asprashya, Antya, Bahya, Antyavasin, Antyaja, Achhut, depressed classes, Harijans, scheduled castes and ex-untouchables. Getting to the root of the matter is a difficult task because there is no historical record or evidence maintained by the Dalits themselves. All that is available in writing is what has been recorded by their rivals, which, naturally, cannot be taken as a reliable source or material for reconstructing the history of the Dalits. Historical roots cannot only provide clues to the lost identity of the Dalits, they can also help us in answering a number of other pertinent questions: Who are the Dalits? Where did they originate? How have they come into their current status and who is responsible for this?

The Ancient Period

The *Rig Veda* is the earliest written literary source for the history of India. A large part of the text is addressed to Lord Indra. The *Rig Veda* talks of a fierce war having been taken place among different groups. Two opposing forces may be seen in the *Rig Veda*. First, those to whom the various hymns of the *Rig Veda* are addressed, and second, those against whom they are directed. Ramprasad Chandra has made an important observation about this: 'These hymns reveal two hostile peoples in the land of the Seven Rivers now called the Punjab – the Deva worshipping Arya and the Deva-less and riteless Dasyu or Dasa.'[1] In order to examine these two opposing groups more closely, let us look at these relevant verses from the hymns of the *Rig Veda*:

1. *Vi janihayaran ye ch dasyvo …*[2]
   You (Indra) know well the Aryas and Dasyus …
   … hativi dusyun prarya Vaarnamavata.[3]
   … He (Indra) killed the Dasyus and protected the Aryans.
2. *Vadhihi dasyu dhanini …*[4]
   You (Indra) killed the rich Dasyu …
   Akarma dasyurabhi no amanturanya-varto amanus.[5]
   All around us are the ritual-less Dasyu, inhuman, who are following alien laws.
   anaso dasyu …[6]
   The noseless Dasyu …
3. *Sa jatubharma chhadadadhana ojo.*
   puro vimindannacharada vi dasi.
   vidana vajirna dasyuve hetimas narya
   saho vadhrya sumnamindar …
   dasyu hatyaua.[7]
   Armed with his thunderbolt, Indra went about destroying the forts of the Dasas.
   O Indra, throw your thunderbolt at the Dasyus,
   Increase the power and glory of the Arya
   O Indra, throw your thunderbolt at the Dasyus,
   Increase the power and glory of the Aryas.
   Sa vartrahendra karsunayoni
   purandaro dasiraraiyada vi …
   hatavi dasyuno pura ayasinin tarita.[8]
   Indra the vartra-killer, fort-destroyer,
   Scattered the Dasas
   Who dwelt in darkness …
   He killed the Dasyus
   and broke the forts made of iron.
4. *Ddasa cha vartra hatamayrani cha*
   Sudasmindravruna vasavatama.[9]
   Indra and Varuna killed the Dasas and the Aryas (अर्य),
   Who were Sudas' enemies and helped him with favour.

Yo no Dasa ayro vapurustutadeva
Indra yudhve chiketati.[10]
O most respected Indra, the godless people,
Whether Dasas or Aryas ('अर्य),
Who want war with us.

5. *Yatha deva asureshu sadramugaresu chakirre.*[11]
Even the gods kept faith in the mighty Asuras.
Hatyaya deva asurana …[12]
When the gods killed the Asuras …

6. *Apasedhana raksaso yatudhanansthada deva …*[13]
Driving off the Rakshasas and Yatudhanas, the god is present
Jahi nyatrina pani varko hisa.[14]
You (Soma) kill Pani. He is like a wolf.

These verses of the *Rig Veda* definitely deal with two different groups of people, the Aryas and the groups opposing them, such as the Dasas, Dasyus, Aryas (अर्य), Asuras, Rakshasas, Vartra and Pani. The Dasas and Dasyus are described as the enemies of Indra and the Devas. The cities of both the Dasas and the Dasyus have been described as having been razed to the ground by Indra and the Devas. While these references suggest that the Dasa and Dasyus were the same, there are other references that suggest that they were different. This is clear from the fact that the Dasas are referred to separately in fifty-four places and the Dasyus in seventy-eight places. Why should there be so many separate references if they did not form two distinct entities? The probability is that they refer to two different communities.

According to the authors of the Vedic index of names and subjects, 'Arya is the normal designation in Vedic literature from the *Rig Veda* onwards of an Aryan, a member of the three upper classes: Brahmin, Kshatriya or Vaisya – the Arya stands in opposition to Dasa, but also to the Sudra.'[15] Regarding the Dasyus, on the basis of some passages of the *Rig Veda* (1.51.8; 1.103.3; 2.18.19; 3.34.9; to name a few), the authors of the Vedic index entertain the possibility of their being indigenous people, who are assigned special negative traits in the *Rig Veda*, which are nowhere applied in the same text to the Aryas. The Dasyus, according to the *Rig Veda*, are '*anas*' (without face), '*anaso*' (noseless), to mention some descriptors.[16] The distinction between the Aryas and the Dasyus is affirmed by V.S. Apte as well.[17]

Some verses in the *Rig Veda* also highlight some traits of the Dasyus and Dasas, which distinguish them culturally from the Aryas. The *Rig Veda* says that the Dasyus were 'rich' and 'well-to-do'; they lived in 'well-fortified houses and cities'. They are also contemptuously said to be 'ritual-less, inhuman, following alien laws'. They had their own religious and social customs and rites, which were alien to the Aryas. They are described as '*anaso*' or 'noseless', which means their appearance differed from that of the Aryas. Their colour (of both the Dasas and the Dasyus) is described as 'dark with dusky skin'.

The verses indicate the existence of other non-Aryan people, too, with whom the Aryans waged war. These included the Asuras, the Rakshasas, the Pani and Arya (अर्य). The *Rig Veda* uses two words – Arya (अर्य) with a short 'a' and Arya (अर्य) with a long 'a'. The word Arya (अर्य) with a short 'a' is used in the *Rig Veda* at eighty-eight places and in four different senses:

- As an enemy at 43 places;
- As a respectable person at as many as 42 places;
- As an owner, or as a Vaishya or as a citizen in just two places; and
- As a name for India.

In contrast, the word Arya (अर्य) with a long 'a' is used at only thirty-one places.

The one indisputable conclusion which follows from the above discussion is that the term Arya (अर्य), as it occurs in the *Vedas*, was used to denote a group opposed to the Aryans. This group was probably an advance guard of mixed Indo-Aryan people who came to India and, in the course of time, became victims of an Aryan conspiracy.

However, the proposition that the Dasas and the Dasyus were the same as the Shudras is a figment of the imagination. No evidence can be cited in support of this wild guess. As has been said before, Dasa occurs in the *Rig Veda* fifty-four times and Dasyu, seventy-eight times. The Dasas and the Dasyus are sometimes spoken of together, while the word Shudra occurs just once and that too in a context in which the Dasas and the Dasyus find no mention. In the light of these considerations, it is difficult to conclude that the Shudras are the same as the Dasas and the Dasyus.

Another fact to be noted here is that the words 'Dasas' and 'Dasyus' are conspicuous in their complete absence in later Vedic literature. This means they were completely ignored by the Vedic Aryans, who did not consider them to be human beings or part of their society. But, it is quite different when it comes to the Shudras. Though the early Vedic literature is silent on them, the later Vedic literature is full of them. This clearly shows that the Shudras were different from the Dasas and the Dasyus.

In his book, *Who were the Shudras?*, Ambedkar[18] raises some pertinent questions on the identity of the Shudras as well as their pitiable designation as the fourth varna of Indo-Aryan society. His answers are summarized as follows:

- The Shudras were one of the Aryan communities of the Solar race.
- There was a time when the Aryans recognized only three varnas: the Brahmins, the Kshatriyas and the Vaishyas.
- The Shudras did not form a separate varna. They were a part of the Kshatriya varna in Indo-Aryan society.
- There was a continuous feud between the Shudra kings and the Brahmins in which the Brahmins were subjected to many tyrannies and indignities.
- Due to the deep-rooted hatred felt towards the Shudras as a result of their tyranny and oppression, the Brahmins refused to perform the *upanayana* ceremony for the Shudras.
- As a result, the Shudras, who were actually Kshatriyas, were degraded socially, fell below the rank of the Vaishyas and thus came to form the fourth varna.

On the basis of Ambedkar's analysis, it can be concluded that the problem of untouchability took the form of a conflict between two hostile groups. Even today, one can observe the bitter relationship between the Savarnas and the Dalits and the hatred and contempt shown by the former to the Dalits.

Status of Untouchables in Brahminic Literature

Untouchability, with its manifold manifestations, is rooted in notions of purity and pollution, which are believed to have developed in the later Vedic period, along with the emergence of Brahminic literature such as the *Smritis, Samhitas* and the *Upanishads*. An examination of the *Dharma Sutras* reveals that they spoke about a class whom they called the Asprashya. The *Dharma Sutras* also used a variety of other terms such as the Antya, Antyaja, Antyavasin and Bahya. These terms were also used by the later *Smritis*. It is necessary to give an idea of the use of these terms by the different *Sutras* and *Smritis*. It is explained on next page.[19]

Terms such as Asprashya (not to touch), Antya (last/at the end), Bahya (outside the pale of the *chaturvarna*, hence outcaste), Antyavasin (those who live at the end) and Antyaja (born at the end), used in different *Sutras* and *Smritis*, are significant. The segregation they denote was a natural corollary of the ardently preached and widely shared beliefs of purity and pollution, and the terms themselves testify to the practices prevalent in those times. Perhaps, all this meant a conscious perpetuation of an old state of affairs and created a definite barrier to free mixing in the future. These terms also show that the Dalits were living in separate quarters and were pushed to the corners of villages by victorious invaders.

1. *Asprashya*	*Dharma Sutra*	*Smriti*
	Vishnu v. 104	*Smirti*
2. *Antya*	*Dharma Sutras*	*Smriti*
	1. Vasishta (16–30)	1. Manu iv.79; viii.68
	2. Apastambha (iii.I)	2. Yajnavalkya 1.148.197
		3. Atri 25
		4. Likhita 92
3. *Bahya*	*Dharma Sutras*	*Smriti*
	1. Apastambha 1.2.39.18	1. Manu 28
	2. Vishnu 16.14	2. Narada 1.155
4. *Antyavasin*	*Dharma Sutras*	*Smriti*
	1. Gautama xxxi; xxiii.32	1. Manu iv.79; x.39
	2. Vasishta xvii. 3	2. Shanti Parvan of the *Mahabharata* 141; 29–32
		3. *Madhyamangiras* (quoted in Mitakshara on yaj. 3.280)
5. *Antyaja*	*Dharma Sutra*	*Smriti*
	1. Vishnu 36.7	1. Manu iv.61; viii.279
		2. Yajnavalkya 12.73
		3. *Brihadyama Smriti (*quoted by Mitakshara on Yajnavalkya III. 260)
		4. *Atri Smriti* 199
		5. *Veda Vyas Smriti* 1.12.13.

The enumeration of the Antyavasins occurs in the *Smriti* known as the *Madhyamangiras* and that of the Antyajas in the *Atri Smriti* and *Veda Vyas Smriti*. Who they were is apparent from the following table:

Antyavasin	*Antyaja*	
Madhyamangiras	*Atri Smriti*	*Veda Vyas Smriti*
1. Chandala	1. Nata	1. Chandala
2. Shvapaka	2. Meda	2. Shvapaka
3. Kshatta	3. Bhilla	3. Nata
4. Suta	4. Rajaka	4. Meda
5. Vaidehika	5. Charmakar	5. Bhilla
6. Magadha	6. Buruda	6. Rajaka
7. Ayogava	7. Kayavarta	7. Charmakar
		8. Virat
		9. Dasa
		10. Bhatt
		11. Kolika
		12. Pushakar

The above table shows that these generic terms developed into a specific caste name in the texts of the later Vedic period. In the *Chhandogyopanishad,* it is stated that if one who has realized the true nature of the Brahmin offers the remnants of the food used for the Agnihotra sacrifice even to a Chandala it is offered as an oblation in that sacrificial fire.[20] In fact, such food offered to a Chandala is an abomination. It is also stated in so many words that the breed of the Chandala is a degraded one, ranked with that of the dog and the pig. Before 800 BC, thus, we find the idea of ceremonial purity fully developed and operative in relation to the despised and degraded group of people called the Chandalas. The concept of the Panchamas referred to in the *Narada Smriti* speaks of slaves as the fifth class or order.

The *Dharmasutra* writers declared the Chandalas to be the progeny of the most hated of the reverse order of mixed unions of a Brahmin woman with a Shudra man. Kautilya, a practical administrator, provides for a number of these so-called mixed castes. He exhorts them to marry among themselves and follow the customs and avocations as far as possible of their ancestors.

There was a group separately recognized by Vasishtha, which was called the Antyavasin, whom he declared to be the progeny of a Vaishya woman and a Shudra man. According to Manu, however, the Antyavasin had much more depraved origins – they were the progeny of a Chandala man and a Nishada woman. His work was confined to the cremation ground and, according to one commentator, he was to be identified with the Chandalas. Both Baudhayana and Vasishtha mention a degraded caste called Shvapaka. Baudhayana declares the group to have risen from the union of an Ambashtha man with a Brahmin woman at one place, while at another, he says they were the result of the union of an Ugra man with a Kshatriya woman. Manu says the Shvapaka were the progeny of a Kshatriya man and an Ugra woman – he gives a derivation that is just the opposite of Baudhayana's second derivation. He also lists two other groups – Sopaka and Pandusopaka – whom he derives from a Chandala father and Kukkusa and Vaideha mothers, respectively. He prescribes to the Sopaka the vocation of the hangman and to the Pandusopaka, that of a cane-worker. It is to be noted that though both Baudhayana and Manu speak of the Shvapaka as a group, yet Manu in describing its particular vocation calls it the Svapacha. Kautilya calls the group Shvapaka and says that they originated from the union of an Ugra man and a Kshatriya woman. This derivation agrees with Baudhayana's second derivation and is just the opposite of that of Manu.

Patanjali, the great grammarian who lived around 150 BC, has mentioned the female of Svapacha group being called a Svapacha and not Svapach.[21] However, the exact avocations and status of the Svapachas during Patanjali's time are not known. He also speaks of the Mritapas in combination with the Chandalas. Kautilya, who rigorously excluded the Chandalas from all social contact, does not prescribe similar exclusion for the Svapachas. But, Manu is insistent that the Svapachas should be grouped with the Chandalas and treated as their absolute equals. He says they should live outside the village and use the shrouds of corpses for their clothing, broken pots to cook their meals, iron for their ornaments and dogs and donkeys as their wealth. They should work as hangmen, who are prohibited entry into villages and towns during daytime, or as undertakers of unclaimed corpses. They should be stamped with some mark to distinguish them from the rest of the community.

As stated above, Patanjali, who belonged to an earlier age than Manu, does not group the Chandalas and the Mritapas together or lay down any norms for them. And it is not impossible that this manner of looking at the Chandalas and the Mritapas could date back to Panini's times, 500 BC. We learn that both the Chandalas and the Mritapas resided within the limits of the towns and villages of the Aryas as did other Shudras, such as carpenters, blacksmiths, washermen and weavers. The social distinction in status between such groups as carpenters, blacksmiths, washermen and weavers on the one hand and the Chandalas and the Mritapas on the other lay not in the fact of touchability or untouchability, but the distinctions are made only in the use of the vessels of these people. The Chandalas and the Mritapas were technically Apapatras.

It is noteworthy that the technical term, Apapatra, used by Patanjali to characterize the Chandalas and the Mritapas is also used by *Dharmasutra* writers such as Baudhayana, but without specifying the groups implied by the term. Baudhayana exhorts Brahmins not to recite the *Vedas* within the hearing of the Shudras or the Apapatras. Apastamba (*Dharmasutra* II, 17, 20) enjoins that they should not be permitted to see the performance of a funeral sacrifice. From these contexts, it may be inferred that the Apapatras meant the same people to whom the term was applied by Patanjali and even earlier by Panini.

We may conclude that the social position of the classes of people called the Chandalas, the Svapachas and the Mritapas deteriorated slowly but surely between the ages of Panini and Manu. In the former age, they lived within the limits of the village, in which other orders and castes also lived. During the era of Manu (x: 51–2), they were not only excluded from the village, but also assigned duties that clearly showed that they were looked upon as vile specimens of humanity.

The following question arises from the Brahminic literature: Were inter-mixing, inter-dining and inter-marriage prevalent among the various varnas? Certainly not, because it was a closed society at that time. All the terms used in the Brahminic literature for the untouchables were meant to demoralize them.

The Buddhist birth stories called the *Jatakas*, which narrate the conditions prevailing east of Allahabad around the 2nd century BC, describe the Chandalas as the lowest caste. But occasionally, in the enumeration of the castes in the *Jatakas*, another group called the later Vedic Pukkusa is presented as lower than the Chandalas. The references to the Chandalas are specific and almost invariably show them as a despised group. Even to see the members of this group was to see evil, to avert which one must at least wash one's eyes. They are described as occupying sites outside regular villages and towns whether in the west near Taxila or in the centre near Ujjain. They could be detected by their special dialect and their hereditary occupation, sweeping.

The Chinese pilgrim, Fa Hien, a contemporary of Chandragupta II, who lived in India between 405 and 411 AD, states that the Chandalas lived apart from others '... i.e., in separate quarters'.[22] Another Chinese traveller, Yuan Chaung, who visited the region in 629 AD, reiterates that these people were forced to live outside the city.[23]

The Medieval Period

Alberuni visited India in 1020 AD and left a valuable account of his travels. He classifies the Doms and the Chandalas as two of the groups 'not reckoned among any caste or guild. They are occupied with dirty work, like the cleansing of the villages and other services. They are considered as one sole class and distinguished only by their occupation.' Hemachandra, the grammarian, writing about a century later, tells us in his *Deshinamamala*[24] that the Dumba (Dom or Dumba) was a local word for the Svapachas. He also says that the Chandalas carried a stick in their hands to warn people of their coming so that they could avoid their touch; the stick had a specific local name, Jhajjhari.

Kalhana, the Brahmin historian of Kashmir, in his *Rajatarangini,* which was completed in 1150 AD, mentions not only the Chandalas and the Doms, but also the Charmakars or Chamars, who were described as untouchables or the Asprishyas.

About a century and a half before Kalhana, Alberuni had left a record of a very different situation of the untouchables. But, even that situation was only slightly different from the one of utter degradation posited by Manu. First, one noted that all the four orders were described not only as living together in the same towns and villages, but as also 'mixed together in the same housing and lodgings'.

According to Alberuni's information and findings, there were two other classes of people, who were 'not reckoned among any caste'. The first group noticed by him was formed of the people following certain crafts, were eight in number, and were grouped as the Antyajas. Within this group, which formed eight guilds and had to live nearby but outside the villages and the towns of the four castes, there were two sub-divisions. The jugglers, basket and shield makers, sailors, fishermen and hunters of wild animals and birds could intermarry freely, though they belonged to separate guilds. But, none of their members would condescend to have anything to do with the fullers, shoemakers and weavers. The latter three, forming the second sub-division of the Antyajas, would either marry among themselves or the ones with closer similarities.

The sixth class of people (the Antyajas being the fifth) was, according to Alberuni, composed of four groups, of which two, the Domas (Dombas) and the Chandalas, are the two groups about which we know so much from Patanjali, Hemachandra and Kalhana. They were occupied in 'dirty work like the cleansing of the villages and other services'. They were considered 'as one sole class and distinguished only by their occupation'. The Doms' other occupation was to play the flute and sing.

During the Bhakti movement, which swept India from the eighth to the eighteenth centuries, the untouchables were honoured as saints and poets. Nandanar (700–900 AD), a Shaivite saint from Tamil Nadu, and his contemporary, Tiruppan, became one of the twelve Vaishnavite Alvars. The first expression of concern for the Dalits during the Bhakti period comes in the fourteenth and fifteenth centuries in the form of religious reforms. Ramananda, a Hindu reformer, preached equality and chose disciples even from among the untouchables. One of his twelve disciples was Ravidas, a Chamar from Banaras. He founded a sect of the Chamars known as the Raidas or Ravidasis, which follows the teachings of Ramananda. The Bhakti movement also gave rise to the poet saints of Maharashtra, among them were Chokhamela and his entire family, who were part of the Mahars of the 14th century and who inveighed against untouchability.

The Bhakti tradition rejected the authority of the *Vedas*, priesthood and ritual practices, yet failed to recover the lost identity of the untouchables. The revolt continued in various forms till the 18th century. However, each of the revolting group was reabsorbed into the Hindu fold. Perhaps, the last poet saint in this stream was Narsi Mehta, a Gujarati, who coined the term, Harijan. 'Harijan' literally means 'people of god'. There is considerable debate on the meaning of the term. In fact, the term was initially used only to refer to the children of the Devadasis, the female temple dancers. Symbolically speaking, they were the children of god. The Devadasis (*deva* means god and *dasi* means servant) were dedicated to the service of gods and goddesses and the sexual union between the agents (the priests and the nobility of the village) and the servants of god was mystified and even invested with an aura of divinity. However, the children of the Devadasis had a stigmatized identity among the general population because of their ambiguous paternal identity. The term, Harijan, surfaced again when Gandhi picked it up and popularized it in 1933 as part of India's freedom movement, but it was totally rejected by the more aware Dalits, who saw in this terminology yet another attempt to segregate them subtly from the rest of the society.

Duarte Barbosa,[25] a Portuguese traveller who visited India in the 16th century, talks of various categories of people of low station on the Malabar coast. He lists eleven classes of 'Tevars' (probably today's Ezhavas, known as the Tyyas in north Kerala), who earned their livelihood through all kinds of labour, but mainly as serfs of the Nairs, the higher class Hindus. Below them, Barbosa cites the Poleas (or Pulayas), who are described as an 'even lower sect' and regarded as excommunicated and 'accursed'. They live in 'swampy fields and places where respectable people cannot go'; they plough and sow the fields and may not speak to the Nairs except from a shouting distance. They can be killed without attracting any penalty. And, there exists yet an even lower category, the Pareas or the Parayars, who live in uninhabited places and are regarded as being so low that a person can get excommunicated merely by looking at them. They live on roots and wild animals.

Later, in the 20th century, the Ezhavas were to set themselves apart from the other low castes and endeavour to better their conditions. On the other hand, Barbosa describes the Pulayas and Parayars as 'excommunicated' (a highly significant term from the lips of the 16th century Europeans), 'accursed', living in the wilderness, and so on.

The British Era

The policies of the British, though not intended to benefit the untouchables at first, were a blessing in disguise. The benefits can be called the unintended positive effects of a policy that was not specifically geared to that purpose. Simultaneously, the enumeration of the population or the census reports and the efforts of the British colonial government to collect systematic information about the many aspects of India's inhabitants and society provided an opportunity to the untouchables, not just to know about themselves, but also about their counterparts in various parts of the country.

The first British census of India was undertaken during 1871–72. The British census officials were not clear whether the untouchables were to be categorized as Hindus or as a sui generis group of people. This remained a problem from the first to the last British censuses in India. The census directors were concerned about who the untouchables were and what relation they had with the other Indian communities. Consequently, in 1871–72, the Chamars, since long recognized as the largest untouchable caste in the country and found in large numbers in the Bengal province, were described as 'semi-Hinduised Aborigines' in the census. In other provinces, untouchable castes such as the Mahars and the Pariahs were included in the category of untouchables as 'outcaste' or as an unrecognized caste.[26]

In the 1901 Census,[27] some lower castes that were below the twice-born Brahmin groups were categorized thus:

- Those from whom the Brahmins will accept water;
- Those from whom some of the higher castes will accept water;
- Those who are not untouchables, but from whom the Brahmins will not accept water;
- Those who are untouchables, but do not take beef, whose touch defiles and from whom the higher castes will not accept water; and
- The beef-eating group, unclean, impure and filthy, whose touch defiles.

For the first time, the 1911 Census divided the so-called Hindu society into three categories:

- Hindus;
- Animists and tribals; and
- Depressed classes or untouchables.

As a result, the 1911 Census, which invested a separate identity on the untouchables, acquired a new political dimension.

While the 1911 Census primarily separated the Hindus into those who were 100 per cent Hindu and those who were not 100 per cent Hindu, it included into the category of the untouchables and tribes those who[28]

1. deny the supremacy of the Brahmins;
2. do not receive mantra from a Brahmin;
3. deny the authority of the *Vedas;*
4. do not worship Hindu gods;
5. are not served by good Brahmins as family priests;
6. have no Brahmin priests at all;
7. are denied access to the interiors of Hindu temples;
8. cause pollution by touch or by appearing within a certain distance;
9. bury their dead; and
10. eat beef and do not revere the cow.

Of these ten tests, those numbered 1, 3, 4 and 9 differentiate between Hindus and animists and tribals. The rest differentiate between Hindus and untouchables.

The 1920s witnessed major changes and challenges to the untouchables. A new set of self-conscious identities, consisting of radical untouchables claiming that they were the original inhabitants of the land and the sons of the soil came to the forefront. This culminated in an Adi (original) ideology that came to be prefixed to their regional identity. Those from the Telugu-speaking areas of the Madras Presidency presented themselves as Adi-Andhras, the Tamil-speaking untouchables claimed themselves to be the Adi-Dravidas, and those from Karnataka called themselves the Adi-Kannadas. The Telugu-speaking untouchables called themselves the Adi-Hindus, but a large section of them gave to this a militant, anti-Brahmin interpretation. For them, Hinduism was not a religion. As early as in 1917, the first provincial Adi-Andhra Mahasabha claimed that the so-called Panchamas were the original sons of the soil and they were the rulers of the country.[29] In modern-day Uttar Pradesh, too, the untouchables organized themselves on the basis of an Adi-Hindu identity under the leadership of the outcaste ascetic, Acchutananda, who argued that the untouchables were in fact Adi-Hindus, the original or the Nagas or Dasas of the North and the Dravidas of the South of the subcontinent and they were the undisputed heavenly owners of Bharat. All others were immigrants, including the Aryans who had conquered the original populations.[30] Similar arguments were advanced by the Punjabi untouchables, who organized themselves under the banner of the Adi-Dharm movement.

During the period between 1919 and 1935, new titles and phrases were coined to denote the untouchables. The existence of the depressed classes was recognized in the text of the Government of India Act of 1919.

In 1916, when M.B. Dadabhoy moved a resolution in the Legislative Council on the amelioration of the depressed classes, attempts were made to apply the term, 'depressed classes', to criminal and wandering tribes, aboriginal tribes and Hindu untouchables.[31] In 1917, the then educational commissioner, Sir Henry Sharp, in his seventh quinquennial review of the progress of education in India for 1912–17, used the term, depressed classes, to denote only the Hindu untouchable castes. But, he noted that the term was also used to denote the educationally and economically backward Hindu castes, who were 'not absolutely outside the pale of castes'.[32] The franchise committee of 1918–19 divided the Hindu community into three classes: Brahmins, non-Brahmins and Hindu others.[33] In 1928, in reply to a question in the Legislative Assembly by Lala Lajpat Rai as to what classes were considered to be depressed besides or in addition to the untouchables, J. Crerar, the home member, replied that the classes generally considered as depressed in addition to the untouchables were the hill tribes, aboriginals and criminal tribes.[34] In the same year, when the statutory commission asked the government to give a critical account of the total number of depressed classes in British India, the government stated that no caste or tribe had been officially defined as depressed and whether or not any group of the community was socially depressed was a matter of local custom.[35] The statutory commission used the term, depressed classes, to mean only the Hindu untouchable castes – castes that cause 'pollution by touch or by the approach within a certain distance and excluded from its scope the Aboriginals who are definitely outside the Hindu fold'.[36] The central committee also wanted to confine the term, depressed classes, to the Hindu untouchable castes.[37] In their memorandum to the second session of the Round Table Conference (1931), Ambedkar and Rao Bahadur Srinivasan held that 'the Depressed Classes shall be strictly defined as meaning persons belonging to communities which are subjected to the system of untouchability'. They suggested the following alternative nomenclatures for depressed classes: non-caste Hindus, protestant Hindus or non-conformist Hindus.[38]

In 1930, the statutory commission defined that, in origin, these castes seemed to be partly functional, comprising those who followed occupations held to be unclean or degrading, such as scavenging and leather-working, and partly tribal, such as the aboriginal tribes taken into the Hindu fold and transformed into an impure caste.[39] In the 1931 Census, the then Census Commissioner, J.H. Hutton,[40] identified the following disabilities for the depressed classes:

- whether the caste or class in question could be served by Brahmins or not;
- whether the caste or class in question could be served by the barbers, water carriers, tailors, etc., who served caste Hindus;
- whether the caste in question could pollute a high caste Hindu through contact or proximity;
- whether the caste or class in question was one from whose hands a caste Hindu could accept water;
- whether the caste or class in question was debarred from using public conveniences such as roads, ferries, wells or schools;
- whether the caste or class in question was debarred from the use of Hindu temples;
- whether in ordinary social intercourse, a well-educated member of the caste or class in question would be treated as an equal by high caste men with the same educational qualifications;

- whether the caste or class in question was depressed merely on account of its own ignorance, illiteracy or poverty and, but for that, would be subject to no social disability; and
- whether the caste or class in question was depressed on account of the occupation followed and whether, but for that occupation, it would be subject to no social disability.

It was argued that the figures given by the Census Commissioner were for the depressed classes and not for the untouchables, and that the depressed classes included other classes besides the untouchables. According to Ambedkar, 'The term 'Depressed Classes' was used as a synonym for the Untouchables and the term Depressed Classes was used instead of the term Untouchables because the latter, it was felt, would give offence to the people meant to be included under the term. That it was used to denote only the Untouchables and it did not include the Aboriginals or the criminal tribes was made clear in the debate that took place in the Imperial Legislative Council in 1916 on the resolution moved by Dadabhoy.'[41]

The term, 'exterior castes', appeared for the first time in the 1931 Census. The Census Superintendent of Assam suggested changing the nomenclature, depressed classes, to exterior castes. His argument was that it was a broader title because its connotation did not limit itself to 'outcaste' people (which meant people who were outside the caste system). The exterior castes would include also those who had been cast out because of some breach of caste rules. In 1931, a special committee was also set up to draw a 'schedule' of the castes and classes covered under the depressed classes. One of the Round Table Conferences was convened at the time in London.

The franchise committee of 1932, which attempted to define the term, depressed classes, for the purpose of representation, held that this term should be applied to those who would be considered untouchables according to the following test of the 1911 Census:

- Those who are denied access to the interiors of ordinary Hindu temples; and
- Those who cause pollution
  - by touch; and
  - by appearing within a certain distance.

It may be noted that the communal award that provided for reservation of seats for the depressed classes was to be based on the report of the franchise committee.[42] The Poona Pact also did not attempt any definition of the depressed classes, but its thrust was to apply the term, depressed classes, to the Hindu untouchables as this pact was an intra-Hindu affair.

The white paper published in March 1933 substituted the term, scheduled castes, for depressed classes, and without fixing any criteria for the definition of the said castes, enumerated a list of the castes and tribes that were to be included in this category.

More pertinent to our discussion here as well as to the struggles of the untouchables, is the term, scheduled castes, which 'was first coined by the Simon Commission'. The term, scheduled castes, taken literally, connotes 'the Schedule of Castes or the castes put under a schedule'. This term was embodied in Section 305 of the Government of India Act of 1935[43] (Ghurye, 1990). Section 24, a part of the First Schedule of the Government of India Bill of 1935, defined scheduled castes as 'such castes, races and tribes corresponding to the classes of persons formerly known as the Depressed Classes as the council may specify'.[44] Section 26(1) also substantially accepted the above definition and defined scheduled castes as Section 24 did.

Subsequently, according to the First, Fifth and Sixth Schedules of the Government of India Act of 1935,[45] the council issued the Government of India (Scheduled Castes) Order on 30 April 1936,[46] which contained a list of castes, races or tribes that were to be treated as SCs. The list of the castes in the government order and the list in the white paper of 1933 corresponded with the list of the depressed classes drawn up during the 1931 Census.

Over time, this scheduled caste identity became a constitutional identity for the term untouchables is used for all legal and bureaucratic purposes now. Its constitutional adoption led to precision with regard to the castes, classes or groups of castes that were to be categorized as such. It gave a definite and distinct identity to the castes so clubbed without necessitating any interference with the social structures of Hindu society.

The Post-independence Era

The term, Dalit, is comparatively more recent in origin, although not as recent as some scholars suggest.[47] But, the recent theological research shows that concepts such as Dalit, Dal and Dalah have been used extensively in Hebrew.[48] The Dalit concept came into vogue in 1970 in Maharashtra with the launching of the Dalit Panthers Movement. Dalit is a Marathi word, apparently derived from Sanskrit. In an 1831 dictionary, Dalit is defined as 'ground or broken or reduced to pieces generally'.[49] Apparently, it was used in the 1930s as a Hindi and Marathi translation for depressed classes, a term that the British used for what are now called the scheduled castes. In 1930, there was a newspaper in Poona, called *Dalit Bandhu* (*Dalit Brothers*), which was specifically aimed at the depressed classes. The word was also used by Ambedkar in his Marathi speeches.

In the early 1970s, the term, Dalit, was used and popularized by the Dalit Panthers Movement, a militant organization of untouchable youths in Maharashtra. They defined the term with broader connotations and used it collectively for the SCs, STs, neo-Buddhists, workers, landless and poor peasants, women and all those who were economically exploited.[50] For them, Dalit was a symbol of change and revolution, believing in humanism and rejecting the existence of god, rebirth, existence of the soul, the Hindu sacred books that teach discrimination, fate and heaven. Dalits reject religion and priesthood because these have made them slaves. Therefore, being a Dalit is the most secular identity a person could ever have. It denotes a class, rather than a caste. Thanks to the Dalit Panthers Movement, the Dalit Sahitya Movement came into existence and the term came to be legitimized and reinforced. According to some Dalit leaders, the term, Dalit, provides a sense of pride and self-assertion. It is essentially a label to help Dalits achieve a sense of cultural identity. To be a Dalit, they believe, is no more a shameful thing. 'Dalitness' is a source of confrontation and a matter of appreciating the tactility of one's being. However, nowadays, Dalit is being increasingly used as a synonym for the untouchables.

The clearest definition of Dalit in its contemporary usage comes from a letter written to Eleanor Zelliot by Gangadhar Pantawane, a Professor of Marathi at the Marathwada University, Aurangabad, and founder editor of *Asmitadarsh* (*Mirror of Identity*), the chief organ of Dalit literature: 'To me, Dalit is not a caste. He is a man exploited by (the) social and economic traditions of this country. He does not believe in god, rebirth, soul, holy books, teaching separatism, fate and the heavens because they have made him a slave. He does believe in humanism. Dalit is a symbol of change and revolution.'[51]

According to Nandu Ram,[52] though Dalit represents a broader social category of people, it has become a nationwide phenomenon in more recent years and is widely used to denote all untouchables, irrespective of traditional and parochial caste distinctions. It has also become a symbol of their social identity. Nandu Ram states, 'But contrary to a heuristic understanding of the term, Dalit is currently used for and by the Untouchable castes all over the country. Even social scientists have started referring to the Dalits and the Untouchables or the Scheduled Castes interchangeably.'

Conclusion

We may conclude that the terms, Dalits and untouchables are used interchangeably. The broader inclusion of landless and poor peasants, women, STs and other backward castes (OBCs) as Dalits may be intended, but these do not share the same social heritage as the SCs. The OBCs, too, may call themselves Pichhadi Jati, rather than Dalits. So, the term in common parlance has remained synonymous only with the SCs.

Notes

1. Chanda, Ramprasad. 1969. *The Indo Aryan Races: A Study of the Origin of Indo-Aryan People and Institutions.* Calcutta: Indian Studies, p. 3.
2. *Rig Veda.* 1.51.8: All the *Rig Veda*'s Sanskrit text is taken from the *Rig Veda* in the Devanagri script, edited by Shriram Sharma Acharya and published in four volumes by the Sanskrit Sansthan, Bareilly (Uttar Pradesh) in 1985.
3. Ibid., 3.34.9.
4. Ibid., 1.33.4.
5. Ibid., 10.22.8.
6. Ibid., 5.38.10.
7. Ibid., 1.103.3.4.
8. Ibid., 2.20.7.8.
9. Ibid., 7.83.1.
10. Ibid., 10.38.3.
11. Ibid., 10.151.3.
12. Ibid., 10.157.4.
13. Ibid., 1.35.10.
14. Ibid., 6.51.14.
15. MacDonell, Arthur Anthony, & Arthur, Berriedal Keith. 1912. *Vedic Index of Names and Subjects, Vol. 1.* London: Murray p. 64.
16. Ibid., p. 347.
17. V.S. Apte, 1988. The Concise English Sanskrit Dictionary. New Delhi: Moti Lal Banarsidass Publishers Pvt. Ltd. pp. 229, 494.

18. B.R. Ambedkar, 1990. *Writing and Speeches,* Vol. 7. (Ed.) Vasant Moon. Mumbai: Education Department, Maharashtra.
19. Ibid., Vol. 5.
20. Quoted from G.S. Ghurye 1990. *Caste and Race in India*. Mumbai: Popular Prakashan. p. 309.
21. Panini, III, I, 134. Quoted from G.S. Ghurye. ibid., p. 311.
22. James Legge, 1991. *The Travels of Fa-Hien*. Delhi: Munshiram Manohar Lal Publisher Pvt. Ltd. p. 43. (First Published in 1886)
23. T. Waters, 1904. *On Yuan-Chaung's Travels in India,* Vols 1 and 2. London: Royal Asiatic Society.
24. G.S. Ghurye, op. cit. p. 313.
25. D. Barbosa, 1970. *A Description of the Coast of East Africa and Malabar in the Beginning of 16th Century*. London: Hakluyt Society. p. 137.
26. *General Census Report 1871–72*. p. 22, 26.
27. *General Census Report 1901*.
28. D.N. Sandanshiv, 1986. *Reservations of Social Justice*. Mumbai: Current Law Publishers. p. 24.
29. M.B. Gautam, 1991. *Bhagyodayam: Maadari Bhagyareddy Varma's Life Sketch and Mission*. Hyderabad: Adi Hindu Social Service League.
30. R.S. Khare, 1984. *The Untouchable as Himself: Ideology Identity and Pragmatism among the Lucknow Chamars*. Cambridge: Cambridge University Press. p. 85.
31. Home Public, A Proceedings, July 1916, Nos 130–131, Extracts from proceedings of the Indian Legislative Council. Letter dated 16 March 1916 Quoted from Atul Chandra Pradhan. 1986. *The Emergence of the Depressed Classes*. Bhubaneswar: Bookland International.
32. Quoted in the Report of the *Indian Franchise Committee,* Vol.1. Para 279. p. 109. 1932.
33. Ibid.
34. Memorandum submitted to the Indian Statutory Commission by Government of India. *ISC* Vol. V, Part II. p. 1353.
35. Op. cit. Vol. I, *Survey*. p. 40.
36. Op. cit.
37. Indian Central Committee, Report. Cmd. 3451, p. 43. Vol. 1 1927.8vo London. HMSO.
38. B.R. Ambedkar, 1990. *What Congress and Gandhi have done to the Untouchables,* Vol. 9, Appendix II. Mumbai: Education Department, Maharashtra.

39. *Indian Statutory Commission Report,* Vol. 1. 1930. Kolkata: Government of India Central Publication Branch. p. 37.
40. *Census Report 1931.*
41. B.R. Ambedkar, 1990. *Writing and Speeches,* Vol. 5. (ed.) Vasant Moon. Mumbai: Education Department, Maharashtra. p. 242.
42. Pattabhi Sitaramayya, 1946–1947.*The History of Indian National Commission,* Vols I and II. Bombay: Padma Publication. See Clause 9 of the Communal Award, op. cit., Appendix VI. p. 657.
43. G.S. Ghurye, op. cit.
44. Reform Office, File No. 20/1935F. Letter from the Government of India to the Secretary of State for India No. 1,075, dated 26 April 1938.
45. Government of India Act 1935, Schedule 1, Part I, Section 26 (I).
46. Reform Office, KW to File No. 27/3/35F.
47. T.K. Oommen, 1994. Panchamas to Dalits: The Context and Content of Identity'. In *The Times of India,* 11 May.
48. James Massey, 1994. *Towards Dalit Hermeneutics: Re-reading the Text, the History and Literature.* Delhi: 1994.
49. Molesworth. 1975. *Marathi-English Dictionary* (Reprint of 1831 edition).
50. P.G. Jogdand, 1991. *Dalit Movement in Maharashtra.* New Delhi: Kanak Publications.
51. E. Zelliot, 2001. *From Untouchable to Dalit: Essays on Ambedkar Movement.* New Delhi: Manohar Publishers & Distributors.
52. Nandu Ram, 1995. *Beyond Ambedkar: Essays on Dalits in India.* New Delhi: Har Anand Publications.

3

The Dalit Profile

An Overview

According to the 2001 Census, the Dalit (scheduled caste, or SC) population in the country was 16.66 crore – 16.23 per cent of the total population. Punjab had the highest percentage of SCs (28.85), followed by Himachal Pradesh (24.7) and West Bengal (23). More than 80 per cent of the Dalit population can be found in ten states. Here is the statewise SC population:

Table 3.1 Distribution of Dalit (Scheduled Caste) Population

State	*Dalit (Scheduled Caste) Population (in Crore)*
Uttar Pradesh	3.52
West Bengal	1.85
Bihar	1.31
Andhra Pradesh	1.23
Tamil Nadu	1.19
Maharashtra	0.99
Rajasthan	0.97
Madhya Pradesh	0.92
Karnataka	0.86
Punjab	0.70
Total	13.54

Source: Annual Report (2008–09), Ministry of Social Justice and Empowerment.

Table 3.2 States and Union Territories in Terms of Percentage of Dalit Population (in Descending Order)

Category in Terms of Percentage of Dalit Population	*S. No.*	*States/UTs*	*Percentage of Dalits in Total Population of State/UT*
>20%	1	Punjab	28.9
	2	Himachal Pradesh	24.7
	3	West Bengal	23.0
	4	Uttar Pradesh	21.2
15–20%	5	Haryana	19.4
	6	Tamil Nadu	19.0
	7	Uttarakhand	17.9
	8	Chandigarh (UT)	17.5
	9	Tripura	17.4
	10	Rajasthan	17.2
	11	NCR of Delhi	16.9
	12	Orissa	16.5
	13	Karnataka	16.2
	14	Andhra Pradesh	16.2
	15	Puducherry (UT)	16.2
	16	Bihar	15.7
	17	Madhya Pradesh	15.2
10–15%	18	Jharkhand	11.8
	19	Chhattisgarh	11.6
	20	Maharashtra	10.2
5–10%	21	Kerala	9.8
	22	Jammu and Kashmir	7.6
	23	Gujarat	7.1
	24	Assam	6.9
	25	Sikkim	5.0
<5%	26	Daman and Diu (UT)	3.1
	27	Manipur	2.6
	28	Goa	1.8
	29	Dadra & Nagar Haveli (UT)	1.9
	30	Arunachal Pradesh	0.6
	31	Meghalaya	0.5
	32	Mizoram	0.03
	33	Nagaland	0.0
	34	Andaman & Nicobar Islands (UT)	0.0
	35	Lakshadweep (UT)	0.0

Source: Annual Report (2008–09), Union Ministry of Social Justice and Empowerment.

Table 3.2 shows that the highest percentage of Dalit (SC) population is in Punjab (28.9). Four states – Punjab, Himachal Pradesh, West Bengal and Uttar Pradesh – have Dalits as more than 20 per cent of their population. Tamil Nadu, Uttarakhand, Tripura, Rajasthan, Orissa, Haryana, the National Capital Region of Delhi and the union territory of Chandigarh all have a higher percentage of Dalit population than the national average of 16.2 per cent. The four North-eastern states of Arunachal Pradesh, Meghalaya, Mizoram and Nagaland, and the Andaman and Nicobar Islands and the Lakshadweep Islands have less than 1 per cent of their population as Dalits. In fact, in Nagaland and the two islands groups, there are no Dalits at all.

Government Schemes for Dalits: An Overview

Since independence, a number of programmes have been implemented for the development of the Dalits (SCs), seeking to empower them educationally, economically and socially.

Educational Empowerment Schemes

Centrally-Sponsored Schemes

(i) Post-Matric Scholarships

The objective of this scheme is to provide financial assistance to SC students at the post-matriculation or post-secondary level to enable them to complete their education.

The financial assistance includes a maintenance allowance, reimbursement of the non-refundable compulsory fees charged by educational institutions, bank facilities and other allowances. The scholarships are available for studying in India only and are awarded by the governments of the states and union territories to which the applicants belong.

(ii) Pre-Matriculation Scholarships for Children of those Engaged in Unclean Occupations

This scheme was started during 1977–78 and is implemented through the state governments. Initially, it covered only children who were in a hostel. In 1991, day scholars were also brought under its purview. There is no income ceiling or caste restriction for eligibility under the scheme. There are special provisions for disabled students from the target group, which includes the children of:

- scavengers of dry latrines;
- sweepers who have traditional links with scavenging;

- tanners;
- flayers; and
- manhole and open drain cleaners.

  The scheme offers financial assistance in two components:
- monthly scholarships (for ten months); and
- annual ad hoc grant (to cover expenses such as stationery and uniforms).

(iii) Babu Jagjivan Ram Chhatrawas Yojana

This scheme provides hostel facilities to SC boys and girls studying in middle and higher secondary schools and colleges and universities.

State governments, union territory governments and central and state universities and institutions are eligible for this central assistance, both for fresh construction of hostel buildings as well as for expansion of existing hostel facilities. NGOs and deemed universities in the private sector can avail of this scheme only for the expansion of their existing facilities.

(iv) Central Assistance for Construction/Expansion of Hostels for Dalits (SCs)

Table 3.3 below shows the pattern of funding available for hostels for both boys and girls:

Table 3.3 Pattern of Funding for Hostels

Institute/Organization	*Boys' Hostels*	*Girls' Hostels*	*Assistance Available*
State government	50% (SG): 50% (CG)	100% (CG)	New construction and expansion of existing hostels
UT administration	100% (CG)		
Central university	90% (CG): 10% (universities)		
State university/institute	45% (SG): 45% (CG): 10% (NGO/deemed university)		
NGO/deemed university	45% (SG): 45% (CG): 10% (NGO/deemed university)	90% (CG): 10% (NGO/deemed university)	Only expansion of existing hostels

SG: state government; CG: central government; NGO: non-government organization

In addition to the admissible central assistance under the scheme, there is also a one-time grant of ₹ 2,500 per student to meet basic furniture needs.

(v) Free Coaching for SCs and OBCs

The objective of this scheme is to provide quality coaching for the Group A and Group B examinations conducted by the Union Public Service Commission (UPSC), State Boards, the Railway Recruitment Board and the State Public Service Commissions as well as the officer's grade examinations conducted by banks, insurance companies and public sector undertakings (PSUs), and finishing courses/job-oriented courses, such as soft skills, for employment in the private sector in fields such as IT and biotechnology.

This scheme is implemented through reputed coaching institutions and centres run by the state governments, UT administrations, universities and private bodies.

(vi) Merit Upgrade of SC Students

The aim of this scheme is to upgrade meritorious SC and ST students by providing them with facilities for their all-round development through education in residential schools. This is proposed to be done by:

- removing their educational deficiencies;
- facilitating their entry into professional courses by upgrading their merit; and
- generating self-confidence and self-reliance in them.

(vii) Target Group: Class 9–12 SC Students

This scheme provides full central assistance to the states and union territories through an annual package grant of ₹ 15,000 per student. Special allowances such as reader's allowance, transport allowance and escort's allowance are given to students with disabilities.

(viii) Rajiv Gandhi National Fellowships

This scheme provides financial assistance to SC students who are pursuing research leading to an MPhil, PhD or equivalent research degree in universities, research institutions and scientific institutions.

The Universities Grants Commission (UGC) is the nodal agency for implementing this scheme. As many as 1,333 research fellowships (junior research fellows) are awarded annually to SC students. If there are not enough SC candidates to avail of the fellowships in a particular year, the fellowships not availed of are carried forward to the next academic session. If the number of candidates exceeds the number of available fellowships, the UGC decides the awards on the basis of the marks of the candidates in their postgraduate examinations.

The sums of money disbursed under the fellowships have been revised upwards in consonance with annual inflationary effects in order to make the fellowship more beneficial.

(ix) Top-Class Education for Meritorious Students

The objective of the scheme is to promote qualitative education amongst SC students by providing full financial support for pursuing studies beyond class 12.

Its salient features are:

- There are 125 institutes of excellence spread all over the country in the list of identified institutes.
- The identified institutes include all the Indian Institutes of Management (IIMs), Indian Institutes of Technology (IITs), National Institutes of Technology (NITs) (earlier known as RECs), commercial pilot training institutes and reputed medical/law and other institutes of excellence.
- All the identified institutes are allotted ten awards/seats each, except the commercial pilot training institutes, which are allotted five awards/seats each.
- The courses of study covered are engineering, medicine/dentistry, law, management and other specialized streams.
- SC students whose total family income is up to ₹ 2 lakh per annum are eligible for the scholarship.

The scholarships include:

- Full tuition fee and other non-refundable charges (there is a ceiling of ₹ 2 lakh per annum per student towards the fees in private institutes and ₹ 3.72 lakh per annum per student in private commercial pilot training institutes);
- Living expenses of ₹ 2,220 per month per student;
- Books and stationery expenses worth ₹ 3,000 per annum per student; and
- Up-to-date computers with all accessories limited to ₹ 45,000 per student as a one time assistance. Living expenses and the cost of books, stationery and computer are subject to actual expenditure.

(x) National Overseas Scholarships

The National Overseas Scholarship is meant to provide assistance to selected SC students for pursuing a Master's degree course or a PhD programme abroad, but only in the specified fields of engineering, technology and science.

The scheme provides for the actual fees charged by the institutions, passage and visa fees, insurance premium, annual contingency allowance and incidental journey allowance. Only one child of a family is eligible to benefit from the scheme. Prospective awardees should not be more than 35 years old.

The rates of the various components of the scholarship have been enhanced. At present, the rate of annual maintenance allowance is US$ 14,000 per student in the US and all other countries, except Britain, where it is £9,000 per student. The annual contingency allowances for books, essential apparatus, study tours and typing and binding of thesis, among other such things, is US$ 1,375 for students in the US and all other countries and £1,000 in Britain. The incidental journey allowance is US$ 17 or its equivalent in rupees. There is also an equipment allowance of ₹ 1,200. The awardees are permitted to undertake research and teaching assistantships. The scheme provides financial assistance for a maximum period of four years for a PhD programme and three years for a Master's programme. The income ceiling from all sources of the employed candidate or his/her parents/guardians has been raised from ₹ 18,000 per month to ₹ 25,000 per month. The number of awards has been increased from 20 to 30 from the selection year 2007–08. As much as 30 per cent of the awards each year have been earmarked for women candidates from the selection year 2007–08. If unutilized by women candidates, the awards become available to male candidates belonging to the SCs, denotified, nomadic and semi-nomadic tribes, landless agricultural labourers and traditional artisans.

Schemes for Economic Empowerment

Centrally-Sponsored Schemes

(i) Special Central Assistance (SCA) to SCs Sub-Plan (SCSP)

The strategy of the Scheduled Castes Sub-Plan (earlier called the Special Component Plan for SCs) was started in 1979. As per the guidelines issued by the Planning Commission in October 2005 and December 2006 to the states and central ministries and departments, they were required to earmark out of their annual plans funds in proportion to the SC population of their state for the implementation of this scheme. The guidelines also mandated that the funds earmarked under the scheme by the states were commensurate with the overall 16.2 per cent share of SCs in the total population. Since this was not the case in most states, following this directive, the percentage of funds earmarked for this purpose has increased from 11.1 per cent in 2004–05 to 15.1 per cent in 2007–08. However, the fund allocation under the SCSP is not yet taking place on the requisite scale in the central ministries.

The Ministry of Social Justice and Empowerment, through a letter of 19 September 2008 to the Ministry of Finance, took up the issue of starting a separate budget head for the SCSP by all central ministries, under which they would show only the funds allocated to the scheme. Accordingly, on 8 December 2008, the Ministry of Finance issued the necessary instructions to the financial advisors of all the central ministries.

The Special Central Assistance (SCA) scheme for the SCSP is a central sector project that was started in 1980. Under the SCA scheme, 100 per cent grants are given to the states and union territories as an additional incentive to implement the SCSP. The main objective is to give a thrust to the economic development of SC families living below the poverty line.

Central assistance under the scheme is released to the states and union territories on the basis of the following criteria:

SC population of states and UTs	40%
Relative backwardness of states and UTs	10%
Percentage of SC families in states and UTs covered by composite economic development programmes in the state plan to enable them to cross the poverty line	25%
Percentage of SCP to the annual plan compared to number of SC population of states and UTs	25%

Following are the salient features of the scheme:

- Funds under the scheme are provided as an additional incentive to states and union territories implementing the SCSP.
- The main thrust is on the economic development of the SC population and to raise them above the poverty line through self-employment or training.
- Amount of subsidy admissible under the scheme is 50 per cent of the project cost, subject to a maximum of ₹ 10,000 per beneficiary.

- Up to 10 per cent of the total funds released to the states and union territories can be utilized for infrastructure development in villages that have an SC population of more than 50 per cent.
- At least 15 per cent of the SCA scheme was to be utilized by the states and the union territories for SC women.

(ii) Assistance to State Scheduled Caste Development Corporations

The centrally-sponsored scheme for participating in the equity share of the Scheduled Castes Development Corporations (SCDCs) in the ratio of 49:51 was introduced in 1979. At present, there are SCDCs functioning in 27 states and union territories.

The main functions of the SCDCs include identification of eligible SC families and motivating them to undertake economic development schemes, getting financial institutions to offer sponsorships and credit support, providing financial assistance in the form of margin money at low cost and providing subsidy to reduce the repayment liability and enabling the necessary tie-ups with other poverty alleviation programmes. The SCDCs are playing an important role in providing credit and inputs by way of margin money loans and subsidies to the target group.

The SCDCs finance employment oriented schemes covering:

- agriculture and allied activities, including minor irrigation;
- small-scale industries;
- transport; and
- trade and services.

The SCDCs finance projects by dovetailing the loan component from the National Scheduled Castes Finance and Development Corporation (NSFDC) and banks along with margin money from their own funds and subsidies from the SCA scheme.

Central Schemes

(i) National Scheduled Castes Finance and Development Corporation

The National Scheduled Castes Finance and Development Corporation (NSFDC) was set up in February 1989 under Section 25 of the Companies Act, 1956. The broad objective of the NSFDC is to provide central financial aid and assistance in the form of concessional loans to all SC families living below the poverty line (2008–09, ₹ 40,000 per annum in rural areas and ₹ 55,000 per annum in urban areas) for their economic development and economic empowerment through various schemes.

The authorized share capital of the NSFDC is ₹ 1,000 crore and the paid-up capital is ₹ 476.80 crore. During 2008–09, ₹ 45 crore was released as equity to it. From 1 April 2004 to 28 February 2009, the NSFDC had disbursed ₹ 737 crore, covering 2.48 lakh beneficiaries.

The NSFDC functions through a channel finance system in which its concessional loans are routed to the beneficiaries through state channelling agencies appointed by the respective state and union territory administrations.

NSFDC schemes are of two types: (a) creadit-based, and (b) non-credit-based.

(a) Credit-based schemes are shown below in Table 3.4:

Table 3.4 NSFDC Credit-based Schemes

Scheme	*Unit Cost*	*Annual Interest Rate Chargeable to*	
		State Channelling Agencies	*Beneficiaries*
Term loan	Up to ₹ 5 lakh	3%	6%
Term loan	Above ₹ 5 lakh and up to ₹ 10 lakh	5%	8%
Term loan	Above ₹ 10 lakh and up to ₹ 20 lakh	6%	9%
Term loan	Above ₹ 20 lakh and up to ₹ 30 lakh	7%	10%
Mahila Kisan Yojana	Up to ₹ 50,000	2%	5%
Micro Credit Yojana	Up to ₹ 30,000	2%	5%
Mahila Samriddhi Yojana	Up to ₹ 30,000	1%	4%

(b) Non-credit-based schemes (e.g., Skill Development Training Programmes): Through its state channelling agencies, the NSFDC sponsors skill development training programmes for educated unemployed youth in the target group in emerging areas such as apparel technology, computer technology, electronic engineering, mobile phone repairs, BPOs/call centres and automobiles repairs. These programmes are conducted by reputed government and semi-government institutions. The trainees are provided free training and a stipend of ₹ 500 per month to meet their incidental expenses. They are also provided placement assistance and entrepreneurial guidance to start their own ventures with concessional finance from the NSFDC and the state channelling agencies. In 2008–09, the total expenditure on skill training programmes was ₹ 1.34 crore, benefiting 1,622 youth.

(ii) National Safai Karamcharis Finance and Development Corporation

The National Commission for Safai Karamcharis Act of 1933 defines a *safai karamchari* as 'a person engaged in, or employed for, manually carrying human excreta or any sanitation work'.

The target groups of the National Safai Karamcharis Finance and Development Corporation (NSKFDC) are scavengers (people wholly or partially employed in manual handling of human excreta, and their dependents) and *safai karamcharis* (people engaged in or employed in any sanitation work, and their dependents).

There is no income limit fixed for availing of this financial assistance. However, the NSKFDC accords priority to the economic development and rehabilitation of scavengers and, amongst scavengers, to those whose income is below the poverty line; women and disabled people among the target group get higher priority.

The authoriszd share capital of the NSKFDC was enhanced from ₹ 200 crore to ₹ 300 crore in February 2009. During 2008–09, ₹ 30 crore was released as equity to it. The paid-up capital of the NSKFDC as on 31 March 2009 was ₹ 230 crore. It implements schemes promoting self-employment or those promoting alternative occupations through concessional finance and skill development schemes. Since its inception, the NSKFDC has disbursed ₹ 445 crore, covering 1.73 lakh beneficiaries.

The NSKFDC schemes are also of two types: (a) credit-based, and (b) non-credit-based.

(a) Credit-based schemes are shown below in Table 3.5:

Table 3.5 NSKFDC Credit-based Schemes

Scheme and Amount of Loan	*Interest Chargeable from*	
	State Channelling Agencies	*Beneficiaries*
Term loans up to ₹ 10 lakh	3%	6%
Educational loans up to ₹ 15 lakh	3%	6%
Micro-credit finance up to ₹ 30,000	2%	5%
Mahila Samridhi Yojana up to ₹ 30,000	1%	4%
Mahila Adhikarita Yojana up to ₹ 50,000	2%	5%
Skills training	100% grants with stipend of ₹ 500 per month	

(b) Non-credit-based schemes (e.g., Skill Development Training Programmes): Skill development training is imparted to eligible members of the target group for self-employment ventures and to improve their employability. Assistance is provided in the form of 100 per cent grants of up to ₹ 1 lakh pre-trade. Apart from providing free training, each candidatc also receives a monthly stipend of ₹ 500.

Social Empowerment Schemes

Centrally-Sponsored Schemes

These schemes offer assistance to states and union territories in implementing the Protection of Civil Rights Act, 1955, and the Scheduled Castes and Scheduled Tribes (Prevention of Atrocities) Act, 1989.

Under these schemes, financial support is provided to the states and union territories by way of:

- strengthening the administrative, enforcement and judicial machinery;
- promoting inter-caste marriages;
- generating awareness; and
- undertaking relief and rehabilitation measures for the benefit of the affected people.

Central Sector Schemes

(i) Central Assistance to Voluntary Organizations Working for the Welfare of SCs

The basic objective of this scheme is to provide grants-in-aid to voluntary organizations to assist them in undertaking projects that will help SC people obtain gainful employment or start income generating activities on their own.

Financial assistance is provided under this scheme to the extent of 90 per cent of the total approved expenditure given to eligible voluntary organizations with a cap of ₹ 10 lakh per project. Projects are funded in 39 different activities, mostly relating to the educational and vocational sectors, such as running mobile dispensaries, residential and non-residential schools, small hospitals and computer training centres. Aid is also provided for paying honorariums and stipends and purchase of books, uniforms, furniture and rent.

(ii) National Awards to NGOs and Human Rights Activists for Outstanding Work in Combating Atrocities and Eradication of Untouchability

In 2006, the Union Ministry of Social Justice and Empowerment instituted four national awards (one for each region) worth ₹ 2 crore for individual activists and worth ₹ 5 lakh for non-governmental organizations, to be given annually for outstanding fieldwork in the area of eradicating untouchability and in combating offences of atrocities under the Protection of Civil Rights Act, 1955, and the Scheduled Castes and Scheduled Tribes (Prevention of Atrocities) Act, 1989.

(iii) National Commissions

(a) National Commission for Scheduled Castes: The National Commission for Scheduled Castes and Scheduled Tribes, instituted under Article 338 of the Constitution in 1980, was bifurcated into two commissions, the National Commission for Scheduled Castes and the National Commission for Scheduled Tribes after the 89th Constitutional (Amendments) Act of 2003.

The National Commission for Scheduled Castes (NCSC) is responsible for monitoring the safeguards provided to the SCs and for reviewing issues concerning their welfare. The functions of the NCSC as enumerated in Article 338 (5) of the Constitution are:

- To investigate and monitor all matters relating to the safeguards provided for the SCs under this Constitution or under any other law for the time being in force or under any order of the government and to evaluate the working of such safeguards.
- To inquire into specific complaints with respect to the deprivation of the rights and safeguards of the SCs.
- To participate and advise on the planning process of socio-economic development of the SCs and to evaluate the progress of their development under the union and any state.
- To present to the President, annually and at such other times as the Commission may deem fit, reports on the working of those safeguards.
- To make in such reports and recommendations as to the measures that should be taken by the Union or any state for the effective implementation of those safeguards and other measures for the protection, welfare and socio-economic development of the SCs.
- To discharge such other functions in relation to the protection, welfare and development and advancement of the SCs as the

President may, subject to the provisions of any law made by Parliament, by rule specify.

The NCSC has wide powers to protect the safeguards and promote the interest of the SCs.

The erstwhile National Commission for Scheduled Castes and Scheduled Tribes (NCSCST) had submitted seven annual reports and four special reports under Clause 6 of Article 338 of the Constitution. All these reports were presented to both Houses of Parliament.

The NCSC has 12 state offices, one each in Agartala, Ahmedabad, Bangalore, Chandigarh, Chennai, Guwahati, Hyderabad, Kolkata, Lucknow, Patna, Pune and Thiruvananthapuram.

(b) National Commission for Safai Karamcharis: The National Commission for Safai Karamcharis Act, 1993, was enacted in September 1993. The Act defines the term, '*safai karamchari*', thus, '*safai karamchari* means a person engaged in or employed for manually carrying human excreta or any sanitation work.'

Section 3 of the Act envisages the establishment of a National Commission for Safai Karamcharis to perform the following functions:

- To recommend to the Centre-specific programmes of action towards the elimination of inequalities in status, facilities and opportunities for *safai karamcharis* under a time-bound action plan.
- To study and evaluate the implementation of the programmes and schemes relating to the social and economic rehabilitation of *safai karamcharis* and make recommendations to the Centre and states for better coordination and implementation of such programmes and schemes.
- To investigate specific grievances and take suo moto notice of matters relating to the non-implementation of
  - — programmes or schemes in respect of any group of karamcharis;
  - — decisions, guidelines or instructions aimed at mitigating the hardship of *safai karamcharis*;
  - — measures for the social and economic uplift of *safai karamcharis;* and
  - — the provisions of any law in its application to *safai karamcharis.*
- Besides, the commission also
  - — takes up such matters with the authorities concerned or with the central or state governments;

— makes periodical reports to the Centre and states on any matter concerning *safai karamcharis*, taking into account any difficulties or disabilities encountered by them; and
— looks into any other matter which may be referred to it by the Centre.

The National Commission for Safai Karamcharis was first constituted as a statutory body in August 1994. After that, the tenure of the Commission was extended as a non-statutory body through resolutions from time to time. So far, the Commission has submitted seven reports and the action taken memoranda thereon have been placed before parliament.

(iv) Foundations

(a) Dr Ambedkar Foundation: The main objective of the Dr Ambedkar Foundation is the implementation of programmes and activities that further the ideology and message of Dr B.R. Ambedkar among the masses both within the country as well as abroad. The Foundation has been entrusted with the responsibility of managing, administering and carrying out the long-term schemes and programmes identified during the centenary celebrations of Dr Ambedkar.

The general body is the supreme body of the Dr Ambedkar Foundation. It is headed by the union minister for social justice and empowerment. There are 11 ex-officio members representing the disciplines of education, social work and administration, and 32 members nominated by the Ministry of Social Justice and Empowerment from among eminent members of society such as social workers, educationists and journalists.

- *Dr Ambedkar Chair:* To propagate the ideology and philosophy of Dr Ambedkar and carry out research work on Ambedkar, ten Dr Ambedkar chairs have been instituted in thrust areas such as the legal system, education, social change and development, social policy and social action, social work, sociology, economics, anthropology, the Dalit movement and its history, Ambedkarism and social change and social justice at various universities/institutions. The yearly grant to each chair is ₹ 10 lakh.
- *Dr Ambedkar Samajik Samta Kendra Yojna:* This scheme envisages the construction of Ambedkar community centres, research centres and libraries. The Ambedkar Foundation provides financial assistance to these projects according to the classification of the cities in which they are being set up.

- Publication of a monthly magazine, *Samajik Nyay Sandesh*.
- *Dr Ambedkar Medical Aid Scheme:* This scheme envisages assistance to SC patients, whose annual family income is less than ₹ 50,000 and who require surgical operations for life-threatening ailments in the kidneys, heart or liver, cancer or any other serious diseases, including knee and spinal surgeries. This scheme was revised recently to make it more broad based in terms of the hospitals and diseases covered under it. In addition to the local member of Parliament, now, district magistrates, collectors, deputy commissioners of districts and health and social welfare secretaries of states and union territories can also recommend cases for medical assistance. The medical aid now stands increased to ₹ 1 lakh from ₹ 75,000 and 50 per cent is given before the surgery.
- Celebration/Observation of Dr Ambedkar's birth anniversary/ Mahaparinirvan Diwas of Dr Ambedkar.
- *Collected Works of Ambedkar:* Dr Ambedkar's writings have been translated into nine languages, Hindi, Malayalam, Tamil, Telugu, Bengali, Oriya, Punjabi, Urdu and Gujarati.
- *Dr Ambedkar National Merit Scholarship Scheme for Secondary Examination:* The Ambedkar Foundation offers merit scholarships to recognize, promote and assist meritorious SC and ST students who wish to pursue higher studies. The scheme provides a one-time cash award. There are four awards for each of the 29 boards for SCs and STs. The scheme also offers 250 special merit scholarships of ₹ 10,000 each to SC and ST students as one-time grant as under:
    - students securing the highest marks: ₹ 60,000;
    - students securing second position: ₹ 50,000;
    - students securing third position: ₹ 40,000; and
    - girl students securing the highest marks, if they do not fall in the above three categories: ₹ 40,000.
- *Dr Ambedkar National Scholarship Scheme for Meritorious Students of the Scheduled Castes in the Higher Secondary Examination:* The Ambedkar Foundation formulated a scheme during 2007–08 for merit scholarships to recognize, promote and assist meritorious SC students pursuing higher studies at the senior secondary level.

  SC students whose family income from all sources is ₹ 1 lakh or less in the preceding financial year are eligible for the scholarship.

The students should have appeared in any of the recognized state or Central Board of Secondary Education (CBSE) exams and scored not less than an aggregate of 50 per cent marks.
The scholarships (₹ 60,000, ₹ 50,000 and ₹ 40,000) are awarded to the three students scoring the highest marks in the regular Class 12 examination conducted by the relevant education board or council in three streams, arts, science (maths and biology) and commerce. After these first three positions of merit, the next three girl students securing the highest marks in each stream will be given a special scholarship of ₹ 20,000 each. There are 12 awards for each of the 29 boards.

- *Dr Ambedkar National Relief Scheme for SC Victims of Atrocities:* The scheme is in the nature of a contingency arrangement to provide instant monetary relief to the victims of heinous offences under the Scheduled Castes and Scheduled Tribes (Prevention of Atrocities) Act, 1989. The relief amount is provided directly to the victims or their family members or dependents by the Dr Ambedkar Foundation once an FIR is lodged under the Act and after being apprised of the fact by the respective state or union territory administration. Up to ₹ 2 lakh is paid to each victim with the approval of the union minister (Ministry of Social Justice and Empowerment) and the chairperson of the Dr Ambedkar Foundation. During 2008–09, ₹ 11.25 lakh were given as financial aid to eight victims of atrocities in Madhya Pradesh, Uttar Pradesh and Rajasthan.

(b) Babu Jagjivan Ram National Foundation: Another national foundation – Babu Jagjivan Ram National Foundation – was established in the memory of Jagjivan Ram (Dalit leader) in order to propagate his ideology, philosophy and mission and to carry forward more widely the services he rendered to the underprivileged and the nation.

The Foundation, which is based in New Delhi, functions as an autonomous body under the Union Ministry of Social Justice and Empowerment. It is registered as a society under the Societies Registration Act, 1860, with a one time corpus grant of ₹ 50 crore. An additional ₹ 4 crore was provided to start the Foundation's activities and meet initial establishment costs. The union minister for social justice and empowerment is the chairperson of the governing body of the Foundation.

The salient features and objectives of the Foundation are:

- To propagate the ideology, philosophy and mission of Jagjivan Ram;
- To collect, acquire, maintain and preserve the personal papers of Jagjivan Ram and other historical material pertaining to him;

- To encourage and promote study and research on his life and work;
- To publish, sell and distribute books, papers, pamphlets and information in pursuance of the objectives of the Foundation;
- To acquire, preserve and protect places connected with him and raise memorials to him;
- To propagate his ideals and memory through the print and electronic media by promoting Dalit artists, who do not have such opportunities;
- To encourage and promote Dalit artists through specially designed developmental schemes for their social, cultural, educational and economic development;
- To implement special schemes for the eradication of untouchability and caste-based prejudice in society;
- To undertake and implement the various schemes and programmes assigned from time to time by the central and state governments;
- To organize the birth and death anniversaries and other commemorative events of the life of Jagjivan Ram; and
- To undertake all such activities that are not specially mentioned in the aims and objectives listed above, but which promote these objectives.

On 5 April 2008, a Sarva Dharam Prarthana Sabha was organized at Samta Sthal, the *samadhi* of Babu Jagjivan Ram in New Delhi, to commemorate the leader's birth centenary. The meet was attended by the vice-president of India, the prime minister, the Congress president and several dignitaries and social activists.

The closing ceremony was held at the Balayogi Auditorium in the Parliament Annexe, where the keynote address was delivered by the President of India, while the Prime Minister was the chief guest.

On 6 July 2008, the death anniversary of Jagjivan Ram, another Sarva Dharam Prarthana Sabha was organized at Samta Sthal, which was attended by the Prime Minister and other prominent dignitaries.

On 7 July 2008, a third Sarva Dharam Prarthana Sabha was organized at the birthplace of Jagjivan Ram, Chandwa in Arrah district, Bihar.

A programme to set up a Babu Jagjivan Ram Chair in various universities has been initiated.

(v) Reservation in Education and Employment

(a) Reservation in Education: The Central Education Institute (CEI) (Reservation in Admission) Act, 2006, came into effect from the academic session of 2008–09. The Act provides for the reservation of 15 per cent seats for SC students, 7.5 per cent seats for ST students and 27 per cent seats for other backward classes (OBCs), excluding the creamy layer, in central educational institutions (other than those exempted under Section 4 of the Act).

(b) Reservation in Employment: Instructions were issued by the Union Ministry of Home Affairs on 21 September 1947, providing for 12.5 per cent reservation in direct recruitments made by open competition and 16.66 per cent in the open competition category for SC candidates. With the increase in the percentage of the SC population, the need has been felt to increase the reach of such reservations. According to the 1961 Census, the percentage of SC population was 14.7 per cent. Accordingly, on 25 March 1970, the percentage of reservation for SCs in direct recruitment in the open competition category was increased from 12.5 per cent to 15 per cent. But, the percentage of reservation in direct recruitment other than by open competition was kept unchanged at 16.66 per cent. The percentage of reservation for SCs and STs in public sector employment has remained unchanged since then. The reservation policy was extended mutatis mutandis to central public sector enterprises too.

Improvement in Certain Key SC Indicators

Impact on Targeted People

Though the SCs continue to lag behind the general population in terms of most socio-economic indicators, the gap between them and the general population is reducing slowly, as is evident from the following discussion:

Increase in Literacy

The literacy data available from the decennial censuses indicate that the gap between the SCs and general population has shrunk. During the decade between 1991 and 2001, literacy levels among the SCs increased by 17.28 percentage points as compared to 12.79 percentage points among the total population. The more remarkable increase has been in female literacy among the SCs. Nevertheless, low levels of literacy among rural SC women remain a cause of concern.

Table 3.6 Literacy Percentage of Total Population and Dalit Population in 1991 and 2001

Census Year	*Total*			*Dalits (Scheduled Castes)*		
	Male	*Female*	*Total*	*Male*	*Female*	*Total*
1991	64.13	39.29	52.21	49.91	23.76	37.41
2001	75.00	54.00	65.00	66.64	41.90	54.69

Source: Census of India, 1991 and 2001, RGI, New Delhi.

Decrease in Poverty

The poverty ratio among the SCs has declined during the period between 1999–2000 and 2004–05. However, the pace of decline has been slower than the decline in the overall poverty numbers. More than one-third of the SC population, both in rural and urban areas, are still living below the poverty line. The poverty gap between the SCs and the total population has shrunk between 1999–2000 and 2004–05.

Table 3.7 Percentage of BPL Population by Type of Residence, General and Dalits in 1999–2000 and 2004–05

Category	*1999–2000*		*2004–05*		*% Decline (1999–2000 to 2004–05)*	
	Rural	*Urban*	*Rural*	*Urban*	*Rural*	*Urban*
Total*	27.09	23.62	28.30	25.70	–1.21	–2.08
SC	36.25	38.47	36.80	39.90	–0.55	–1.43
Gap	9.16	14.85	8.50	14.20	–0.66	–0.65

* Includes SC population.

Source: Planning Commission.

Occupational Mobility

There are indications of occupational diversification taking place among the SCs. As per the 2001 Census, the dependence of the SCs on agriculture declined from 74.50 per cent in 1991 to 61.24 per cent in 2001. More importantly, the share of agricultural labourers among them came down significantly from 49.06 per cent to 39.16 per cent during the same period. The decline in dependence on agriculture was accompanied by an almost commensurate increase in the other workers' category, which is predominantly in the services sector.

Table 3.8 Occupational Diversification among Dalits

(in percentage)

Category	*Total*		*Dalits (Scheduled Castes)*	
	1991	*2001*	*1991*	*2001*
Cultivators	39.74	33.11	25.44	22.08
Agricultural Labourers	19.66	20.29	49.06	39.16
Household Industry	02.56	03.90	02.41	03.71
Other workers	38.04	42.70	23.08	35.05

Source: Census of India, 1991 and 2001, RGI, New Delhi.

The sad fact, however, is that despite the number of developmental programmes initiated for the amelioration of the SCs, most of them are still to taste the fruits of development even after so many years of independence.

Reference

Annual Report 2008–09. New Delhi: Union Ministry of Social Justice and Empowerment.

4

Constitutional Safeguards for Dalits

Only in 1950 did Indian society enter into a covenant with itself to be secular, democratic and egalitarian, to rid itself of its highly rigid, caste-based, hierarchical structure with the ascending rigidity of privileges and descending order of disabilities that had been in practice for some three millennia. The overwhelming majority of Indian society had been subjected to various kinds of social discrimination, economic deprivation and total powerlessness through the ages. The victims of this entrenched backwardness broadly comprise the present scheduled castes (SCs), scheduled tribes (STs) and other backward castes (OBCs).

Though all these categories are collectively known by the generic term, backward classes, the nature and magnitude of their backwardness are not the same. The Dalits (SCs) and STs are the most backward of these groups.

The learned men who framed the Indian Constitution considered it necessary to make special provisions to enable these deprived segments of people to join the mainstream by providing for their equitable share in the governance process through a policy of reservations in elected bodies, public services and education, protection against social and economic exploitation, and enhanced and specific financial allocation for expediting their socio-economic development. This chapter deals with the definition of the legal and administrative concepts of SCs and their constitutional safeguards.

Definition and Specification of Scheduled Castes

Definition of Scheduled Castes

The SCs are defined in Article 366 (24) of the Constitution as 'such castes, races or tribes or parts or groups within such castes, races or tribes as are deemed under Article 341 to be Scheduled Castes for the purpose of the Constitution'.

Specification of a Caste as a Scheduled Caste

Article 341 deals with the specifications of a caste as a scheduled caste and reads as under:

Article 341 Scheduled Castes

1. The President may with respect to any State or Union Territory and where it is a State after consultation with the Governor thereof, by public notification, specify the castes, races or tribes or parts or groups within castes, races or tribes which shall for the purpose of this Constitution be deemed to be SCs in relation to that State or Union Territory, as the case may be.
2. Parliament may by law include in or exclude from the list of SCs specified in a notification issued under the clause: (i) any caste, race or tribes or part of or group within any caste, race or tribes, but save as aforesaid a notification issued under the said clause shall not be varied by any subsequent notification.'

So far, six constitutional orders have been issued, specifying SCs in 26 states and five union territories:

- The Constitution (Scheduled Castes) Order, 1950.
- The Constitution Union Territories Scheduled Castes Order, 1951.
- The Constitution (Jammu and Kashmir) Scheduled Castes Order, 1956.
- The Constitution (Dadar and Nagar Haveli) Scheduled Castes Order, 1962.
- The Constitution (Pondicherry) Scheduled Castes Order, 1964.
- The Constitution (Sikkim) Scheduled Castes Order, 1978.

These constitutional orders have been amended by Acts of Parliament from time to time, the last being in 2007. A total of 1,208 castes have so far been specified as meeting the scheduled castes criteria and procedures for specifying a caste as a scheduled caste.

The criteria followed for inclusion of a community in the SC list is extreme social, educational and economic backwardness, arising out of the traditional practice of untouchability.

The government laid down detailed procedures (modalities) for deciding claims for inclusion, exclusion and modifications in the list of SCs and STs in June 1999 (subsequently modified in June 2002), which involves the following steps:

- The proposal is first recommended by the state or union territory administration.
- The proposal is then recommended by the Registrar General of India (RGI).
- The proposal is then further required to be recommended by the National Commission for Scheduled Castes.
- After the proposal is recommended by the above agencies, it is placed before the union cabinet.
- After the government approves it, the proposal is put up in the form of a bill in parliament for consideration and passing.
- After the bill becomes an Act, necessary amendments are carried out in the orders specifying the list of SCs.
- In the case of claims recommended by a state or union territory administration, but not agreed to by the Registrar General of India, the concerned state or union territory administration is asked to review and further justify its recommendations in the light of the Registrar General's comments. On receipt of further clarification from the state or union territory administration, the proposals are referred to the Registrar General for comments. If the Registrar General does not agree in the second round, too, the proposal is rejected at the level of the union ministry.
- Cases on which the state or union territory government and the Registrar General are in agreement, but which the Commission does not support, are rejected by the union ministry.

The Directive Principles of State Policy

Part IV of the Constitution contains the Directive Principles of State Policy. It is the duty of the state to follow these principles both in the matter of administration as well as in the making of laws. Most of the Directive Principles aim at the establishment of the economic and social democracy which is pledged in the preamble to the Constitution.

Article 38 provides that the state will secure a social order for the promotion of welfare of the people:

(i) The state strives to promote the welfare of the people by securing and protecting as effectively as it may a social order in which justice – social, economic and political – shall inform all the institutions of national life.

(ii) The state shall, in particular, strive to minimize the inequalities in income and endeavour to eliminate inequalities in status, facilities and opportunities, not only amongst individuals but also amongst groups of people residing in different areas or engaged in different vocations.

Article 46 says that 'the state shall promote with special care the educational and economic interests of the weaker sections of the people, and in particular of the Scheduled Castes and Scheduled Tribes, and shall protect them from social injustice and all forms of exploitation'.

Fundamental Rights

Part III of the Constitution contains the Fundamental Rights.

The Fundamental Rights, laid down in Article 16 (4), empower the state to make any provisions for reservations in appointments or posts in favour of any backward classes, which, in its opinion, is not adequately represented in the services under the state.

Article 16 (4A) specifies that nothing shall prevent the state from making any provisions for reservation in matters of promotion to any class or classes of posts in the services under the state in favour of the SCs and STs, which, in the opinion of the state, are not adequately represented in the services under the state.

Article 16 (4B) specifies that nothing shall prevent the state from considering unfilled vacancies of a year, which are reserved for being filled up in that year in accordance with any provisions for reservation made under Clause (4) or Clause (4A) as a separate class of vacancies to be filled up in any succeeding years and such class of vacancies shall not be considered together with the vacancies of the year in which they are being filled up for determining the ceiling of 50 per cent reservation on total number of vacancies of the year.

Article 14 deals with equality before law and states that the state shall not deny to any person equality before the law or equal protection of the laws within the territory of the country.

Article 15 prohibits discrimination against any citizen on grounds only of religion, race, caste, sex and place of birth:

(a) The state shall not discriminate against any citizen on grounds only of religion, race, caste, sex, place of birth or any of them.
(b) No citizen shall, on grounds only of religion, race, caste, sex, place of birth or any of them, be subject to any disability, liability, restriction or condition with regard to
    (i) access to shops, public restaurants, hotels and places of public entertainment; or
    (ii) use of wells, tanks, bathing *ghats*, roads and places of public resort maintained wholly or partly out of state funds or dedicated to the use of the general public.
(c) Nothing in this Article shall prevent the state from making any special provision for women and children.
(d) Nothing in this Article or in Clause (2) or Article 29 shall prevent the state from making any special provision for the advancement of any socially and educationally backward classes of citizens or for the SCs and STs.

Article 17 abolishes untouchability and its practice in any form is forbidden. The enforcement of any disability arising out of untouchability shall be an offence punishable in accordance with law.

Article 23 prohibits traffic in human beings and begging and other similar forms of forced labour and provides that any contravention of this provision shall be an offence punishable in accordance with the law. It does not specifically mention SCs and STs, but since the majority of bonded labourers belong to SCs and STs, this provision has special significance for them.

Article 24 provides that no child below 14 years shall be employed to work in any factory or mine or engaged in any other hazardous employment. There are central and state laws to prevent child labour. Since a substantial portion of the child labour engaged in hazardous employment belong to SCs and STs, this provision is also significant for the SCs and STs.

Article 29 (1) provides that any section of the citizens in the territory of India or any part thereof having a distinct language, script or culture of its own shall have the right to conserve the same. This provision has special significance for the STs as many of them have distinct languages.

Article 29 (2) says that no citizen shall be denied admission into any educational institutions maintained by the state or receiving aid out of state funds on grounds of religion, race, caste, language or any of them. This provision is relevant for the SCs and STs because some institutions have denied admission to these groups in the past.

Article 25 (2)(b) provides that Hindu religious institutions of a public character shall be open to all classes and sections of Hindus. The term, Hindu, includes people professing the Sikh, Jain and Buddhist faiths. This provision is relevant as some sects of Hindus claim that the SCs and STs have no right to enter their temples.

Other Constitutional Provisions

Article 164 (1) provides that in Bihar, Madhya Pradesh and Orissa, there will be a minister in charge of tribal welfare, who may, in addition, be in charge of the welfare of the SCs, the other backward castes (OBCs) or any others. With the creation of the states of Jharkhand and Chhattisgarh, both of which have high concentration of tribals, Article 164 (1) needs to be amended.

Article 243 (D), which came into existence with the 73rd Constitution Amendment Act, 1992, provides that

(a) seats shall be reserved for
   - (i) the Scheduled Castes, and
   - (ii) the Scheduled Tribes.
   - (iii) In every panchayat and the number of seats so reserved shall bear, as nearly as may be, the same proportion to the total number of seats to be filled by direct election in that panchayat as the SC population in that panchayat area or of the STs in that panchayat area bears to the total population of that area and such seats may be allotted by rotation to different constituencies in a panchayat.
   - (iv) Not less than one-third of the total number of seats reserved under Clause (1) shall be reserved for women belonging to the SCs or, as the case may be, to the STs.
   - (v) Not less than one-third (including the number of seats reserved for women belonging to the SCs and STs) of the total number of seats to be filled by direct election in every panchayat shall be reserved for women and such seats may be allotted by rotation to different constituencies in a panchayat.
   - (vi) The offices of the chairpersons in the panchayat reserved at the village or any other level shall be reserved for the SCs, STs and women in such manner as the legislature of a state may, by law, provide:

     provided that the number of offices of chairpersons reserved for the SCs and STs in the panchayats at each level in any state shall bear, as nearly as may be, the same proportion to the total number of such offices in the panchayats at each level as the population of the SCs in the state or of the STs in the state bears to the total population of the state;

provided further that not less than one-third of the total number of offices of chairpersons in panchayats at each level shall be reserved for women;

provided also that the number of offices reserved under this clause shall be allotted by rotation to different panchayats at each level.

Similarly, *Article 243 (T)* provides for the reservation of seats:

(a) Seats shall be reserved for the SCs and STs in every municipality and the number of seats so reserved shall bear, as nearly as may be, the same proportion to the total number of seats to be filled by direct election in that municipality as the population of the SCs in the municipal area bears to the total population of that area and such seats may be allotted by rotation to different constituencies in a municipality.

(b) Not less than one-third of the total number of seats reserved under Clause (1) shall be reserved for SC women or ST women.

(c) Not less than one-third (including the number of seats reserved for women belonging to the SCs and STs) of the total number of seats to be filled by direct election in every municipality shall be reserved for women and such seats may be allotted by the rotation of different constituencies in a municipality.

(d) The offices of chairpersons in the municipalities shall be reserved for the SCs, STs and women in such manner as the legislature of a state may, by law, provide.

(e) The reservation of seats under Clauses (1) and (2) and the reservation of offices of chairperson (other than the reservation for women) under Clause (4) shall cease to have effect on the expiration of the period specified in Article 334.

(f) Nothing in this part shall prevent the legislature of a state from making any provisions for reservation of seats in any municipality or effects of chairperson in favour of backward classes of citizens.

Soon after independence, it was found that there had been large alienation of tribal lands to non-tribals for paltry sums of money. Thus, the tribals faced severe problems of land alienation. The Constitution-makers foresaw these difficulties and made special provisions regarding the governance of tribal affairs and tribal lands.

The Fifth Schedule of the Constitution under *Article 244* provides for legislation for the special problems of scheduled areas.

Article 244 lays down that

(a) the provisions of the Fifth Schedule shall apply to the administration and control of the scheduled areas and scheduled tribes in any state other than in Assam, Meghalaya, Tripura and Mizoram; and

(b) the provisions of the Sixth Schedule shall apply to the administration of the tribal areas in Assam, Meghalaya, Tripura and Mizoram.

The Fifth Schedule contains provisions regarding administration and control of the scheduled areas and scheduled tribes. Eight states of India have scheduled areas: Andhra Pradesh, Bihar, Gujarat, Himachal Pradesh, Madhya Pradesh, Maharashtra, Orissa and Rajasthan. All these states have Tribes Advisory Councils and the governors of these states have special responsibilities and powers.

The Fifth Schedule, under Article 244 (1), provides special provisions for legislation for the special problems of scheduled areas. Para (5) of the Schedule authorizes the governor to direct by public notification that any particular Act of Parliament or of the Legislative Assembly of the state shall not apply to the scheduled area or any part thereof or shall apply to the said area, subject to such exceptions and modifications as he may specify. Para 5 (2) authorizes the governor to make regulations for peace and good government in the scheduled areas of the state in particular in respect of matters specified therein. The exact version of the law applicable to scheduled areas is:

(a) Notwithstanding anything in this Constitution, the governor may by public notification direct that any particular Act of Parliament or of the legislature of the state shall not apply to a scheduled area or any part thereof in the state, subject to such exceptions and modifications as he may specify in the notification and any direction given under this sub-paragraph may be so as to have retrospective effect.

(b) The governor may make regulations for the peace and good government of any area in a state, which is for the time being a scheduled area. In particular and without prejudice to the generality of the foregoing power, such regulations may

   (i) prohibit or restrict the transfer of land by or among members of STs in such areas;

(ii) regulate the allotment of land to members of the STs in such area;

(iii) regulate the carrying on of business as money-lender by persons who lend money to members of the STs in such area.

(c) In making many such regulations as is referred to in sub-paragraph (2) of this paragraph, the governor may repeal or amend any Act of Parliament or of the Legislature of the state or any existing law, which is for the time being applicable to the area in question.

(d) All regulations made under this paragraph shall be submitted forthwith to the President and, until assented to by him/her, shall have no effect.

(e) No regulations shall be made under this paragraph unless the governor making the regulations has, in the case where there is a Tribes Advisory Council for the state, consulted such council.

In addition to the above-mentioned eight states, Tamil Nadu and West Bengal, which do not have any scheduled areas, also have the statutory Tribes Advisory Councils.

Article 275 (1) provides that such sums as parliament may by law provide shall be charged on the Consolidated Fund of India in each area as grants-in-aid of the revenues of such states as parliament may determine to be in need of assistance, and different sums may be fixed for different states.

Provided that these shall be paid out of the Consolidated Fund of India as grants-in-aid of the revenues of state, such capital and recurring sums as may be necessary to enable that state to meet the costs of such schemes of the development as may be undertaken by the state with the approval of the government for the purpose of promoting the welfare of the Scheduled Tribes in that state or raising the level of administration of the rest of the areas of that state.

A similar provision exists in this Article for paying such special grants to the states covered under the Sixth Schedule from the Consolidated Fund of India. The Sixth Schedule contains the provisions relating to the administration of the tribal areas in Assam (North Cachar Hills district). There are autonomous district councils and autonomous regional councils in these areas, which have a long tradition of self-management systems. These autonomous councils not only administer the various departments and their development programmes, but they also have the power to make laws on a variety of subjects, as, for example, land, forest, shifting cultivation, village and town administration, including village and town police, public health and sanitation, inheritance of property, marriage and divorce and social customs.

Article 330 provides for reservation of seats for the SCs and STs in the House of the People:

1. Seats shall be reserved in the House of the People for:
   (a) the Scheduled Castes,
   (b) the Scheduled Tribes, except the Scheduled Tribes in the autonomous districts of Assam, and
   (c) the Scheduled Tribes in the autonomous district of Assam.

The number of seats reserved in any state or union territory for the SCs and STs under Clause (1) shall bear, as nearly as may be, the same proportion to the total number of seats allotted to that state or union territory or part of the state or union territory, as the case may be, in respect of which seats are so reserved, bears to the total population of the state or union territory.

Article 332 provides for reservation of seats for SCs and STs in the state assemblies:

1. Seats shall be reserved for the SCs and STs, except those STs in the autonomous districts of Assam, in every state assembly.
2. Seats shall be reserved also for the autonomous districts in the Assam assembly.
3. The number of seats reserved for the SCs and STs in any state assembly under Clause (1) shall bear, as nearly as may be, the same proportion to the total number of seats in the assembly as the population of the SCs in any state or of the STs in the state or part of the state, as the case may be, in respect of which seats are so reserved, bears to the total population of the state.

3A. Notwithstanding anything contained in Clause (3), until taking effect under Article 170 of the readjustment, on the basis of the first census after 2000, of the number of seats in the state assemblies of Arunachal Pradesh, Meghalaya, Mizoram and Nagaland, the seats which shall be reserved for the STs in the assembly of these states shall be:
   (a) If all the seats in the assembly of such state in existence on the date of coming into force of the 57th Constitution Amendment Act of 1987 (hereafter in this clause referred to as the existing assembly) are held by members of the STs, all the seats except one,

(b) In any other case, such number of seats as bearing to the total number of seats, a proportion not less than the number (as on the said date) of ST members in the existing assembly bears to the total number of seats in the existing assembly.

3B. Notwithstanding anything contained in Clause (3), until the readjustment, under Article 170, takes effect on the basis of the first census after 2000 of the number of seats in the assembly of Tripura, the seats which shall be reserved for the STs in the assembly shall be, such number of seats as bears to the total number of seats, a proportion not less than the number, as on the date of coming into force of the 72nd Constitution Amendment Act, 1992, of ST members in the assembly in existence of the said date bears to the total number of seats in that assembly.

(1) The number of seats reserved for an autonomous district in the Assam assembly shall bear to the total number of seats in that assembly a proportion not less that the population of the state.

(2) The constituencies for the seats reserved for any autonomous district of Assam shall not comprise any area outside that district.

(3) No person who is not a member of a Scheduled Tribe of any autonomous district of Assam shall be eligible for election to the assembly from any constituency of that district.

Article 334 provides for reservation of seats and special representation to end the foregoing provisions:

(a) the reservation of seats for the SCs and STs in the House of the People and in the state assemblies; and

(b) the representation of the Anglo-Indian community in the House of the People and in state assemblies by nomination shall cease to have effect on the expiration of 70 years from the commencement of this Constitution. This reservation has been extended by amending the Constitutions every ten years. The provision of reservation in the Lok Sabha and state assembles has been extended to all 2020.

Provided that nothing in this Article shall affect any representation in the House of the People or in any state assembly until the dissolution of the then existing house or assembly, as the case may be.

Article 335 deals with the claims of the STs and SCs to public sector services. Accordingly, the claims of the SC and ST members shall be taken into consideration constantly with the maintenance of the efficiency of administration, in the making of appointments to services and posts in connection with the affairs of the Union or of the state. The Department of Personnel and Training, vide OM No. 36012/23/96–Estt. (RES) dated 22 July 1997, withdrew instructions issued for providing lower qualifying marks for promotion for SC and ST candidates in response to a Supreme Court judgment in the case of *S. Vinod Kumar vs Union of India*. Parliament, vide the 82nd Constitution Amendment Act in 2000, amended the provisions contained in Article 335 and inserted the following provision: 'Provided that nothing in this Article shall prevent in making of any provisions in favour of the members of the Scheduled Castes and Scheduled Tribes for relaxation in qualifying marks in any examination or lowering the standards of evaluation for reservation in matters of promotion to any class or classes of services or posts in connection with the affairs of the Union or of a state.'

What people constitute the SCs and STs is defined in Articles 366 (24) and 366 (25). How these people are identified and decided is contained in Articles 341 and 342.

Article 366 (24) defines the SCs as those castes, races or tribes or parts of or groups within such castes, races or tribes as are deemed under Article 342 to be SCs for the purposes of this Constitution.

Article 366 (25) defines STs as those tribes or tribal communities as are deemed under Article 342 to be STs for the purposes of this Constitution.

Article 341 provides that:

1. The President may with respect to any state or union territory, and where it is a state after consultation with the governor thereof, by public notification, specify the castes, races or tribes which shall for the purposes of this Constitution be deemed to be SCs in relation to that state or union territory, as the case may be.
2. Parliament may by law include in or exclude from the list of SCs specified in a notification issued under Clause (1) any caste, race or tribe, but save as aforesaid, a notification issued under the said clause shall not be varied by any subsequent notification.

Article 342 provides:

1. The President may with respect to any state or union territory, and where it is a state, after consultation with the governor thereof, by public notification, specify the tribes or tribal communities, which shall for the purposes of this Constitution be deemed to be STs in relation to that state or union territory, as the case may be.

2. Parliament may by law include in or exclude from the list of Scheduled Tribes specified in a notification issued under Clause (1) any tribe or tribal community or part of or group within any tribe or tribal community, but save as aforesaid, a notification issued under the said clause shall not be varied by any subsequent notification.

Article 338 provides for a National Commission for Scheduled Castes (NCSC):

1. The Commission shall consist of a chairperson, vice-chairperson and other members so appointed shall be such as the President may by rule determine.
2. The chairperson, vice-chairperson and other members of the Commission shall be appointed by the President by warrant under his hand and seal.
3. The Commission shall have the powers to regulate its own procedures.
4. It shall be the duty of the Commission to:
    (a) investigate and monitor all matters relating to the safeguards provided for the SCs under this Constitution or under any other law for the time being in force or under any order of the government and to evaluate the working of such safeguards;
    (b) inquire into specific complaints with respect to the deprivation of rights and safeguards of the SCs;
    (c) participate and advise on the planning process of the socio-economic development of the SCs and to evaluate the progress of their development;
    (d) present to the President, annually and at such other times as the Commission may deem fit, reports upon the working of those safeguards;
    (e) make in such reports recommendations as to the measures that should be taken by the Union or any state for the effective implementation of those safeguards and other measures for the protection, welfare and socio-economic development of the SCs and STs, and to discharge such other functions in relation to the protection, welfare and development and advancement of the SCs;
    (f) the President shall cause all such reports to be laid before each House of Parliament along with a memorandum explaining the action taken or proposed to be taken on the recommendation relating to the Union and the reasons for the non-acceptance, if any, of any of such recommendations; and

(g) where any such report, or any part thereof, relates to any matter with which any state government is concerned, a copy of such report shall be forwarded to the state governor who shall cause it to be laid before the legislature along with a memorandum explaining the action taken or proposed to be taken on the recommendations relating to the state and the reasons for the non-acceptance, if any, of any of such recommendations.

The Commission shall, while investigating any matter referred to in sub-clause (a) or inquiring into any complaint referred to in sub-clause (b) of Clause (5), have all the powers of a civil court trying a suit and in particular in respect of the following matters, namely:

(i) summoning and enforcing the attendance of any person from any part of the country and examining him or with;
(ii) requiring the discovery and production of any documents;
(iii) receiving evidence on affidavits;
(iv) requisitioning any public or copy thereof from any court or office; and
(v) issuing commissioning for the examination of witnesses and documents.

Thus, the Union and every state shall consult the Commission on all major policy matters affecting the SCs. In Article 338, references to the SCs shall be construed as including references to such other backward classes as the President may, on receipt of the report of the Commission, appoint under Clause (1) of Article 340 by order specify and also to the Anglo-Indian community.

References

Bakshi, P.M. *The Constitution of India.* India: Universal Law Publishing House.

Broken People. 1999. New York, NY: Human Rights Watch.

National Commission for Scheduled Castes and Scheduled Tribes, Sixth Report, 1999–2000 and 2000–01.

Sharma, G.S. 1975. *Legislation and Cases on Untouchability and Scheduled Castes in India*. Bombay: Allied Publishers.

5

Systematic Exclusion of Dalits

The Dalits, or the Scheduled Castes (SCs), constitute one of the most disadvantaged groups in Indian society. They are a stigmatized people and are, on this account, excluded from mainstream society and made to suffer numerous disabilities, which are regulated through religious beliefs and practices. In other words, they experience the systematic exclusion that is inbuilt in our hierarchical social system. It excludes them from interaction and access to social resources through social arrangements, normative value systems and customs. This chapter has been organized into four sections. After this introductory section the second section looks at how the children of inter-varna marriages used to demoralize the original inhabitants of this country (the untouchables). The third section deals with experiences of discrimination faced by the SCs in various walks of life and perceptions of untouchability. The final section contains concluding remarks.

Policy makers, political parties, academics, non-governmental organizations and human rights bodies are under the comfortable illusion that untouchability is a thing of the past, which we got rid of by planned development and social reforms. Therefore, this matter has been off the national agenda in recent years.

Although the Constitution of India officially outlaws untouchability, it continues to be in practice in many parts of the country even after six decades of independence. Abuse of their basic human rights is an everyday experience for the SCs, who endure discrimination, violence, insults and humiliation regularly. In countless villages, they are excluded from mainstream society. They are prevented from exercising their voting rights. They are prohibited from taking water from village wells and from entering temples. They are forced to eat and drink from separate vessels in public restaurants and sit separately in the village panchayats. They are forced to render services such as manual scavenging, excavating, cremating dead bodies and removing carcasses.

Imposed Identity

The Hindu social order does not recognize the individual as the centre of social purposes. The social order is based primarily on varna and not on individuals. There are four varnas – Brahmins, Kshatriyas, Vaishyas and Shudras. However, there is a further social category beyond these varnas – these are variously referred to as the Panchamas, the outcastes, the Dalits or the scheduled castes. Thus, Hindu society is not an individual Brahmin, Kshatriya, Vaishya or Shudra – it includes all of them.

Hindu dharma is based on the theory of karma, three *gunas* (qualities) and the transmigration of the soul. All these three theories are applied to justify the social order. By karma (action) are caused the various conditions of men – the highest, the middle and the lowest. It is as a consequence of the many sinful acts committed by one's body, voice or mind that a person becomes a bird, a beast or a low caste person, respectively, in his/her next birth. There are three *gunas* predominating in the body. The study of the *Vedas*, austerity, knowledge and purity are marks of the good or higher qualities, whereas cruelty and covetousness are marks of the dark or lower qualities.

Through each of these qualities, a human being obtains various transmigrations. It is the preponderance of certain kinds of qualities that determines the birth of a man as a Brahmin, a Shudra or an untouchable. People who have sinned enter an inferior existence or womb, while those who lead an ideal life obtain cessation of birth and death, or nirvana, which is the ultimate aim of all souls.

The doctrine that the different varnas were created from different parts of the divine body has generated the belief that it must be divine will that they remain separate and distinct. It is this belief that has created among individual Hindus an instinct to be different from each other.

The varna is often claimed not only to be of the nature of castes, but up to a point, to be castes. A Brahmin and a Kshatriya at any point of time represent a particular caste, while the term Vaishya, in recent years, is being associated with some particular caste groups with some qualifying adjectives. As a matter of fact, none of the four terms for varna now represent anything but groups of castes.[1]

The Hindu social order is a ladder of castes placed one above the other, together representing an ascending scale of respect and a descending scale of contempt. As opposed to the principles of liberty, equality and fraternity, according to Ambedkar,[2] the Hindu social order is based on the principle of graded inequality, fixed occupation and fixing of people with their respective castes. In this social order, the lowest social group has been labelled under various names, from the early Asprashya (untouchable) to the present day legalized label of scheduled castes and the more recent Dalit. In the annals of Indian history, the SCs have had different identities imposed upon them: Chandalas, Avarna, Antyavasin, Bahya, Achhut, Asprashya, Parihas, to name a few. Untouchability, with its manifold manifestations, is rooted in the notions of purity and pollution, which is believed to have developed in the later Vedic period, when Brahminic literature emerged in the form of the *Smritis, Samhitas* and the *Upanishads*. This Brahminic literature uses a variety of terms such as Asprashya, Antya, Antyaja, Antyavasin and Bahya for the untouchables. These terms, as they are used in the different Brahminic books, are significant. Segregation was the natural corollary to the ardently preached and widely shared belief in pollution and several terms such as *Asprashya* (not touchable), *Antya* (the last or at the end), *Bahya* (outside the pale of the *chaturvarna,* hence outcaste), *Antyaja* (born at the end), *Antyavasin* (those who live at the end) testify to the current practices.[3] Perhaps, all this meant a conscious perpetuation of an old state of affairs and created a definite barrier to free mixing in the future. These terms also show that the SCs used to live in separate quarters and that they were pushed to the corners of the habitation clusters by their fellow villagers.

Other terms were also used in Brahminic literature to humiliate and morally demoralize the SCs. These are the terms used in the different Hindu scriptures.

Pratiloma Sons

Brahminic literature throws up the question whether varna – intermixing, inter-dining and inter-caste – marriages were prevalent at that time. Certainly not, because society was a very closed one then. Table 5.1 shows that these generic terms developed into specific caste names only in the later Vedic period along with the emergence of Brahminic literature such as the *Smritis, Samhitas* and the *Upanishads*. The children of inter-varna marriages used to demoralize and exclude the original inhabitants of this country (the untouchables) from the mainstream. Such hatred can be found and observed even today against the untouchables by the Savarnas (the higher castes).

Table 5.1 Development of Generic Terms into Specific Caste Names

Authority	*Parentage*		*Parentage*
	Father	*Mother*	*Sons*
Baudhayana Dharmasutra	Shudra	Brahmin	Chandala
	Shudra	Kshatriya	Ksatta
	Shudra	Vaishya	Magadha
	Kshatriya	Brahmin	Suta
Gautama Dharmasutra	Shudra	Brahmin	—
	Shudra	Kshatriya	Vaidehaka/Pulkasa
	Shudra	Vaishya	Valdahaka/Ayogava
	Vaishya	Brahmin	Magadha/Ksattri
	Vaishya	Kshatriya	Magadha/Dhariva
	Kshatriya	Brahmin	Suta
Vaikhanasa Smarta Sutra	Shudra	Brahmin	Chandala
	Shudra	Kshatriya	Pulkasa
	Vaishya	Brahmin	Magadha
	Kshatriya	Brahmin	Suta
Arthasastra of Kautilya	Shudra	Brahmin	Chandala
	Shudra	Kshatriya	Ksatta
	Shudra	Vaishya	Ayogava
	Vaishya	Brahmin	Vaidehaka
	Kshatriya	Brahmin	Suta
Manusmrti	Shudra	Brahmin	Chandala
	Shudra	Kshatriya	Ksatta
	Shudra	Vaishya	Ayogava
	Vaishya	Brahmin	Vaideha
	Vaishya	Kshatriya	Magadha
	Kshatriya	Brahmin	Suta

Source: Mukherjee, Prabhati. 1988. *Beyond The Four Varnas.* Delhi: Motilal Banarasi Dass, pp. 47–49.

Forms of Untouchability Practices

Untouchability can be observed in the actual behaviour, ideas, beliefs and feelings of individuals. It is observed that in contemporary times, the practice of untouchability has modified itself to become more subtle.

Table 5.2 below shows the main untouchability practices prevailing in various parts of India:[4]

Table 5.2 Untouchability Practices in India

Untouchability Practices	*Forms of Each Practice*
Denial of drinking water	If a village has a common water source for both SCs and Savarnas, the following forms of untouchability are seen to be observed:
	The SCs are not allowed to draw their own water. The Savarnas draw the water for them and pour it into their pots. They have to wait until a higher caste Hindu comes to the water source and is favourably inclined towards drawing water for them.
	The SCs are not supposed to touch the pots of the Savarnas.
	The SCs can get water only after all the Savarnas have fulfilled their own water needs.
	In most villages, separate wells and bore-wells continue to exist for the SCs and the Savarnas. In case of acute shortage of water, Sarvarnas can use the SCs' water source. But, it is not the other way around. If the Savarna castes want water from the SCs' bore-well, they have to first cleanse the bore-well and its surroundings.
	If a village has a natural lake, pond or tank, the SCs are supposed to draw their water from downstream, where the Savarnas do not go.
Pouring drinking water into their hands	Mostly confined to the workplace.
Prohibited from entering a Savarna house	SCs are not allowed to enter the houses of the Savarnas and they are compelled to stand far away from their houses.
	SCs can only go to certain parts of a Savarna's house: the outer extension of the house and outside the threshold, but not the interior parts. At the time of harvest, SCs are sometimes allowed to enter to store their agricultural products in a Savarna's house.
Segregation at feasts	On the occasion of a marriage or a function in a Savarna family, SCs are usually not invited, and if they are invited, they can eat only after the Savarnas have finished.
	In some places, SCs are supposed to bring their own plates. Sometimes, they are told to wash their own plates after they have dined.
	Almost all the time, SCs are served at a distance from the hosted premises.
	Sometimes, they are given their food in towels or in their upper garments.

Cont'd...

...Cont'd

Discrimination in schools	SC students have to sit separately at the back of the class. SC students are often abused by their caste name. They are not allowed to eat together with the Savarnas. There are separate water facilities for SC students. There is discrimination between SC and Savarna teachers. Savarna children are not admitted to schools in SC hamlets.
Ban on sitting in public places	SCs are not allowed to sit in public places. SCs have to sit separately at some distance from the other castes. Often, they are allowed only to stand, that too with folded hands. SCs are allowed to sit at lower level.
Ban on walking in Savarna localities	SCs are not allowed to walk wearing footwear of any kind in the vicinity of the Savarnas. They are not allowed to use an umbrella in Savarna localities. They are not allowed to ride cycles or in rickshaws and, in certain cases, even in bullock carts.
Forced services	Drum beating for funerals and festivals/jatras. Grave digging. Cremation of dead bodies. Chappal making. Removal of animal carcasses. Scavenging. SCs are supposed to sweep the whole village at the time of festivals and jatras.
Denial of services	(a) Laundry services Denial of laundry service. Even laundry shop owners refuse to iron the clothes of SCs. (b) Barber services SCs are denied the hairdressing services. If a family member is cutting the hair of SCs, he cannot perform the same service for the Savarnas. If such services are rendered to SCs in an SC locality, the service provider must purify himself immediately on coming back to his house. (c) Denial of entry into shops SCs are prohibited from entering shops. Where they are allowed into a shop, they cannot touch anything.

Cont'd...

...Cont'd

	They have to stand in separate lines and not touch any Savarnas.
Untouchability in giving and receiving things in the shop	SCs are not allowed to touch any items. They have to indicate with a small stick the items they desire to buy.
	SCs have to stand outside the shop and the exchange takes place by throwing the money and the purchased item.
	Sometimes, a separate tray is kept for the SCs, through which the exchange takes place.
Discrimination in health services	SCs have to stand in a separate line.
	Physical touch is avoided both during check-ups and while prescribing medicines.
	Health workers seldom visit the SC areas in a village.
	SCs are asked to come to the main village for treatment.

Perceptions of Untouchability

It is observed that untouchability is not only about not touching certain kinds of people; it is a much more complex phenomenon that is fundamentally evil, despicable and anti-human. It is a prejudice much stronger than racial prejudice and more dangerous because it is invisible. In the course of time, the avoidance of physical contact has disappeared in most villages and urban areas, but behavioural attitudes and the forms of untouchability have changed accordingly. Untouchability can be observed in actual behaviour in the idea and belief systems of Indian society, as also in the feelings of individuals. These may differ according to the demographic or social characteristics of the individuals or they may be uniform. The same group may behave differently in a different situation. Different groups of individuals may not always observe untouchability in the same situation.

It is argued that untouchability is but a virulent form of poverty and illiteracy, and once these problems are eliminated, the problem of untouchability will also come automatically to an abrupt end. Economic and educational development may help in minimizing the gravity of the problem of untouchability, but it cannot root it out. In a caste-based society, it is social inequalities that are predominant, not economic ones.

Hindu society is based on the caste system; caste and its relative status occupy importance, not the economic status of a particular caste. So far as access to social, religious, economic and political activities are concerned, literacy has no relevance since there is a very high percentage of discrimination against even literate SCs. Even SCs who are rich, educated and possess some social status are often subjected to the same humiliation as poor and illiterate SCs.

Therefore, it can be said that even though untouchability is linked with poverty and illiteracy, it will not be eradicated with the removal of these. Untouchability is an independent institution, coupled with prejudice against and hatred for a section of society. Had it originated because of poverty and illiteracy, it would have been equally active against poor and illiterate caste Hindus, but this is not so. For the SCs, untouchability is the cause and poverty and illiteracy are its effects. Even though poverty and illiteracy have made untouchability more severe and complicated and the three are intermixed to a great extent, they are by no means one and the same.

In his book, *Caste in India*, J.H. Hutton[5] says that untouchability is the consequence of ritual impurity. He explains, 'The origin of the position of the exterior castes is partly racial, partly religious and partly a matter of social custom. There can be little doubt that the idea of untouchability originates in taboo.'

Christoph Von Fürer-Haimendorf[6] believes that untouchability is an urban development and the result of unclean and ritually impure occupations. Once untouchability developed in urban or semi-urban settlements, its gradual spread to the villages was inevitable for it is the towns that set the standards everywhere.

Stephen Fuchs[7] proposes a new theory regarding the origin of untouchability. He says there is sufficient evidence to prove that both the Aryans and the Dravidians, on their arrival in India, still belonged to an animal breeding culture. They must have brought along also their aversion to manual work and to foreign people. The Aryans, during their slow advance through Northern India, and the Dravidians, wandering down the west coast into South India, encountered on their way a multitude of earlier settlers who either submitted passively to their conquest or were defeated in fierce battles. As conquerors, they managed to impose many of their cultural values and prejudices on the people in India. A new dimension – ritual purity – was added to their inherited attitudes to manual work and racial purity and they gradually developed this unique Hindu caste system, which is intimately connected ideologically with the concept of untouchability.

F.G. Bailey[8] says, 'Caste is a system of ranks which is related to differential control over the productive resources.' Each person in the caste system performs economic, political and ritual roles and, except for certain anomalies, there is a high degree of coincidence between the political and economic ranks and the ritual ranking of caste. The anomalies are apparent mainly at the uppermost and lowermost ranks of the ritual ladder. A Brahmin of scant economic means does not fall to a low ritual rank, nor can a wealthy untouchable attain a high ritual rank. The ritual rank of the caste groups between these two extremes tends to follow their economic rank in the village community.

Dumont criticizes Bailey's interpretation of the caste system, saying ritual purity is the code of the caste system. It has no differential control over productive resources.

According to Dumont,[9] caste represents the institutionalization of hierarchical values. In his holistic conception of caste, hierarchy is expressed in a cultural code of relative purity and impurity in a continuously graded status order; the extremes of this order are the Brahmins – the most pure people – at the top and the untouchables – the least pure people – at the bottom. The Brahmins and the untouchables are conceptually opposed in a number of ways that contribute to their archetypal purity and impurity. The Brahmin lives at the centre of the village and is a 'god on earth', while the untouchable lives outside the village and is apparently excluded from religious life.

Dumont, however, sees the Brahmins and the untouchables as also being complementary to each other – the completion of a 'whole' by two equally necessary but unequally ranked parts. The impurity of the untouchables is conceptually inseparable from the purity of the Brahmins because the execution of impure tasks by some is necessary for the maintenance of purity of others. Society is a totality made up of two unequal but complementary parts.

Social and religious separation pervades the entire caste system. The most notorious separation is that of untouchability. The members of the four main varnas, which constitute the mouth, arms, thighs and feet of the creator, Brahma, do not accept water that has been handled by castes that are outside Brahma's auspicious body. The untouchable castes are not admitted into society because their bodies and minds are considered impure, dull or otherwise unfit for initiation.

Dumont's position has been severely criticized by several anthropologists and sociologists such as Gerald Berreman (1971), Kathleen Gough (1973) and Joan Mencher (1974).[10] Dumont has been widely criticized for using Brahminical sources to understand Hindu society, which commits him to only a Brahminical view of it; the untouchables may conceive of the society differently.[11]

Many anthropological writings have been devoted to the cultural traditions of the low-caste groups. They have emphasized the differences between the socioreligious ideology of the upper castes and lower castes, especially the untouchables, who have traditionally been kept outside the varna system (Juergensmeyer, 1982; Burghart, 1983; Khare, 1984; Appadurai, 1986; Deliege, 1992).[12] They have analysed Hindu society from bottom up.

Gough points out that cultural differences between the high and low castes are due to political and economic variables generated by the upper castes. The untouchables have a distinctive social and cultural sub-system. Similar views are shared also by Joan Mencher (1974), Bernard Cohn (1955), Robert Miller (1966) and Gerald Berreman (1971). According to all of them, the untouchables are seen to have demystified caste and its accompanying ideology, thus seeing the caste system in an objective and culture-free way for what it really is – a system of oppression. Mencher feels that the caste system is a system of exploitation of the lower castes.

Bernard Cohn[13] also regards the untouchables as the bearers of an alternate social and cultural system, different from the upper caste culture. In his analysis of the untouchables (the Chamars of North India), he finds the untouchables to be different from the high castes, that is, the social and spatial separation between the untouchables and the high castes. Because the untouchables cannot hear, let alone learn the *Vedas*, or be given religious services by the Brahmins, or enter high caste temples, they suffer from a kind of communication block. The result of this communication block, however, is not a form of lack of culture, but the retention of a historically prior pre-Aryan little tradition. Unlike the great tradition of the higher castes and of the Brahmins in particular, the little tradition of the untouchables contains a 'pre-Aryan and non-Brahminic religion', which emphasizes the propitiation of the goddesses of disease and the use of mediums and exorcists.

Miller[14] has studied the untouchable Mahars of Central India. He writes that the Mahars have built a tradition that can hardly be called a distinctive variant of the great tradition cognate to those of the four major varnas. In fact, the Mahars are building on a counter great tradition, which has always existed in India as an antithesis to the Brahminical great tradition. In this counter tradition, 'equality is opposed to inequality', the individual's ability is opposed to ritualism, and escape from the system is opposed to movement within the system.

Ambedkar[15] also propounded a thesis on the origin of untouchability. The original distinction between the Hindus and the untouchables, before the advent of untouchability, was the distinction between tribesmen and broken men from alien tribes. It is the broken men who subsequently came to be treated as the untouchables. Untouchability sprang from two roots:

- Contempt and hatred for the broken men as for Buddhism by the Brahmins; and
- Continuation of eating beef by the broken men after it had been given up by the others.

Ambedkar tries to explain what he means by broken men. He proposes an inventive hypothesis. When primitive society began, it was still nomadic and warring. They began to attack the settled tribes as the latter were wealthier. The settled tribes also had grain, which the nomads wanted. The settled men needed defenders as they had lost their warlike spirit. They employed the 'broken men' and defeated the nomads and other stray people who needed protection and shelter. These became the mercenaries of the settlers, but were not allowed to stay within the settlement. They were kept at a distance because they belonged to different tribes. They were treated with disrespect, both as broken men and as mercenaries.

The practice of untouchability made Ambedkar suffer at the hands of the upper castes as a child and even as a youth. Elsewhere, slavery and serfdom had vanished, but the practice of untouchability continued to exist in India. The caste system owed its origin to the Vedic ideals of Varnashrama Dharma. 'The root of untouchability is the caste system, the root of (the) caste system is the religion attached to Varna, and the root of Varnashrama is Brahminical religion, and the root of (the) Brahminical religion is authoritarianism and political power.'[16]

Hinduism divides society into four varnas, which include an occupational hierarchy as each caste is allotted a particular work. In other words, there is not so much a division of labour as a division of labourers. Ambedkar says, 'The caste system is not merely division of labour, it is division of labourers. It is a hierarchy in which the division of labourers is graded one above the other.'[17] The concept of god and related Hindu religious customs tend to preserve the caste system till today. Religious doctrines make the untouchables believe that they are born to suffer and are fit only to do menial jobs. 'Besides caste hierarchy and economic backwardness, psychologically also people of lower caste were brainwashed through religious propaganda.'[18] He adds, 'Caste does not result in economic efficiency, caste cannot and it has not improved the race. Caste has, however, done one thing – it has completely disorganised and demoralised the Hindus.'[19]

Ambedkar wanted that everyone should be treated equally and that there should be no discrimination just because one happened to be born an untouchable. He said, 'The religion which teaches man to behave with another man in an inhuman manner is not religion but infamy. The religion which does not recognise a human being as a human being is a curse. The religion in which the touch of animals is permitted but the touch of a human being pollutes, is not a religion but the mockery of religion.'[20]

The Hindu religion is based on the principle of caste hierarchy and graded inequality. If the concept of caste is removed, there is no Hindu religion. For a Hindu, caste is more important than anything else. Ambedkar said, 'A Hindu's public life is caste. Virtue has become caste-ridden and morality has become caste-bound.'[21]

The religious doctrines have been accepted as the code of conduct for all of the society. If that is so, how can one make the untouchables understand that it is religion which is making them lead a miserable life in the garb of caste? Ambedkar said, 'It is not possible to break the caste without annihilating the religious notions on which the caste system is founded.'[22] He added that socioreligious disabilities have dehumanized the untouchables and their interests are at stake and, therefore, the interests of the whole humanity. The caste Hindu has a code which the SCs are required to follow. This code lays down the acts of omission and commission that the caste Hindus treat as offences:[23]

- The SCs must live in separate quarters away from the habitation of the Hindus. It is an offence for the SCs to break or evade the rule of segregation.
- The quarters of the SCs must be located towards the south of the main settlement of the caste Hindus since the south is the most inauspicious of the four directions. A break of this rule shall be deemed to be an offence.
- The SCs must observe the rule of distance, pollution or shadow of pollution as the case may be. It is an offence to break the rule.
- It is an offence for a member of the SCs to acquire wealth.
- It is an offence for a member of the SCs to build a pucca house.
- It is an offence for a member of the SCs to wear a clean dress, shoes, watch or gold ornaments.
- It is an offence for an SC to ride on a horse or a palanquin through the village.
- It is an offence for an SC to sit on a chair in the presence of a caste Hindu.

- It is an offence for an SC to take a procession through the areas where caste Hindus live.
- It is an offence for an SC to speak a cultural language.
- The SCs must do the menial jobs of the caste Hindus. It is an offence for the SCs to refuse such jobs or to demand minimum wages for doing it.

The caste Hindus internalized these codes through the socialization process. Even today, these codes exist, though they are more visible in the rural areas; they continue to exist in cities and towns, too, but are generally less visible. They have been internalized in the state of mind of every caste Hindu. Due to this code, caste Hindus have never shown any fellow feeling for the SCs and have continually excluded them from the social mainstream. Although the SCs are dependent on the caste Hindus, they are regularly ill-treated and humiliated by them. If Hindu society plays its part in maintaining the established order, so do the Hindu officials of the state. Between them, they have made the established order impregnable.

Although untouchability was abolished by the Constitution of India, a report issued by the National Commission for Scheduled Castes underscores that untouchability, imposition of social disabilities on persons by reason of their birth in certain castes, is still practised in many forms throughout the country. Untouchability is prevalent not only in its physical form, but also dwells deep in the minds of the people. The main causes for the continuance of untouchability even after six decades of independence are:[24]

- the deep-rooted caste system;
- carrying on of unclean occupations by the SCs;
- illiteracy;
- lack of awareness among the SCs; and
- rigidity and bias created by religious literature.

We find these basic facts true for SCs across most levels:

- the SCs find themselves at the bottom of most of the human development indices.
- their social and economic backwardness is clearly related to their religion sanctioned exclusions from all walks of public life.
- discrimination is not a thing of the past, but an everyday reality.

Table 5.3 below summarizes the types of exclusion faced by the SCs:

Table 5.3 Types of Exclusion Faced by the Scheduled Castes

Sources of Deprivation/ Exclusion	*Types of Identities*	*Nature of Oppression*	*Needs*
Lowest status in the caste hierarchy	Untouchables	Social repression	Social equality
Powerlessness	Subject	Political disenfranchisement	Political participation
Poverty	Slave	Economic exploitation	Bargaining for better economic conditions
Lack of culture	Not a human being	Cultural repression	Cultural revolution and negation of Brahminism
Lack of education	Ignorant/ illiterate	Repression at various levels	Equal educational facilities

Ambedkar did not stop at mere speeches and writing. He entered into direct action. All the agitations he spearheaded took place when India's freedom struggle was on. He believed that the India's freedom struggle was 'a struggle for power as distinguished from freedom so long as the cause of the freedom was not the cause of the untouchables' and refused to join it.

In 1927, a conference was convened at Mahad in Maharashtra. All the arrangements were made and it was announced that the untouchables would use the water from the common tank at Mahad. On the appointed day, Ambedkar took water from the Chowdar tank and drank it. Immediately, all the untouchables who were assembled there also followed their leader and took water from the tank. He said, 'At the outset, let me tell those who oppose us that we did not perish because we could not drink water from the Chowdar tank. We now want to go to the tank only to prove that we are also human beings.'[25]

A temple entry conference was also arranged in Mahad that same year. The untouchables were not traditionally allowed to enter the temple. The Savarnas wanted to build a separate temple for the untouchables. Ambedkar said, 'The most important point we want to emphasise here is not the satisfaction you get from the worship of the image of god, but the plain fact that a temple is not defiled by the presence of an untouchable nor is the purity of the image affected by it. That is why we oppose the idea of separate temples for us and insist on entering them.' Ambedkar addressed the conference and said that the untouchables were determined to enter the temple and asked that

Hindu society be organized on two main principles – equality and absence of casteism.

But, the struggle was not over. Mahad witnessed another scene of rebellion. Ambedkar had always been against the *Manusmriti* since it was a charter of rights for caste Hindus and would have kept the untouchables slaves forever. He was of the opinion that the teachings of Manu were detrimental to the welfare of the untouchables. Moreover, Ambedkar was a rationalist and did not believe in the principles of the *Manusmriti*. Therefore, in December 1927, he burnt the *Manusmriti*. This was a great blow to the orthodox Hindus.

Ambedkar represented the untouchables at the Round Table Conferences from 1930 to 1932 and succeeded in getting a separate electorate for them. But, this move was thwarted and he was forced to sign the Poona Pact, which provided for a joint electorate with reservations, to save the life of Mahatma Gandhi. Ambedkar did not have any faith in the joint electorate because he believed that any untouchables elected through reservation with the help of the other castes would not be able to work for their own community. He said all untouchable representatives must identify themselves with the party and forget their own community. In a joint electorate, the SC representatives were only silent spectators and not active participants in protecting the interests of their community members. It is because 'they have to depend on the mainstream of political parties to attract caste Hindus and other voters. This dependence in reality meant subservience to the caste Hindu leaders who dominate the mainstream political parties,' said Ambedkar.

Ambedkar's only aim in life was to alleviate the deteriorating conditions of the untouchables. When he cooperated with the British or the Congress, it was only to get social justice for the untouchables. He said, 'Ours is a battle, not for wealth or for power, but it is a battle for freedom. It is a battle for the reclamation of human personality.'

Conclusion

We may conclude that untouchability or imposition of social disabilities or exclusion of persons by reason of their birth into certain castes is still practised in many forms throughout the country. And this practice is not just visible in physical forms, but also exists as deep-rooted beliefs in the minds of people. The main causes for the continuance of untouchability even after 60 years of independence are the deep-rooted caste system and the rigidity and bias created by religious and Brahminical scriptures. Therefore, Ambedkar called upon Hindus to annihilate the caste system, which he saw as a great hindrance to social solidarity and to set up a new social order based on the ideals of liberty, equality and fraternity, in consonance with the principles of democracy. He advocated inter-caste marriages as one of the solutions to the problem. He stressed that belief in the *Shastras* was the root cause for the flourishing of the caste system. He, therefore, called for freeing every man and woman from this thraldom by cleansing their minds of the pernicious notions found in the *Shastras*. He actively promoted inter-dining and inter-marrying among the various castes. He advocated that society be based on reason and not on the atrocious traditions of the caste system.

Notes

1. Kumar, Rabindra. 2002. 'Atrocities on Dalits: Structural Dysfunction', *Fourth Word Journal*, No. 16. Bhubaneswar: NISWASS.
2. Ambedkar, B.R. 1990. Writing and Speeches, Vol. 3. Mumbai Education Department, Maharashtra.
3. Ibid.
4. The data on forms of untouchability were collected by the students of NISWASS, Bhubaneswar, during their studies of Scheduled Castes (Gokha, Ganda, Ghasi and Kandara).
5. Hutton, J.H. 1963. *Caste in India.* Bombay. Oxford University Press.
6. Fürer-Haimendorf, Christoph von. 1950. 'Foreword'. In Stephen Fuchs, *The Children of Hari: A Study of the Nimar Balahis in the Central Provinces of India*. Vienna: Verlog Herald quoted in S.M. Michael (ed.) 1999. *Untouchables: Dalits in Modern India.* Colorado (USA): Lynne Rienner Publishers Inc.
7. Fuchs, Stephen. 1981. *At the Bottom of Indian Society: The Harijan and Other Low Castes*. Delhi: Munshiram Manoharlal.
8. Bailey, F.G. 1957. *Caste and Economic Frontiers.* Manchester: Manchester University Press.
9. Dumont, Louis. 1988. *Homo Hierarchicus.* Delhi: Oxford University Press
10. Dumont, Louis. 1970. *Religion, Politics and History in India*. Paris and The Hague: Mouton
11. Berreman, Gerald. 1971. 'The Brahminical View of Caste'. In Dipankar Gupta (ed.) 1992. *Social Stratification*. Delhi: Oxford University Press, pp. 80–92. Gough, Kathleen. 1973. 'Harijan in Thanjavur'. In K. Gough and H.P. Sharma (eds) *Imperialism and Revolution in South Asia*. New

York: Monthly Review Press. Mencher, Joan P. 1974. 'The Caste System Upside Down'. In Dipankar Gupta (ed.) 1992. op. cit.

12. (A) Freeman, J. 1979. *Untouchable: An Indian Life History*. London: Allen and Unwin. Burghart, Richard. 1983. 'Sociology of India: An India Cultural Approach to the Study of "Hindu Society"'. In *Indian Sociology*, No. 17. Lynch, Owen M. 1977. 'Method and Theory in the Sociology of Laws: Dumont, A Reply'. In Kenneth David (ed.) 1977. *The New Wind: Changing Identities in South Asia.* The Hague: Mouton.

    (B) Juergensmeyer, Mark. 1982. *Religion as Social Vision: The Movement Against Untouchability in Twentieth Century Punjab*. Berkeley: University of California Press. Khare, R.S. 1984. *The Untouchable as Himself: Ideology, Identify and Pragmatism among the Lucknow Chamars*, Cambridge: Cambridge University Press.

13. Cohn, Bernard. 1954. *The Chamar of Senapur: A Study of the Changing Status of a Depressed Caste*. Quoted in S.M. Michael (ed.) *Dalits in Modern India: Vision and Values.* New Delhi: Vistaar Publications.
14. Miller, Rober. 1966. 'Button, Button: Great Tradition, Little Tradition, Whose Tradition?' In *Anthropological Quarterly*, No. 39, pp. 26–42. Quoted in S.M. Michael (ed.) op. cit.
15. Ambedkar, B.R. 1990.*Who were Untouchables? Writing and Speeches, Vol. 7.* Mumbai: Education Department, Maharashtra.
16. Biswas, Oneil. 1988. *A Phenomenon Named Ambedkar.* New Delhi: Blumoon Books, p. 28.
17. Ambedkar, B.R. 1990. *Writings and Speeches,* Vol. 3. Mumbai. Education Department, Maharashtra, p. 67.
18. Ambedkar, B.R. 1990. *Writings and Speeches,* Vol. 1. Mumbai. Education Department, Maharashtra, p. 67.
19. Ibid., p. 50
20. Ibid.
21. Ibid.
22. Ibid.
23. Ambedkar, B.R. 1993 *Writings and Speeches,* Vol. 5. Mumbai. Education Department, Maharashtra.
24. Government of India, *Fourth Report 1996–97 and 1997–98,* Vol. 1. National Commission for Scheduled Castes and Scheduled Tribes, Government of India.
25. Keer, Dhananjay. 1987. *Dr Ambedkar's Life and Mission*. Reprint. Mumbai: Popular Prakashan.

6

The Mahadalits of Bihar

Myth and Reality

The Scheduled Caste (SC) population of Bihar is 13,048,608 as per the 2001 Census, constituting 15.7 per cent of the total population (82,998,509) of the state. Bihar is the third largest state in terms of SC population. The growth of the SC population during 1991–2001 was 30.7 per cent, which is 2.1 per cent higher than the growth of the total population (28.6%). The state has 23 SCs and all of them were enumerated in the 2001 Census. Overall, the state accounts for 1.3 per cent of the total SC population in the country.

The SCs are overwhelmingly rural, with 93.3 per cent of them living in hamlets. Among the districts of Bihar, Gaya has the highest proportion of SCs (29.6%) followed by Nawada, Aurangabad, Kaimur, Vaishali and Nalanda. Kishanganj district has the lowest proportion of SC population (6.6%).

Out of the 23 SC groups, the Chamars are the most populous caste with a population of 4,090,070, constituting 31.3 per cent of the total SC population in the state. The Chamars are followed by the Dusadhs, who number 4,029,411 (30.90%). The next four SCs in descending order are the Musahar, Pasi, Dhobi and Bhuiya castes. Along with the Chamars and Dusadhs, these six castes constitute 93.2 per cent of the total SC population of Bihar. Five castes – the Chaupals, Banatars, Haris, Kanjars and Rajwars – number 100,111 to 213,795, constituting 5.8 per cent of the state's SC population. The remaining 12 castes, along with the generic castes, constitute the residual 1.1 per cent of the total SC population. Eight castes together form less than 19,000 (see Table 6.1).

The Chamars constitute a whopping 58–67 per cent of the total SC population in the Gopalganj, Siwan, Buxar and Kaimur districts. The Dusadhs total up to 54 per cent each in the Vaishali and Begusarai districts. The Pasis and Bhuiyas are concentrated primarily in Gaya district, whereas the Musahars and Dhobis have the maximum concentration in the Purnia and East Champaran districts, respectively.

Table 6.1 Distribution of SCs in Bihar

Name of Castes	*Total People*	*Male*	*Female*	*% age among SCs*
Bantar	1,01,223	52,403	48,820	0.78
Bauri	2,097	1,074	1,023	0.02
Bhogta	12,659	6,723	5,946	0.10
Bhumij	2,333	1,197	1,136	0.02
Bhuiya	5,68,403	2,93,027	2,75,376	4.37
Chamar	40,90,070	21,22,732	19,67,338	31.41
Chaupal	1,00,111	52,021	48,090	0.77
Dabgar	3,590	1,813	1,777	0.03
Dhobi	647,491	3,36,880	3,10,611	4.97
Dom	1,55,383	80,855	74,528	1.19
Dusadh	40,29,411	21,07,535	19,21,876	30.94
Ghasi	674	365	309	0.01
Halalkhor	3,960	2,069	1,861	0.03
Hari	1,81,748	94,035	87,713	1.40
Kanjar	1,620	860	760	1.40
Kurariar	6,566	3,366	3,200	0.05
Lalbegi	809	445	364	0.01
Musahar	21,12,136	10,93,077	10,19,059	16.22
Nat	38,615	19,976	18,639	0.30
Pan	3,653	1,959	1,694	0.30
Pasi	7,11,389	3,70,599	3,40,790	5.46
Rajwar	2,13,795	1,09,831	1,03,964	1.64
Turi	33,638	17,344	16,294	0.26
Generic Castes	27,234	14,506	12,734	0.21

Source: Economic Survey 2008–09, Bihar.

Development Initiatives

After independence, India adopted two models of development – a liberal and democratic framework of modernization and a scientific and technological one. As a result, it became a welfare state committed to the welfare and development of its people in general and of the vulnerable sections in particular. The preamble to the Constitution of India provides for social, economic and political justice; liberty of thought, expression, belief, faith and worship; equality of status and opportunity; and promotion of all among the citizens. It also provides fraternity assuring the dignity of the individual and the unity and integrity of the nation. The Constitution contains the Directive Principles of State Policy, Fundamental Rights and protection of specific sections under Articles 38, 39 and 46. All these stand testimony to the commitment of the state to its citizens. Deriving from this, the government has adopted a strategy of planned development to reduce inequality of income and status and to offer opportunities to all. The planning era started with the initiation and implementation of the First Five-Year Plan in 1951, which envisaged the establishment of community development programmes for all sections and regions. The central theme of the community development programmes was to help people to help themselves, with special emphasis on the uplift of the weaker sections.

The various measures taken in the First Plan for the development of the weaker sections are listed below:

- Provision for education as an urgent need of these sections, particularly the SCs: Extensive measures have been taken by both the states and the Centre to increase educational facilities for the SCs. The concessions given to them include free tuition, stipends, scholarships, books, stationery and other equipment. There is also a provision for opening educational institutions in areas where the SCs live in large numbers and establishing hostels for their benefits.
- Allotting wasteland to the SCs residing in rural areas.
- Reserving a certain percentage of government positions for the SCs and relaxation in almost all these cases the standards set for age, qualification and experience.
- Providing ₹ 10 crore from state funds for the benefit of the SCs during the Plan period. The Centre also provided ₹ 4 crore as additional financial help. A provision was also made for more

liberal disbursement of money under different heads to institutions working for the SCs. An effort was made to improve efficiency in proper utilization of funds through effective and well-supervised organizations. Similarly, an effort was made to establish community centres to integrate isolated colonies of SCs.

The Second Five-Year Plan (1956–61) aimed at accelerating the rate of growth by initiating a strategy to bring about the necessary structural changes in the economy. In this plan, development programmes were formulated for the SCs with the objective of improving their social status by providing them better educational and economic opportunities. Around ₹ 21.28 crore were earmarked for this purpose. An additional ₹ 6.25 crore were allocated under various central government sponsored schemes for providing SCs with housing and drinking water, for their economic uplift and as aid to voluntary organizations working to remove untouchability.

The Third Five-Year Plan (1961–66) aimed at achieving a 'good social life' for every citizen of India through development based on a socialistic economy. The plan laid down the foundation for self-reliant economic growth. This plan conceived the 'first stage of a more intensive development leading to a self-reliant and self-generating economy'. In addition to this, the plan also earmarked ₹ 40 crore for special programmes aimed at the welfare of the backward classes, out of which, ₹ 30 crore were provided for the uplift of the SCs. About half of this amount was meant for their educational development, while the rest was divided almost equally between schemes for their economic uplift and schemes to provide them health care, housing and other facilities.

These provisions were intended to supplement the benefits that would be available in an increasing measure to the SCs from the general development programmes provided for in the plan. The plan also placed special emphasis on ensuring that SCs obtained their due share of the benefits in each programme. The community development programme, rural work programmes, schemes for land resettlement, the programme for village and small industries and other schemes undertaken in the interest of agricultural labourers had the greatest bearing upon raising the living standards of the SCs.

As already explained, the programmes for the SCs laid out in the Third Plan were intended to provide for certain special schemes. They did not in any sense take the place of the development programmes undertaken for the community as a whole. In the field of education, the main aims were to make special facilities available to SCs through scholarships, provide them with residential facilities at educational institutions, grant them fee exemptions and offer financial assistance to needy students. In order to promote the SCs' economic life, stress was laid on allotment of land, providing assistance in cultivation, training in running small scale industries and improved techniques in traditional crafts. The bulk of the special allocations made in the Third Plan sponsored by the Centre was concerned with the following:

- improving the working conditions of people engaged in unclean occupations, including eradication of the practice of carrying night soil as head loads;
- subsidies for housing for sweepers and scavengers;
- provision of house sites for SCs who were:
  - engaged in unclean occupations, and
  - landless labourers;
- award of post-metric scholarships; and
- aid to voluntary organizations working for the welfare of the SCs.

Under the general housing programmes, funds were earmarked for the acquisition and development of land for house sites for agricultural workers, among whom SCs formed a considerable proportion.

Up to the beginning of the Fourth Five-Year Plan, the main emphasis was on blanket coverage of the population with developmental programmes without any reference to their beneficiaries. Since the sole concern was increased production and economic growth, no attention was paid to who the beneficiaries were and who reaped the fruits of development. Furthermore, the agricultural sector was the main focus of rural development activities and there were hardly any programmes worth the name for landless labourers, artisans or even marginal farmers.

Under this broad policy of planned efforts, the fruits of development accrued mainly to the asset owning classes, or large and medium landholders, and those who owned sizeable assets for other pursuits allied to agriculture. Overall, India registered a high rate of growth in basic agricultural commodities. Briefly, growth took place in the economy as a whole in the aggregate sense, but when perused in a dis-aggregative manner, the longstanding structural disparity in the population persisted on more or less the same scale, instead of showing a declining trend.

Just prior to the launch of the Fourth Plan, economists and planners started quantifying poverty conditions and people living under conditions of absolute poverty in the country. It revealed that a sizeable proportion of the population was stagnating in poverty-ridden conditions and was completely out of the mainstream development process. Such a situation, even after two decades of planned economic development, sounded the alarm bell for the planners, who began to debate what the ultimate objective of development efforts was in a welfare state. This then led to the recognition of the principle of growth with distributive justice.

The two new approaches were adopted in the Fourth Plan. The plan depicted a radical departure in terms of planning philosophy and planning efforts. It identified two broad approaches, which were adopted as an integral part of the planning process. These were:

- Identification of vulnerable and weaker sections of society and creation of gainful employment and avenues for them with financial assistance. One important set of funds was provided by the state in the form of subsidies, against which institutional finance was obtained in the shape of credit on a differential rate of interest. This broad policy approach for helping the weaker sections has now widely come to be known as the 'beneficiary approach'.
- Special component plans were initiated for vulnerable regions that were trapped in climatically and geographically different conditions. The main focus was to accelerate the pace of development in such areas, which were in a relatively disadvantageous position from the viewpoint of resource endowment and infrastructural development. This was aimed to be achieved through additional input of resources specially earmarked for such regions. Since the people living in such areas were also relatively poorer, accelerated development of such regions in an integrated manner was envisaged to speed up the socio-economic development of the people living there. This approach has come to be known as the 'specific area development approach'.

A review on the eve of the launch of the Fourth Plan showed that the nature of plan outlays in the backward classes sector was not fully recognized. In actual practice, the schemes were formulated in an ad hoc manner without a long-term perspective and general development funds for these classes. Therefore, in the Fifth Five-Year Plan, a new strategy was evolved to ensure the flow of benefits from the general sectors to the backward classes. The states were requested for the necessary quantity of funds from identifiable programmes in proportion to the population of the backward communities and tribals, so that the programmes were oriented to their specific needs. It covered aspects of social development in contrast to the primary emphasis on economic activities and ventures in the beneficiary and area development approaches. The main features of the minimum needs programme during the Fifth Plan were as follows:

- to provide universal elementary education to the age group of 6–14 years;
- to make all persons in the 15–35 years' age group literate;
- to train and provide one community health worker in each village to cover and make available services for sanitation, immunization, simple remedies and referral services;
- to assure supply of potable water to all problem villages;
- to connect villages with a population of 1,000 or more with link roads;
- to provide the mid-day meal scheme for children in the 11–16 years' age group and supplementary feeding programmes for undernourished children and their nursing mothers; and
- to provide facilities for the electrification of villages.

The National Minimum Needs Programme (MNP) was intended primarily to provide essential infrastructure and social services to the SCs. Most of these basic necessities could be categorized under the head of social consumption. This theme was another important approach outlined in the Fifth Plan for the amelioration of the living conditions of the SCs.

The above-mentioned programmes in the Fifth Plan were not entirely successful in any significant way in improving the condition of the SCs, except in certain states. The operational level loophole for identifying the weak or the poor were not taken into account. The apparent loophole in the categorization of farmers into small and marginal classes is one example of that. In many instances, large and middle sized farmers sub-divided their cultivable holdings among their family members and thus became eligible for facilities under the beneficiary specific programmes. Another significant revelation was that the implementing agency was oriented solely to targets and achievements, as, for example, the beneficiaries and the benefited, the loans distributed, the subsidies given. Even if a single beneficiary was benefited by a number of programmes, he was counted as many times under 'beneficiaries benefited'. Furthermore, the qualitative aspect of taking into consideration the amelioration of particular beneficiary on a sustained basis was conspicuous by its absence, although it was the ultimate objective of the beneficiary specific programmes. But this was missing from the minds of the implementing agencies. The levels of private consumption expenditure do not quite reflect the improvements in the living standards brought about by public expenditure on social services lumped together under the MNP.

Neither the Fifth Plan nor the MNP initiated under it were significantly successful in improving the condition of the SCs. Therefore, the Sixth Five-Year Plan shifted strategy by introducing the concept of the *Special Component Plan (SCP)*, which allocated specific funds for the socio-economic development of the SCs in addition to the general programmes of economic development undertaken by the Centre and states. The SCP envisages the channelling of fund outlays and benefits from all the sectors of development in the annual plans of the states and union territories and central ministries at least in proportion to their respective SC populations both in physical and financial terms.

In 2007, the SCP was renamed the *Scheduled Castes Sub-Plan (SCSP)* and the emphasis shifted from family welfare to beneficiary oriented development schemes within the general framework of socio-economic programmes specially directed and designed for the benefits of the SCs. The SCSP is neither a single scheme nor a collection of individual schemes, but a comprehensive plan instrument for channelling a reasonable share of development benefits and outlays from every development sector of the state and central plans towards the uplift of the SCs. It envisages identifying schemes under the general sectors of development that are relevant and beneficial to the SCs, quantification of funds from all divisible programmes, and determination of specific programmes under each sector. These family-oriented programmes are expected to cover all the major occupational groups such as agricultural labourers, small and marginal farmers, share-croppers and leather workers through composite income generating programmes. In addition, they also seek to improve the living conditions of the SCs by making environmental improvements to SC clusters by enhancing their access to social, educational and other community services and earmarking fund outlays for these purposes.

It is a known fact that the SCs form the largest single group among agricultural labourers and a substantial number of them are artisans and marginal farmers, who need the benefits of employment and horizontal and vertical occupational mobility and other such programmes under the SCSP.

Thus, the aims of the SCSP are:

- economic development through beneficiary oriented programmes for raising income and creating assets; and
- *basti*-oriented schemes for infrastructure development, educational development, etc.

Monitoring

The Union Ministry of Social Justice and Empowerment, during discussions, regularly impresses upon the states that they should ensure adequate allocations under the SCSP. As incentive, 25 per cent of special central assistance is released to states and union territories on the basis of the percentage allocations made by them under the SCSP as compared to the share of SCs in their total population. The ministry is also monitoring the formulation and implementation of the SCSP by the states and central ministries.

A standing tripartite committee was constituted in 2006 in the Planning Commission to review the implementation of the SCSP's special strategy for SCs and to resolve various policy related issues thereto with respect to the central ministries and the state governments. The committee identified 30 ministries/departments that are service oriented and whose activities are divisible in nature for the effective implementation of the SCSP. Till 2004–05, 16 ministries/departments had formulated their individual SCSPs (Annual Report, 2004–05).

The state of Bihar has also implemented the SCSP for the development of its SCs. *The Bihar State Welfare Department (BSWD)* was set up with the aim of catering to the welfare of the SCs, STs and OBCs in the state. It is implementing various schemes for the educational, economic and social development of the SCs. The following are the functions of the department:

SC Welfare

- award of stipend;
- book loan facility;
- loan for income generation through the SC Cooperative Development Corporation and through banks with subsidies;
- running of hostels;
- running of residential schools;
- assistance to atrocity victims;

- medical aid for chronic diseases;
- legal aid; and
- uniforms to school going girls.

Stipend for People Engaged in Unclean Occupations

Stipend Schemes

BSWD is running a number of stipend schemes for the welfare of SC, ST and OBC students. These schemes have been designed to fulfil the educational needs of the students. The rates of stipend are as given below:

Table 6.1 Stipend Schemes in Bihar

Type of Stipend Scheme	*Rate/Month (in ₹)*
Post-Matric: As per the central rates, which ranges between ₹ 90 and ₹ 740 for different courses	
High School Stipend (Class 7 to 10)	55
Middle School Stipend (Class 5 to 6)	30
Primary School Stipend (Class 1 to 4)	15
Musahar Stipend	30
Hostelers	80

Residential Schools

BSWD also runs 30 residential schools for SC boys, 21 residential schools for SC girls, and 15 residential schools for STs. In addition, 12 residential schools for OBC girls have been sanctioned recently.

Students are admitted to these schools on the basis of merit and provided free boarding, lodging and education.

Uniforms for Girls

This is specially meant for SC and ST school going girls; two sets of uniform are provided every year to each child attending a government school.

Hostel Scheme

BSWD also runs hostels for SCs, STs and OBCs. Only residential facilities are provided in these hostels; the mess facilities are managed by the students themselves.

At present, there are 146 hostels for SCs, 13 hostels for STs and five hostels for OBCs.

Ayurvedic Medical Centres

Ten such centres are being run in Bihar to provide medical facilities to STs in the areas dominated by them where free medical advice and medicines are provided at these facilities. New buildings for these centres are being constructed out of the funds provided by the Eleventh Finance Commission.

Medical and Legal Aid

The medical aid scheme offers cash assistance ranging between ₹ 300 and ₹ 1,000. Similarly, under the legal aid scheme, SCs and STs are provided assistance to contest court cases.

Assistance under the SC, ST Atrocities Prevention Act, 1989/PCR Act, 1955

The SC, ST Atrocities Prevention Act, 1989, was enacted to provide protection to SCs and STs from atrocities committed by other castes. Under the SC, ST Atrocities Prevention Rule, 1995, the home commissioner of the state is the nodal officer for the implementation of the Act. Nine SC/ST police stations are working under the Act in Bihar.

BSWD also provides funds for financial assistance to victims in the cases registered under this act. The district magistrate is the authorized person for this.

Special Central Assistance to Special Component Plan

The Centre provides Special Central Assistance (SCA) grants to the states for the economic development of the SCs. This grant is an addition to the SCSP of the states.

As per the new guidelines issued by the Centre, this scheme is to be implemented along the lines of the Swarnjayanti Gram Swarojgar Yojana and there is a provision to give up to ₹ 10,000 as subsidy to avail of the benefits of the scheme. The state also provide 5 per cent additional subsidy.

Organizational Set-up

The organizational set-up for implementation of SC welfare schemes is as follow:

1. At headquarters level:
   (i) The Bihar State Welfare Department is headed by the Secretary. At the headquarter level, he is assisted by the joint secretary/deputy secretaries/under-secretaries.
   (ii) There is one Directorate of Welfare headed by the director, who is responsible for implementing schemes for SCs, STs and OBCs. He is assisted by one deputy director and a number of assistant directors.
2. At divisional level:
   The office of the deputy director works at the divisional level.
3. At district level:
   The office of the district welfare officer functions at the district level.
4. At sub-divisional level:
   The sub-divisional welfare officers are placed as per sanctioned posts at the sub-divisional level.
5. At block level:
   Block welfare officers are posted to carry out the works at the block level.

After the implementation of Panchayati Raj system, the panchayats have been given the powers to implement the various schemes such as the school stipend schemes.

Fund Flows to SCSP

As we know the funds for the SCSP are allocated in proportion to the SC population of each state. Since the SCs constituted 15.7 per cent of Bihar's total population in 2001, the state is bound to allocate its budget in proportion to their population of the total state plan outlay and also department-wise for the development of the SCs.

Table 6.2 shows the flow of funds to the SCSP from 2002–03 to 2008–09. It is found that the flow of funds out of the total state plan outlay was more uptil 2005–06, but that it has fallen short of the norm fixed by the Centre, i.e., 15.7 per cent (equal to the overall SC population of the state), since 2007–08. This table indicates that the state has violated the norms and one can find instances of lesser allocations, transfer of funds and shortfalls in expenditure, too. The state government has allotted less funds to the SCSP from 2007 to 2009. It is obligatory for a state to allocate funds to the SCSP in proportionate to its SC population, but Bihar has not fulfilled this obligation. It is not only cheating on the SCs, but also violating their human rights.

Table 6.2 Distribution of SCSP Outlay (in ₹ crore)

Year	*Total State Plan Outlay*	*SCSP Allocation*	*SCSP Expenditure*	*% of SCSP Allocation*	*Share of SCP as % of Population (15.7)*	*Diverted*
2002–03	2,724.13	572.48	NA	21.02	441.85	–130.62
2003–04	2,770.00	442.58	NA	15.98	434.89	–7.69
2004–05	4,569.70	718.36	NA	15.72	717.44	–0.917
2005–06	4,735.46	985.57	360.53 (37%)	20.81	790.82	–194.48
2007–08	10,200.00	434.27	NA	4.25	1,632	1,197.73
2008–09	13,500.00	450.00	NA	3.34	2,119	1,668

Note: Percentage and subtraction are based on amount of expenditure.

Source: Handbook on Social Welfare Statistics, 2004, Government of India, New Delhi.

Budget 2007–08

Bihar's total plan outlay for 2007–08 was ₹ 10,200 crore, out of which, as per the SCSP, the SC allocation should have been ₹ 1,632 crore (15.7%). But as per the vote-on-account presented by the Finance Minister in March 2007, the allocation made under the SCSP was only ₹ 1,632 crore (see Table below), which means Bihar's budget denied the SCs ₹ 1,197.73 crore. One can thus discern the priorities of the government – its concern is clearly not the uplift of the SCs.

Out of the 56 departments/ministries in Bihar, only seven allocated funds under the SCSP. Ministries such as Education and Health did not have any allocation for the SCs in their plan outlay. This clearly shows that the SCs in Bihar are particularly way behind their counterparts in the other states. SCs, STs and OBCs contributed only 66 per cent of the total allocation even in the seven ministries/departments that had allocated such funds (see Table 6.3).

Development of SCs

The SCs in the country in general and particularly those in Bihar have been suffering from commulative deprivation through the ages. Therefore, the framers of the Indian Constitution considered it necessary to make special provisions in the statutes to enable them to join the mainstream by providing for their equitable share in governance

Table 6.3 Bihar Budget 2007–08 (in ₹)

Major Heads	*Total Allocation*	*%age due to SCs as per SCSP–15.7*	*Amount Found in Demand of Grants*	*Amount Denied*	*Percentage*
Administration of justice	25,06,35,000	3,93,49,695	0	3,93,49,695	100
Land revenue	40,63,00,000	6,37,89,100	0	6,37,89,100	100
Taxes on sales, trade, etc.	2,00,000	31,400	0	31,400	100
Fiscal services	9,44,00,000	1,48,20,800	0	1,48,20,800	100
Secretariat –general services	28,59,08,000	4,48,87,556	0	4,48,87,556	100
District administration	3,67,78,58,000	57,74,23,706	0	57,74,23,706	100
Civil aviation	8,00,00,000	1,25,60,000	0	1,25,60,000	100
Treasury and accounts administration	12,89,00,000	2,02,37,300	0	2,02,37,300	100
Roads and bridges	18,99,46,50,000	2,98,21,60,050	0	29,82,160,050	100
Police	2,00,00,000	3,14,00,000	0	3,14,00,000	100
Stationary and printing	3,00,00,000	4,71,00,000	0	4,71,00,000	100
Public works	33,54,65,000	5,26,68,005	0	5,26,68,005	100
Other administrative services	58,21,00,000	9,13,89,700	0	9,13,89,700	100
General education	13,71,63,01,000	2,15,34,59,257	0	21,53,459,257	100
Technical education	23,14,34,000	3,63,35,138	0	3,63,35,138	100
Sports and youth services	2,93,00,000	46,00,100	0	46,00,100	100
Art and culture	6,52,00,000	1,02,36,400	0	1,02,36,400	100
Medical and public health	1,38,50,00,000	21,74,45,000	0	21,74,45,000	100

Cont'd...

...Cont'd

Water supply and sanitation	3,48,27,85,000	54,67,97,245	0	54,67,97,245	100
Housing	4,00,00,000	62,80,000	0	62,80,000	100
Urban development	8,57,47,50,000	1,34,62,35,750	0	13,46,235,750	100
Information and publicity	3,65,00,000	57,30,500	0	57,30,500	100
Welfare of SCs, STs and OBCs	1,78,54,55,000	28,03,16,435	1,09,59,18,000	1,70,72,463	60.9
Labour and Employment	23,68,60,000	3,71,87,020	0	3,71,87,020	100
Social security and welfare	7,77,27,30,000	1,22,03,18,610	0	1,22,03,18,610	100
Nutrition	2,99,36,60,000	47,00,04,620	0	47,00,04,620	100
Relief on account of natural calamities	4,66,00,00,000	73,16,20,000	0	73,16,20,000	100
Other social services	2,05,05,000	3,21,92,850	0	3,21,92,850	100
Crop husbandry	2,54,28,25,000	39,92,23,525	37,05,42,560	2,86,80,965	77.40
Soil and water conservation	3,60,00,000	56,52,000	57,60,000	1,08,000	1.87
Animal husbandry	12,82,90,000	20,141,530	0	2,01,41,530	100
Dairy development	44,07,00,000	6,91,89,900	46,50,000	6,45,39,900	93.27
Fisheries	5,50,00,000	86,35,000	0	86,35,000	100
Forestry and wildlife	33,15,40,000	5,20,51,780	0	5,20,51,780	100
Agricultural research	24,00,00,000	3,76,80,000	0	3,76,80,000	100
Cooperation	4,49,00,000	70,49,300	1,00,00,000	+2,9,50,70,000	
Other agricultural programmes	1,50,00,000	23,55,000	0	23,55,000	100
Special Programmes for rural development	1,07,57,50,000	16,88,45,650	0	16,88,45,650	100
Rural employment	7,39,58,16,000	1,16,11,43,112	2,92,18,89,600	+1,76,07,46,488	

Cont'd...

...Cont'd

Other rural development programmes	1,89,65,847,000	2,97,76,37,979	10,00,00,000	1,97,76,379	66.41
Main irrigation	11,42,27,19,000	1,79,33,66,883	0	1,79,33,66,883	100
Major and medium irrigation	1,56,92,29,000	24,63,68,953	0	24,63,68,953	100
Minor irrigation	1,50,00,00,000	23,55,00,000	0	23,55,00,000	100
Command area development	20,00,00,000	3,14,00,000	0	3,14,00,000	100
Flood control and drainage	3,16,60,03,000	4,97,06,2471	0	49,70,62,471	100
Power projects	10,44,33,38,000	1,63,96,04,066	0	1,63,96,04,066	100
Non-conventional sources of energy	4,00,00,000	62,80,000	0	62,80,000	100
Village and small industries	80,72,00,000	12,67,30,400	0	12,67,30,400	100
Industries	2,84,06,00,000	44,59,74,200	0	44,59,74,200	100
Telecommunications and electronic industries	42,65,00,000	6,69,60,500	0	6,69,60,500	100
Industries and minerals	65,47,00,000	10,27,87,900	0	10,27,87,900	100
Road transport	1,20,00,000	18,84,000	0	18,84,000	100
Secretariat economic services	6,80,00,000	1,06,76,000	0	10,67,000	100
Tourism	25,13,02,000	3,94,54,414	0	3,94,54,414	100
Census survey and statistics	3,56,00,000	55,89,200	0	55,89,200	100
Investment in general financial and trading institutions	1,00,00,000	15,70,000	0	15,70,000	100

through reservation in elected bodies, public services and educational courses, protection against socio-economic exploitation, and enhanced, specific financial allocation for expediting their socio-economic development. Here, we try to find out the impact of the SCSP on the development of the SCs.

To measure the development of the SCs, the National Scheduled Castes Commission (1999–2000 and 2000–01) suggested the SC Human Development Index, taking into consideration factors such as literacy rate, infant mortality rate, incidence of atrocities against the SCs, estimates of consumption expenditure, and people living below the poverty line to assess the gap in the socio-economic development of the SCs and other sections of society, which would give them an estimate of the gap between the development of the SCs and the other sections of society and detail the effort still required to be made for the development of the SCs.

Atrocities against SCs

Caste and religion play a vital role in establishing an unequal society. Though the SCs constitute about 15.7 per cent of the state's total population, Brahminism and feudalism are more predominant in Bihar due to the dominating presence of the upper castes. Whenever the SCs try to lead a life with dignity and self-respect, the other castes become uneasy because they want the lower castes to continue to remain downtrodden and do their traditional menial work. They oppose assimilation and integration of the lower castes with the so-called mainstream, citing fears of social adulteration. Their fear is that if the lower castes occupy a higher social position, violating the age-old customs, it will lead to social disturbances. Though the SCs are constitutionally guaranteed political reservation, the caste Hindus seldom accept them and often use that as a pretext to attack the Dalits.

Despite their strong numbers, the SCs have long been victims of social discrimination and subjected to several disabilities and restrictions in their social existence by the dominant upper castes, especially in rural Bihar.

Table 6.4 shows only the number of registered cases of atrocities committed against the SCs. Many more cases go unreported primarily because of the indifferent attitude of the police and the inaccessibility of the courts. What is more shocking is the verbal instructions from the government to the police to not register cases of atrocities against the SCs in order to show that the law and order situation is good in the state.

Table 6.4 Crimes against SCs in Bihar

Year	*Number of Cases Reported*
2001	693
2002	876
2003	1,185
2004	1,785
2005	1,572
2006	1,729
2007	1,932

Source: National Crime Records Bureau.

The table also shows that there has been a gradual rise in the number of atrocities against the SCs in Bihar since 2004. Because of the rising awareness and assertion of the Dalit groups, pressure from conscious Dalit political leaders, human right groups and other like-minded sections, more cases are getting registered now.

Educational Status

There is a general consensus that education is an important aspect of development and, in the recent past, it has been taken as one of the major indicators of development. Education is an important social resource and a means of reducing social inequality. It helps an individual to raise his social status in various ways. The knowledge, skills, values and attitudes acquired through education helps him lead a better life. With this realization, the Centre and states have adopted policies and programmes for the improvement of education facilities for the SCs.

The makers of our Constitution were absolutely aware of the need for the state to promote education amongst all and especially amongst the weaker sections. Hence, a number of safeguards have been provided in the Constitution through Articles 15(4), 29(i) and 350 for the educational development of the weaker sections of society.

Educating the SCs and other weaker sections has been a major part of the governmental efforts since the early 1950s. This includes mainly financial support in the form of school and college scholarships and running hostels and other facilities. The educational backwardness of the SCs is a major fallout of the traditional Hindu social order.

The general condition of education among the SCs is pitiable. It is a matter of common knowledge that the SCs have lagged behind in the

Table 6.5 Caste- and Sex-wise Literacy in Bihar (in %)

Year	*Scheduled Castes*			*All Population*		
	Males	*Females*	*Total*	*Males*	*Females*	*Total*
1961*	11.2	0.9	6.0	29.8	6.9	18.4
1971*	11.9	1.0	6.5	30.6	8.7	19.9
1981*	18.0	2.5	10.4	38.1	13.6	18.1
1991*	24.0	5.4	15.1	42.0	18.1	30.6
2001**	40.2	15.6	28.5	60.32	33.57	47.53

* The literacy rate is calculated on the basis of the number of literates and total population.

** The literacy rate is calculated on the basis of the population for a seven year period.

Source: Census of India.

field of education not only in Bihar, but all over the country. Table 6.5 depicts the literacy rate of the SCs and that of the total population of Bihar. In 2001, only 28.5 per cent of the SCs were literate, while it was a high 60.32 per cent for the rest of the population. The table also indicates the gap in the literacy rates between the SCs and the others between 1961 and 1991. The situation was far more pathetic in the case of the SC women. The level of literacy among SC females was extremely low at 5.4 per cent in 1991, while it was nearly three times higher among the others in Bihar (18.11%). The rate of growth of female literacy among the SCs was also more than that of the total population, yet the gap between the two groups has widened from 1971–81 to 1981–91 to 1991–2001. This has happened despite the so-called progressive educational programmes for SCs in Bihar.

The reasons for this wide gap between the two could be manifold:

1. There has been a general trend among the upper caste men and women to become literate and obtain education right from the beginning as they came in direct contact with the British and modern education.
2. The rising literacy among the SCs is only a recent phenomenon.
3. The SCs have always been engaged in productive achievement – manual labour, where literacy is hardly needed.
4. The SCs have always suffered from subordination as well as untouchability and many other forms of discrimination at the hands of the upper castes.
5. Teachers (belonging mostly to the upper castes) have customarily practised indifferent attitudes towards the SCs.
6. Schools were/are located in the upper caste localities.

Table 6.6 Distribution of Enrolment of Student by Social Category

Social Category	*Educational Level*	*2003–04*	*2004–05*	*2005–06*	*2006–07*	*Percentage Increase in Four Years*
All	Primary (I-V)	97,32,357	1,09,17,135	1,12,33,590	1,25,27,117	28.72
	Upper Primary (VI-VIII)	14,82,470	19,36,213	21,63,453	25,62,318	72.84
	Total (I-VIII)	1,12,14,847	1,28,53,348	1,33,97,043	1,50,89,435	34.55
SC	Primary (I-V)	16,30,643	18,03,005	18,19,098	22,12,091	35.66
	Upper Primary (VI-VIII)	1,70,731	2,36,506	2,50,377	3,36,970	97.37
	Total (I-VIII)	18,01,374	20,39,511	20,69,475	25,49,061	41.51
ST	Primary (I-V)	1,29,224	1,22,421	1,49,785	2,28,181	76.43
	Upper Primary (VI-VIII)	12,240	17,037	22,101	27,666	126.03
	Total (I-VIII)	1,41,574	1,39,458	1,71,886	2,55,847	80.72

Source: Economic Survey 2008–09, Bihar.

Any effort made by the SCs to become literate and achieve even minimum levels of education has been discouraged by the upper castes. In many cases in the past, the Dalits were socially boycotted, severely punished both physically and financially by imposing fines, especially in the rural areas, if they dared to become literate and achieve even minimum levels of education.

Students in School

Post-independence, there has been an explosion in school enrolments in Bihar and in the other states of India. In Bihar, there has been a massive rise – 34.5 per cent – in the number of children enrolled in primary and upper primary schools between 2003–04 and 2006–07. There has been a 41.5 per cent increase in the enrolment of SC children and a 80.7 per cent increase in the enrolment of ST students during the same period. Enrolments have improved significantly at the upper primary levels – an overall increase of 72.8 per cent. For the SCs, the enrolment in upper primary

Table 6.7 Distribution of Enrolment of Students by Categories in Bihar (% in parentheses)

Class	*Social Category*	*2003–04*	*2004–05*	*2005–06*	*2006–07*
Primary 1–4	SCs	16,30,643 (16.75)	18,03,005 (16.51)	18,19,098 (16.19)	22,12,091 (17.65)
	STs	1,29,334 (1.3)	1,22,421 (1.12)	1,49,785 (1.33)	2,28,181 (1.82)
	Non-SC/ST	79,72,380 (80.91)	89,91,709 (82.36)	92,64,707 (82.47)	1,00,86,845 (80.53)
	Total	97,32,357	1,09,17,135	1,12,33,590	1,25,27,117
Upper 5–8	SCs	1,70,731 (11.5)	2,36,506 (12.21)	2,50,377 (11.57)	3,36,970 (13.15)
	STs	12,240 (0.94)	17,037 (0.87)	22,101 (1.02)	27,666 (1.07)
	Non-SC/ST	12,99,489 (87.65)	16,82,670 (86.92)	18,90,975 (87.40)	21,97,682 (85.78)
	Total	14,82,460	19,36,213	21,63,453	2,56,23,187
Total 1–8	SCs	18,01,374 (16.06)	20,39,511 (15.86)	20,69,475 (15.44)	25,49,061 (16.89)
	STs	1,41,574 (1.26)	13,458 (1.08)	1,71,886 (1.28)	2,55,847 (1.69)
	Non-SC/ST	92,71,869 (82.67)	10,67,437 (83.05)	1,11,55,682 (83.27)	1,22,84,527 (81.14)
	Total	1,12,14,817	12,85,33,448	1,33,97,043	1,50,89,435

Source: Economic Survey 2008–09, Bihar.

school has increased by 97.4 per cent, while, for the STs, it has increased by 126 per cent (see Table 6.6). Table 6.7 depicts the real picture of student enrolment among the various categories.

Dropout Rates

It is well known that many children who attend school do not necessarily complete a given level of education. The problem of dropping out is a serious one in our education system and the rate of dropouts is an important indicator of its efficiency. The rate of dropping out is found to be very high in Bihar. It was 51.59 per cent at the primary level, 79.69 per cent at the upper primary level and a massive 83.06 per cent at the secondary level in 2004–05. However, at the primary level, this rate declined by 5 per cent between 2004–05 and 2005–06. The decline has been higher in the case of boys. However, at the upper primary level, there was only a very modest decline of just 1 per cent during the period, while the secondary level had no respite and slipped further by 0.01 per cent (see Table 6.8).

Table 6.8 Distribution of Dropout Rates at Primary, Upper Primary and Secondary Levels

Year	*Primary*			*Upper Primary*	*Secondary*
	Total	*Girls*	*Boys*		
2004–05	51.59	48.62	53.37	74.69	83.06
2005–06	46.55	45.25	47.37	73.37	83.07

Source: Economic Survey 2008–09, Government of Bihar.

Table 6.9 Dropout Rates of SC Students in Classes 1–5, 6–8 and 9–12, 2005–06

Classes	*Boys*	*Girls*	*Total*
1–5	55.52	55.84	55.64
6–8	79.86	80.43	80.06
9–12	89.65	92.05	90.52

Source: Ministry of Human Resources Development, Government of India.

Table 6.9 indicates the dropout rates for SC students in Classes 1–5, 6–8 and 9–12 in Bihar for 2005–06. It reveals higher dropout rates in Classes 9–12 and 6–8 (65.26% and 73.55%, respectively). It also reveals that the dropout rate among boys is 72.32 per cent and among girls, 75.09 per cent, at the Class 9–12 level.

Important factors responsible for the high rate of dropping out, particularly of girls and those belonging to the SCs, are: (i) poverty; (ii) illiteracy of parents; (iii) high opportunity cost of these children; (iv) sociocultural barriers for girls to go to school; (v) poor health and nutritional status of the children; (vi) lack of basic infrastructure in schools; (vii) indifferent attitude of teachers towards SC students; (viii) unsuitable location of the schools – most schools are in Savarna localities; (ix) lack of motivation; and (x) fear of insecurity.

Higher Education

Table 6.10 Reserved Seats for Various Social Groups in Universities and Colleges in Bihar (%)

Category	*Percentage*
Scheduled Castes	10
Scheduled Tribes	1
Economically Backward Classes	16
Backward Classes	12
Women of Backward Classes	3

Table 6.11 Higher Education Institutions in Bihar, 2008–09

Institutions	*Number*
Universities	12
Open Universities	1
Research Institutions	11
Total Number of Colleges/Institutes	504
Government	255
Private (Aided)	4
Private (Unaided)	245
Education/Teacher Training Institutions	15
Medical Colleges	23
Engineering/Technical Colleges	7
Others	63

Source: Economic Survey 2008–09, Bihar.

In keeping with Bihar's policy of affirmative action for the marginalized and oppressed sections of society, reservation is guaranteed in universities and colleges. In addition to caste, community and gender-based reservations, 3 per cent seats are also reserved for the physically challenged within each category (see Table 6.10). This table reveals that even 63 years after independence, the government has not provided for reservation in higher education in proportion to the target population.

Table 6.12 Course-Wise Enrolment of SC Students in Higher Education in Bihar, 2000

Courses		*Enrolment*				
		PhD/ MPhil	*Postgraduate Programmes*	*Bachelor's Programmes*	*Total*	*Others*
Arts	Boys	100	1,998	18,551	20,649	1,94,233
	Girls	5	114	1,527	1,646	33,496
Total		105	2,112	20,076	22,293 (8.92)	2,27,729 (91.08)
Commerce	Boys		465	13,180	13,645	87,323
	Girls		75	995	1,070	20,464
Total			540	14,175	14,715 (12.01)	1,07,787 (87.98)
Science/ Computer/ Applications	Boys		1,023	12,073	13,096	87,999
	Girls		196	1,458	1,654	26,458
Total			1,219	13,531	14,750 (11.4)	1,14,457 (88.58)
Engineering/ Technology	Boys			697	697	5,495
	Girls			112	112	881
Total				809	809 (11.25)	6,376 (88.74)
Medical	Boys			748	748	5,895
	Girls			491	491	3858
Total				1,239	1,239 (11.29)	9,753 (88.70)
Educational/ Teacher Training	Boys			1,303	1,303	7,805
	Girls			22	22	1,088
Total				1,325	1,325 (12.96)	8,893 (87.03)
Others	Boys			3,572	3,572	28,891
	Girls			935	935	7,151
Total				4,507	4,507 (11.11)	36,042 (88.88)

Source: Economic Survey 2008–09. Bihar.

Table 6.12 shows the course-wise enrolment status of SCs in higher education in Bihar. The enrolment of female SC students in general streams such as arts, science and commerce is low at 5–6 per cent, but comparatively higher at 11–15 per cent for male students. Thus, the gender gap is very stark indeed. In medical and engineering, however, the enrolments are the same for male and female SC students. This also reveals that most students are still more interested in traditional subjects such as arts and commerce than engineering/technology. It also shows a clear violation of the constitutional obligation of providing reservation to SCs in proportion to their population.

Consumption Pattern Trends

The standard of living of a household can be understood with the help of its monthly per capita expenditure (MPCE) in both rural and urban areas. The average monthly per capita expenditure of people belonging to any household type are significantly different among the different social groups in Bihar. The average MPCE of SCs and STs is much lower than other groups in both rural and urban areas in Bihar. The average daily per capita expenditure of SCs is ₹ 10.97, as against ₹ 15.25 for the rest of the population in rural areas. Similarly, in urban areas, SCs spend ₹ 14.69, as against ₹ 26.93 for the rest of the population (see Table 6.13).

Table 6.13 Distribution of Average Monthly Per Capita Expenditure for Different Social Groups of Bihar

Social Groups	*Average MPCE*	
	Rural	*Urban*
STs	337.16	524.74
SCs	329.32	440.88
OBCs	384.66	499.52
Others	457.59	808.03
All	384.45	601.58

Source: National Sample Survey, 1999–2000.

Table 6.14 shows the distribution of rural persons by MPCE class separately for different social groups with an 'All Groups' column provided for comparison. It depicts that the MPCE figures for SC and ST groups are much lower than those for the general population. This is revealed by the much higher proportion of people falling in the lower

MPCE ranges for SC and ST groups as compared to the general population. The MPCE level of OBCs is better than those of SCs and STs, but not as high as that of the other groups. It further reveals that 82.4 per cent of the SCs have an MPCE of between ₹ 0 and ₹ 420 (₹ 14), while only 52.9 per cent of the others fall in this range.

Table 6.14 Percentage Distribution of Monthly Per Capita Expenditure in Rural Bihar, 1999–2000

MPCE (₹)	*SCs*	*STs*	*OBCs*	*Others*	*All Groups*
0–225	14.4	14.0	6.1	3.9	7.9
225–255	11.9	13.4	8.0	4.2	8.4
255–300	19.7	17.4	16.6	8.3	15.6
300–340	16.7	18.0	14.8	12.2	14.9
340–380	12.0	12.5	14.4	11.5	13.2
380–420	7.7	6.3	10.2	12.8	10.0
420–470	7.4	6.2	9.7	13.7	9.8
470–525	4.4	4.1	7.4	8.4	6.7
525–615	3.8	3.5	5.9	11.2	6.4
615–775	1.7	3.6	4.4	7.3	4.4
775–950	0.2	0.4	1.5	3.5	1.6
Above 950	0.1	0.5	0.8	3.0	1.1
Average MPCE (₹)	329.32	337.16	384.66	457.59	384.45

Source: National Sample Survey, 1999–2000.

Incidence of Poverty

Table 6.15 BPL Population by Social Groups in Bihar, 2004–05

Social Category	*Rural*	*Urban*
SCs	64%	67.2%
OBCs	37.8%	41.4%
Others	26.6%	18.3%

Source: Annual Report, 2004–05, Ministry of Social Justice and Empowerment, Government of India.

Table 6.15 indicates the incidence of poverty among the various social groups in Bihar. It reveals that 64 per cent of the SCs and 37.8 per cent of the OBCs in rural Bihar are living below the poverty line; the corresponding figures for urban Bihar are 67.2 per cent and 41.4 per cent, respectively. These figures are higher than those for others living below the poverty line.

Work Participation

The work participation rate of SCs is 39.7 per cent, which is marginally lower than the national average of 40.4 per cent. While there has been a marginal decline in the rate of male work participation from 54.4 per cent to 49.2 per cent, the female rate of work participation has increased from 23.3 per cent to 29.5 per cent during 1991–2001. Among the total workers, 71 per cent are main workers and this proportion is almost comparable with the national average of 73 per cent.

Table 6.16 Distribution of Workers in Bihar

Social Categories	*Cultivators*	*Agricultural Labourers*	*Household Industrial Workers*	*Other Workers*
SCs	7.9	77.6	3.3	11.2
STs	21.3	62.5	4	12
All	29	48	3.9	19

Source: Census of India, 2001.

Agricultural labourers constitute the largest proportion – 77.6 per cent – of all workers .(see Table 6.16). This implies that more than three-fourths of the total SC workers are agricultural labourers. This figure is higher than the national average of 45.6 per cent. Other workers constitute 11.2 per cent, which is lower when compared to the national average of 30.5 per cent in respect of all SCs. Workers engaged in household industries constitute 3.3 per cent, which is at par with the SCs' national average of 3.9 per cent.

Land Issues

Land reforms are central to any real battle against Bihar's backwardness. With 90 per cent of the state's population living in villages and 74 per cent of its workforce employed in agriculture, Bihar is still predominantly rural or agrarian. Yet, agriculture accounts for only 33 per cent of its gross domestic product and the landholding pattern remains absolutely skewed. Marginal and small farmers, who constitute roughly 96.5 per cent of total landowners, own about 66 per cent of the total land, while medium and large farmers, who constitute only 3.5 per cent of the landowning community, own roughly 33 per cent of the total land. Citing the figures of the National Sample Survey Organization (NSSO), the Land Reform Commissions report throws up a reverse trend of land concentration: between 1992 and 2003, the proportion of large landowners went down from 0.2 per cent to 0.1 per cent, yet their share in total land area increased from 4.44 per cent to 4.63 per cent.

The proportion of the landless or the near landless among the rural poor has been increasing steadily from 67 per cent in 1993–94 to 75 per cent by the turn of the century. Between 1991 and 2001, migration from Bihar increased by more than 200 per cent; the national average during the same period stood at just 21.5 per cent. Landlessness aggravates poverty and forces people to migrate out of the state in addition to retarding the development of agriculture. Between 1991–92 and 1995–96, agriculture in Bihar grew at a negative rate of 2 per cent per annum, followed by a very sluggish 0.8 per cent annual recovery during the next six years (when, nationally, agriculture grew at 3 per cent per annum). Despite having very fertile soil and copious water resources, agricultural growth remains so sluggish in Bihar that the Land Reform Commission finds it 'evident that there is a structural bottleneck in Bihar agriculture due to a very queer pattern of land ownership and very extortionate system of tenancy at will, which are causing great impediment to an accelerated rate of agriculture growth'.

About 91 per cent of Bihar's SCs live in rural areas, where the main source of income is either cultivation of agricultural land (as self-employed farmers), wage labour or some type of non-farm employment. Therefore, access to land for cultivation is critical. Surplus land through land ceiling and government land are distributed to the SCs on a priority basis. As on March 1999, surplus ceiling land of 3,08,223 acres had been distributed across Bihar. Of these, some 1,81,701 acres were distributed to SCs, 39,937 acres to STs and 86,585 acres to non-SCs/STs. A total of 3,79,518 beneficiaries have been covered so far, of which 2,34,334 were SCs, 43,004, STs and 1,02,180, non-SCs/STs (Kumar, 2000). SC beneficiaries accounted for about 61.74 per cent, the share in area was around 58.95 per cent. The land distributed to SCs per beneficiary comes to 0.78 acre, which was nearer to the average per distribution (0.81 acre.)

Similarly, as on March 1999, surplus government land amounting to 1,33,709 acres were distributed in Bihar. Of these, around 5,47,571.82 acres were distributed to SCs (Kumar, 2002).

SC beneficiaries accounted for about 47.05 per cent of the total, with their share in area coming to around 40.95 per cent. The land distributed to SCs per beneficiary comes to 0.89 acre.

With respect to ownership of agricultural land in rural areas during 1982 and 1992 (land ownership data is not available for earlier rounds of NSSO data), it was observed that about 19.73 per cent of the SC households in Bihar were landless in 1992. This is much higher than the 8.52 per cent in all households in general.

Despite the distribution of land under ceiling and government land, the percentage of SC landless households has increased from 7.92 per cent in 1982 to 19.73 per cent in 1992. Nearly 80.27 per cent of SC households owned some land in 1992. However, of these, nearly 77.08 per cent owned less than 2.49 acres in 1992. The average area owned by the small farmer is 0.89 acres, which is near landless households. The landless and near-landless put together account for nearly 96.8 per cent of the total SC households. This indicates the pitiable condition of the SCs in Bihar (Kumar, 2002).

Land Distribution

Allotment of land is one of the major programmes of the state for improving the economic status of the SCs. A large section of the SC population earns its livelihood by working on land. Under the programme, land is to be distributed for the following reasons: (1) reclamation of cultivable wastelands; (2) distribution of surplus land released through ceiling on agricultural holdings; and (3) land to be made available through the Bhoodan movement and the allotment of cultivable wastelands after proper reclamation. The land available for distribution and utilization among the landless is handed over to the administration for that purpose. There are two types of land: (i) *gair mazarua aam*; and (ii) *gair mazarua khas*. The first type is meant for common use, such as grazing, irrigation, graveyards, etc. The second type of land is cultivable land, which is neither under the zamindars for self-cultivation nor under tenants. This is land that has been captured by powerful landowners. After independence, both types of land came under state control. The village *gram sabha* also has some control over land. However, due to the problems of irrigation maintenance, non-utilization of surplus land collected for distribution and the nexus between the administration and the zamindars, surplus land of both types, though earmarked on paper for distribution among the SCs, remains unused on a large scale.

It was found that only 21.14 per cent of the respondents were allotted agricultural land by the state. The title deeds were issued, allotting them 20 decimals of land each, but only 0.85 per cent of them actually took possession of the land (Kumar, 2002).

The key recommendations of the Land Reform Commission are threefold: (i) do away with the present system of classification of land into six categories with ceiling varying from 15 acre to 45 acres, for all kinds of land; (ii) allot between one acre and 0.66 acre of ceiling surplus land to the lowest quintile of agriculture labourers consisting of 16.68 lakh households each and assign at least 10 decimals of land to the shelter-less households of 5.48 lakh non-farm rural workers each; and (iii) enact a Bataidari Act to ensure secure and heritable right of cultivation to all tenants/sharecroppers with 60 per cent share of the produce (if the landowner bears the cost of production) or 70–75 per cent of the produce (if the *bataidar* bears the cost of production). But Bihar has not implemented this recommendation because of the opposition of the upper caste landlords, who are strong supporters of Bharatiya Janata Party (BJP).

Health Status

Health status is another valid indicator of human development. Good health, by itself, improves the quality of life. The health Profile of a community can be gauged by indicators such as morbidity, mortality, immunization of children and expectant mothers, and longer life expectancy. Table 6.17 shows infant mortality and child mortality by social characteristics.

Table 6.17 Infant and Child Mortality by Social Categories, 1998–99

Social Groups	*Neonatal Mortality*	*Post-Neonatal Mortality*	*Infant Mortality*	*Child Mortality*	*Under-Five Mortality*
SCs	52.8	33.5	86.3	52.0	133.8
STs	56.1	25.6	81.9	37.8	116.6
OBCs	71.0	24.3	75.3	34.1	106.8
Others	43.1	24.0	61.2	29.9	89.3

Source: National Family Health Survey (NFHS 1998–99), Bihar.

The infant mortality rate and child mortality rate among SCs is 86.3 and 133.8 per 1,000 births, respectively, which is much higher than among other communities (see Table 6.17). SC, ST and OBC children depict considerably higher levels of infant mortality and child mortality rates than do the children of the other groups.

The overall sex ratio of the SCs in Bihar is 923 females per 1,000 males, which is lower than the national average of 936 in respect of all SCs.

The Mahadalits Commission

On the eve of Independence Day, 2007, Bihar announced the constitution of a Mahadalits Commission to study the condition of the disadvantaged groups among the SCs. A notification for the constitution of this Commission was issued on 20 September 2007. The Mahadalits Commission was constituted under the chairmanship of Vishwanath Rishi, a former minister; its other members were Baban Rawat, Rajendra Prasad Nat, Chhote Lal Rajbanshi and K.P. Ramaiah, who was the commissioner of the Magadh range, as member secretary.

The major aims of constituting the Commission are to:

1. identify the castes within the SCs who lagged behind in the development process;
2. study the educational and social status of these castes and suggest measures for their uplift;
3. recommend actions to initiate measures for their educational and social uplift along with ways for their employment; and
4. work on any other matter the state entrusts to it.

The Mahadalits Commission submitted its first interim report to the government on 20 November 2007. It identified 18 of the SC 23 castes in the state as lagging in development – these constituted 31 per cent of the total SCs in Bihar. The Commission did not include four SCs – the Paswans (Dusadhs), the Pasis, the Dhobis and the Chamars in the Mahadalits category. These four constitute 69 per cent of the SC population in the state. It suggested ways for the socio-economic and political empowerment of the other SCs groups. The criteria for identification of Mahadalits are representation in government jobs and panchayats, and literacy rates of below 10 per cent (Economic Survey of Bihar). Thus, they are both socially and educationally more backward. The report also said that there were no high school teachers or senior officials from these castes in the state despite reservations in government jobs for them.

Bihar included the Pasis and the Dhobis in the list of Mahadalits on 28 July 2009, following the second recommendation of the

Commission. The Commission observed that out of the 23 SCs in Bihar, 21 were actually deprived in terms of educational, economic, sociocultural and political status. The Commission identified these 21 castes primarily on the basis of their literacy rate (Economic Survey, 2008–09). The Chamars were also included in the list of Mahadalits by the third recommendation of the Commission. While the total literacy rate of Bihar is 47 per cent, and that for all SCs is 28.5 per cent, it is only 16.7 per cent in case of the Mahadalits. It noted that these castes did not benefit from the affirmative actions meant exclusively for the SCs. Following this, the government included 22 of the 23 SC castes of the state in the Mahadalits list.

The other 19 Mahadalit castes are the Bantar, Bauri, Bhogta, Bhuiyan, Chaupal, Dabger, Dom, Ghasi, Halalkhor, Hads, Kanjor, Kuriar, Lalbegi, Musahar, Nat, Pan, Rajwar and Turi.

Recommendations

The Mahadalits Commission recommended special polling stations for the Mahadalits since it was very difficult for these people to get to the main polling stations and exercise their franchise freely. It demanded reservation for them in panchayats and local bodies and exclusive representation in Grade IV jobs. All Mahadalit families were to be covered under the BPL schemes, a grain bank scheme was to be started to provide them grain on loan, they were to be given boiled rice instead of wheat under the rural development schemes, they were to be ensured 200 days of secure employment in a year, they were to be given bank financing on a priority basis, banks were to hold special loan melas for them, they were to be given priority in allotting Indira Awas Patras, schools were to be opened in their areas with free books, scholarships, uniforms and food, and Mahadalit teachers were to be appointed in the schools. These were some of the recommendations.

The government has chalked out an action plan under the label of the Bihar Mahadalit Vikas Mission for the uplift of the Mahadalits. The Mission is registered under the Society Registration Act of 1860 for implementing welfare schemes for these downtrodden castes in keeping with the reports of the Mahadalits Commission. The action plan includes:

1. Three decimal land was to be provided to each landless Mahadalit family for constructing houses under the Mahadalit scheme. (The total number of Mahadalit families was around 10,600 then.)
2. A special Mahadalit Sauchalaya Nirman Yojana was launched, under which each Mahadalit family would receive ₹ 300 from the

Mission for the construction of toilets. (A sum of ₹ 7 crore was released to the Mission for the construction of toilets in the Mahadalit areas.)

3. The government has decided to consider contractual appointments of Mahadalits' dependents by relaxing the eligibility norms for Grade VIII, in the event of their death in harness. Eligible dependents will be asked to attain literacy within a period of two years of the death of their spouse for securing the job on contract.
4. Community centres would be set up in Mahadalit villages with 500 or more population under the community building-cum-workshed construction scheme.
5. Some 10,000 development volunteers will be appointed from Mahadalit families, one in each panchayat of villages with a population of 1,000 and one in each ward in urban areas.
6. Under the Chief Minister's School Uniform Scheme, the state will give ₹ 500 to each Mahadalit student of Classes 1–5 studying in state run schools.
7. Each Mahadalit family will be given ₹ 400 to purchase a transistor radio.
8. Mahadalit settlements will be linked with main roads and preference will be given to children of Mahadalit castes in residential schools for SC boys and girls.
9. Separate SHGs will be created for Mahadalit women to empower them economically.
10. Radio programmes on folk music, dance and stories involving Mahadalits will be made and transmitted.
11. Mobile ayurvedic vans and mobile public distribution system will be introduced in Mahadalit settlements.

Constitutional Validity

Some states have made efforts to bifurcate the SC quota. In 1975, the then Chief Minister of Punjab, Giani Zail Singh, bifurcated the SCs in the state into A and B categories. In 1994, the then Chief Minister of Haryana, Bhajan Lal, created similar A and B categories in his state, as did Rajnath Singh in Uttar Pradesh, but the initiative was lost when an advocate filed a legal case against this quota. In Andhra Pradesh, Chandra Babu Naidu bifurcated the SCs into four – A, B, C and D – categories. This was challenged in the Andhra Pradesh High Court, which upheld the Naidu ministry's step. E.V. Chinnaiah then filed a petition in the Supreme Court in 2004, arguing that there was no constitutional basis for a state to provide a separate quota. A petition was filed by Brajesh Singh Muwal against the SC quota bifurcation in the Punjab and Haryana High Court, too, resulting in these categories being abolished.

Is the division of SCs into Dalits and Mahadalits in Bihar constitutional? Were the SCs divided to enable their socio-economic and educational development or did the move contain some hidden political agenda? Why didn't the Commission include the Dusadhs among the Mahadalits? Are the Dusadhs (the Paswans) politically, economically, socially and educationally more powerful than the other SC groups?

The National Commission for Scheduled Castes declared the formation of the Mahadalits Commission by Bihar to be unconstitutional, stating that the Constitution did not permit a state to take any such step without consulting it.

The Supreme Court also declared such efforts by states as unconstitutional.

The Bihar SC/ST Commission also objected to the use of the word, Dalit, and said that the use of this word itself amounts to an offence against the SC/ST Act, 1989.

The word 'SC' has a legal and administrative connotation. It was adopted by the Government of India Act in 1935. The term 'SC' literally connotes 'schedule of castes or the castes put under a schedule'. This term is embodied in the Government of India Act of 1935 in Section 305. Section 24, part of the First Schedule of the Government of India Bill of 1935, defined the SCs as such castes, races and tribes corresponding to classes of persons formerly known as the depressed classes as His Majesty in Council may specify. Section 26(1), also substantially accepted the above definition and defined the SCs as Section 24 did. The term 'depressed classes' should be applied to those who would be considered untouchable according to the following list of the 1911 Census:

1. those who are denied access to the interior of ordinary temples; and
2. those who cause pollution
   (a) by touch, and
   (b) by appearing within a certain distance.

The SC identity has become a constitutional identity for the term 'untouchables' is used for all legal and administrative purposes. Its adoption led to precision with regard to castes, classes or groups of the castes to be categorized as such.

The term 'Dalit' evolved in the early 1970s. It was used and popularized by the Dalit Panthers, a militant organization of untouchable youths in Maharashtra. The word 'Dalit' is a symbol of change and revolution which believes in humanism and rejects the existence of god, rebirth, soul, the sacred books that teach discrimination, fate and heaven. The rejection of religion and priesthood is because they made the Dalits into slaves. Therefore, Dalit is the most secular identity a person could ever have. It denotes a class rather than a caste.

Bihar did not divide its SCs into Dalits and Mahadalits with good intentions. Using such connotations shows hatred against the SCs. It shows the degrading ritual status of the SCs.

The Constitution provides reservation on the basis of social and educational backwardness. If so, on what basis did the Mahadalits Commission divide the SCs of Bihar? If the criteria used were social and educational backwardness, the condition of the SC castes are as follows:

The SCs are not a homogeneous group. The castes among the SCs reflect hierarchically arranged social status and differential degrees of respect, prestige and influence among them (Kumar, 2002).

The ascribed hierarchy is the fundamental feature among the SCs. It is associated with the principles of purity and pollution, superior and inferior and with the principle of endogamy. Among the SCs also, marriage outside the caste and contact with members outside the group are forbidden. Among the SCs, the Pasis enjoy a higher social status as compared with the Dhobi, Dusadh, Rajwar, Dabgar, Bhuiya and Nat. The lowest among them are the Doms and the Mehtars. Thus, the SCs are heterogeneous groups. But they share a common concern. This common concern is untouchability, which is still practised by upper caste Hindus.

The literacy rate among the SCs of Bihar is dismally low. Their overall literacy rate is 28.5 per cent, according to Census 2001, which is just about half of the national level of 54.7 per cent. Male and female literates constitute 40.2 per cent and 15.6 per cent, respectively. These figures are lower than the national figures (66.6% and 41.9% respectively) (see Table 6.5).

Among the numerically larger castes, the Dhobis register the highest overall literacy as well as female literacy figures, followed by the Pasis, the Dusadhs and the Chamars. The Musahars depict the lowest literacy rates (see Table 6.18).

Table 6.18 Distribution of Literacy Rates among the Scheduled Castes

Literacy Rate	*All SCs in Bihar*	*Dhobis*	*Pasis*	*Dusadhs*	*Chamars*	*Bhuiya*	*Musahar*
All	28.5	43.9	40.6	33.0	32.1	13.3	9
Females	15.6	27.9	25.3	18.5	16.8	6.5	3.9

Source: Office of the Registrar General of India.

Among the literate SCs, 39.7 per cent are either without any significant education or have studied only below the primary level. The proportion of literates who have attained education up to the primary and middle levels constitute 28.4 per cent and 13.1 per cent, respectively. As many as 15.1 per cent literates are educated up to the matric/secondary/higher secondary level; 3.6 per cent have studied up to the graduate and above level; and a meagre 0.1 per cent are non-technical and technical diploma holders (see Table 6.18).

Among the major castes, the Dhobis have the highest proportion of matriculates (19.7%), while the Musahars and the Bhuiyas have the lowest proportion of matriculates (6%). Every seventh Chamar is a matriculate, while every sixth Dusadh and Pasi are matriculates (see Table 6.19).

It may be discerned from the educational levels attained by Bihar's SCs that the dropout rate is high after the primary level as the percentage of middle level literates is less than half of the primary level literates. The number of children attending school decline sharply from the secondary level onwards.

Table 6.19 Distribution of Education among the Major SCs

Names of SCs	*Literate without Educational Level*	*Below Primary*	*Educational levels attained*				
			Primary	*Middle*	*Matric/ Secondary/ Higher Secondary/ Intermediate, etc.*	*Technical and Non-technical Diploma etc.*	*Graduate and above*
All Scheduled Castes	6.6	33.1	28.4	13.1	15.1	0.1	3.6
Dhobis	4.5	28.3	27	14.9	19.7	0.2	5.4
Pasis	5.7	30	27.1	13.4	17.9	0.2	5.6
Dusadhs	6	32	28.5	13.7	16.4	0.1	3.5
Chamars	5.9	33.6	28.5	16.4	15	0.1	3.5
Bhuiyas	15.3	44.1	26.5	7.4	6	Nil	0.6
Musahars	15.3	44	27.8	6.7	5.5	Nil	0.8

Source: Office of Registrar General, India.

Out of the total 38.8 lakh SC children in the age group of 5–14 years, 11.4 lakh attended school – around 29.4 per cent. Alarmingly, as many as 70.6 per cent (27.4 lakh) children in the corresponding age group did not go to school. Among the major SCs, the Dhobis have the highest share of school going children followed by the Pasis, the Dusadhs and the Chamars (see Table 6.20).

Table 6.20 Percentage Distribution of School Going Population Aged 5–14 Years

All Groups	*All SCs*	*Dhobis*	*Pasis*	*Dusadhs*	*Chamars*	*Bhuiyas*	*Musahars*
5–14 years	29.4	45.6	39.4	34.1	33.7	15.1	9.8

Source: Office of the Registrar General of India.

If we take the criteria of economic status to divide the SCs into Dalits and Mahadalits, the economic conditions are as follows:

Table 6.21 Percentage Distribution of SC Workers

Economic Category	*Chamars*	*Dusadhs*	*Musahars*	*Pasis*	*Dhobis*	*Bhuiyas*
Cultivators	7.9	10.3	2.7	12.3	14.8	6.6
Agricultural labourers	80.2	75.9	92.5	46.5	48.1	86.8
HHI workers	2.1	1.6	0.8	12.2	9.6	1.0
Other workers	9.8	12.2	4.0	29.0	27.5	5.6

Source: Office of the Registrar General of India.

Table 6.21 depicts that among the major castes, the Musahars have the highest proportion of agricultural labourers, followed by the Bhuiyas, the Chamars and the Dusadhs, while among the other workers, the Pasis are in the lead, followed by the Dhobis.

Conclusion

It is clear from the above analysis that the Mahadalits Commission has not adopted any meaningful criteria to divide the SCs into Dalits and Mahadalits. It has also not followed the constitutional directive or taken up the criteria of social, educational and economic backwardness to identify which SCs are lagging the most behind. It looks like the Commission had some hidden political agenda. Some social scientists consider this to be the politics of reservation (Rao, 2009). But it is not only the politics of reservation, it is beyond that. The Commission does not want to see the SCs enjoy the benefit of equal distribution of resources. It further shows the intention of the Commission in smaller budgetary allocations for the SCSP and the diversion of allocated funds by the government. There are special provisions or guidelines for the development of disadvantaged sections among the SCs in the SCSP.

Why did Bihar not implement its SC strategies in a proper manner? Sixty-three years after independence, nobody has questioned this. Till date, the state has failed to distribute the fruits of development to the SCs. Suddenly, how did the government, led by the caste Hindus, become so concerned about the development of the SCs? Who will take care of the development of the Mahadalits? What is the status of the Mahadalit Mission? Is it a statutory body or part of the government? Certainly not, it is a registered society. How will this registered society be able to develop the Mahadalits or SCs? If a government which is formed by the elected representatives of the people is not accountable to the people and not able to do justice to the SCs, then how can this registered society be accountable to the development of the SCs? The funds of the SCSP have been misused and diverted by successive governments till date. If the government were indeed keen on the development of the SCs, then the least it can do is to stop the diversion, misuse and improper allotment of funds intended for the SCs.

This is the politics of inclusion and exclusion and divide and rule. In the name of social engineering, the government wants to maintain the Savarna or Manuvadi structure in society. It wants to maintain inequality and upper caste monopoly and spread hatred in society. The Savarna Hindus have a code, which the SCs are required to follow. This code lays down the acts of omission and commission that the caste Hindus treat as offences (Ambedkar). The following is the list of such offences:

1. The SCs must live in separate quarters away from the habitation of the Hindus. It is an offence for the SCs to break or evade this rule of segregation.
2. The quarters of the SCs must be located towards the south of the main settlements of the caste Hindus since the south is the most inauspicious of the four directions; a break of this rule is deemed to be an offence.
3. The SCs must observe the rule of distance, pollution or shadow of pollution, as the case may be. It is an offence to break this rule.
4. It is an offence for SCs to acquire wealth.

5. It is an offence for a member of the SCs to build a pucca house.
6. It is an offence for a member of the SCs to put on a clean dress and wear shoes, a watch or gold ornaments.
7. It is an offence for a member of the SCs to sit on a chair in the presence of a caste Hindu.
8. It is an offence for a member of the SCs to ride on a horse or a palanquin through the village.
9. It is an offence for a member of the SCs to take a procession of SCs through the caste Hindu area.
10. It is an offence for a member of the SCs to not salute a caste Hindu.
11. It is an offence for a member of the SCs to speak a cultural language.
12. The SCs must do 'begari' for the caste Hindus. It is an offence for the SCs to deny this duty or to demand minimum wages for doing this.

The caste Hindus have internalized this code through the socialization process. These codes are visible in the rural areas and invisible in the urban areas. It has become the state of mind in each and every member of the caste Hindus. Due to this code, the caste Hindus have never shown any fellow-feeling for the SCs. Although the SCs are dependent on the caste Hindus, they have always been ill treated and humiliated. If Hindu society plays its part in maintaining the established order, so do the Hindu officials of the state. The two have made the established order impregnable.

The rights of citizenship do not automatically mean the rights of the SCs. A government of the people and for the people cannot mean a government for the SCs. Equal opportunity for all cannot mean equal opportunity for the SCs. Equal rights for all cannot mean equal rights for the SCs.

In every nook and corner of the country, the SCs not only face handicaps, but also various forms of discrimination. The extent to which this is true is known only to the SCs themselves, who labour under umpteen disadvantages. This discrimination is the strongest barrier against the SCs. It prevents them from rising out of it. It has made the life of the SCs one of constant fear of one thing or the other – of unemployment, assault, persecution. All in all, they lead a life of insecurity.

We may conclude that Bihar has not adopted any criteria to divide the SCs rationally, but has arbitrarily included and excluded one caste

(Dusadhs) into the Mahadalits to perpetuate inequality, hatred and prejudice against them and to maintain Manuvadi principles in society. Dusadhs had/have been always challenging the hegemony and tyranny of upper castes and upper Shudras (Kurmies). Because of this, government has excluded them from the Mahadalit lists and tried to weakened them. Under continuous pressure from the Lok Janshakthi Party leader, Ram Vilas Paswan, against the division of the SCs since 2007, the member secretary of the Mahadalits Commission, K.P. Ramaiah, appeared before the media in December 2009 and said, 'We have decided not to follow the policy of bifurcating the castes as done by other states like Punjab, Haryana and in case of the Mallas and Madigas in Andhra Pradesh. The Commission first tackled the smaller castes, which totalled 18 in number. Then, the Pasis and Dhobis who had no numeric representation and no colonies of their own, were added to this list.' Further, he said, the majority of the SCs are marginalized within the social fabric and their economic condition are more or less the same. But later on, the Chamars who had enough numeric representation and colonies of their own were added to this list. It also cleared the intention and hidden agenda of the government.

References

Ambedkar, B.R. 1993. *Writings and Speeches,* Vol. 5. Mumbai. Education Department, Maharashtra.

'Annual Report 2008–09'. New Delhi: Ministry of Social Justice and Empowerment.

'Economic Survey 2008–09'. Government of Bihar.

Jai Bihar. 29 July 2009.

Kumar, Rabindra. 2002. *Impact of Rural Development on Scheduled Castes*. New Delhi: Anmol Publications,

——. 2002. 'Atrocities on Dalits: Structural Dysfunction'. In *The Fourth World*. Bhubaneswar: NISWASS.

——. 2003. 'Evolution of the Concept of Dalit'. In *The Fourth World*. Bhubaneswar: NISWASS.

The Times of India, 15 June 2009.

ZeeNews.com, International Edition. 29 July 2009.

7

Atrocities on the Scheduled Castes

Structural Dysfunction

Atrocities on the Scheduled Castes (SCs) have become an almost regular feature in our society nowadays. Everyday, we come across, in newspapers and other media, a number of crimes such as beating, torture, arson, usurpation, molestation, rapes, killings, etc., of these people by caste Hindus. Such occurrences not only portray the pitiable state of life of the SCs, but also raise several questions. Why are the SCs being murdered, killed, burnt alive, massacred, lynched, discriminated and assaulted in full view of the public? Why should a caste Hindu feel resentful if an SC enters a profession, obtains a position of authority, buys land, enters into commerce, becomes economically independent and occupies a position in the higher echelons of society? Why should all caste Hindus, be they officials or non-officials, make common cause to suppress the SCs? Does this inhuman treatment of the SCs emanate from the Hindu social order, which empowers them to commit these crimes on these hapless people who form a considerable portion of the people of this land?

The Hindu Social Order and the SCs

Social order means the regular and systematic method of social phenomena, which are mutually related. The socialization process and social control maintain order in a society. According to Durkheim, social order is developed not by self-interest, but by collective norms. While opposing a centralized state, Durkheim argues that a society may best be ordered by the division of labour into many groupings, each of which relates the individual to his/her government in specific way.

Durkheim proposes a combination of individualism and collectivism to ensure a stable social order. The existence of social order depends on the collectivization of individuals and the systematic regulation of their behaviour. Communities, groups and associations come under collectivization. These are the organs of social order. Human behaviour is regulated by practices, folklore, values and laws.

The Hindu social order does not recognize the individual as the centre of social purpose. It is based primarily on varna and not on individuals. There are four varnas: the Brahmins, the Kshatriyas, the Vaishyas and the Shudras. And there is another social category beyond the varna – the Panchamas, outcastes, Dalits or SCs. Thus, Hindu society is not the same thing as an individual Brahmin, Kshatriya, Vaishya or Shudra. It includes all of them.

The doctrine that the different varna were created from different parts of the body of the creator has generated the belief that it must be divine will that they remain separate and distinct. It is this belief that has created among individual Hindus an instinct to be different from each other.

The varna is often claimed not only to be of the nature of castes, but, up to a point, to be the castes themselves. A Brahmin or Kshatriya, at any point of time, represents a particular caste, while the term, Vaishya, in recent years, is being associated with a particular caste group with some qualifying adjectives. As a matter of fact, none of the four varnas now represents anything but the various groups of castes.

The Hindu social order is a ladder of castes placed one above the other, together representing an ascending scale of respect and descending scale of contempt. As opposed to the principles of liberty, equality and fraternity, according to Ambedkar,[1] the Hindu social order is based on the principles of graded inequality, fixity of occupation and fixation of people within their respective castes.

In this social order, the lowest social group has been labelled by various names, starting from the Asprashyas or the untouchables to the present-day legalized label, the SCs, and, more recently, the Dalits. While Brahminical scholarship promoted, both in the past and even today, the connotation of the SCs as Achhuts, Bahyas, Antyavasin, Panchama and Asprashyas, Western scholarship promoted their identity as outcastes, ex-untouchables, depressed classes and SCs. This was later legalized by the Indian government. More recently, these unfortunate classes, in the process of carving out their space in our social fabric, have constructed a more assertive *provincial* identity while being remaining within the larger umbrella label of the Dalits.[2]

The SCs are one of the most disadvantaged groups in Indian society. They are a stigmatized people because of which they suffer from numerous disabilities, which are regulated through religious beliefs and practices. If a caste Hindu observes untouchability, it is because his religion enjoins him to do so. If he is ruthless and lawless in resisting the opposition of the SCs against the established order, it is because his religion not only tells him that the established order is divine and therefore sacrosanct, but because it also imposes on him a duty to see that this established order is maintained by all possible means. If he does not listen to the call of humanity, it is because his religion does not enjoin him to treat the SCs as human beings. If he does not feel any qualms about assaulting, looting, burning and committing other criminal acts and inhuman activities against the SCs, it is because his religion tells him that nothing that is done in the defence of the social order is sinful.

As stated in an earlier chapter, the Hindu dharma is based on the theory of karma (action), the three *gunas* (qualities) and the transmigration of the soul. All these theories are applied to justify the social order. By karma are caused the various conditions of men, the highest, the middle and the lowest. As a consequence of the many sinful acts committed by his body or mind, an individual becomes a bird, beast or low caste person, respectively, in his next birth.

There are three *gunas* that predominate the body. The study of the *Vedas*, austerity, knowledge, purity, etc., are marks of virtue, whereas cruelty, covetousness, evil, etc., are marks of vice. Through each of these qualities, an individual obtains various transmigrations of his soul. It is the preponderance of various qualities that determines the birth of a person as a Brahmin, Shudra or untouchable. Those who commit sins are born into inferior existences or wombs, while those who lead an ideal life obtain release from the cycle of birth and death.[3]

Noted philosopher S. Radhakrishnan, who gave a modern interpretation to Indian philosophy, admits that the Hindu social order has degenerated into an instrument of exploitation, tyranny and oppression. It tended to perpetuate inequality and inhumanity and developed the spirit of separatism, hatred and enmity, low and high.[4]

The caste Hindus have a code that the SCs are required to follow and this code lays down the acts of omission and commission that are treated as offences[5] (see Chapter 5 for code and list of offences).

The caste Hindus internalized the code through the socialization process. This code is visible in the rural areas and invisible in the urban areas, but has become a state of mind in each and every caste Hindu. Due to this code, caste Hindus have never shown any fellow-feeling for the SCs. Although the SCs are dependent on the caste Hindus, they have only been ill-treated and humiliated. If Hindu society plays its part in maintaining the established order, so do the Hindu officials of the state. The two have made the established order an impregnable fortress.

The most ironical fact of the current reality is that none of the rights of citizenship extends itself to the SCs. A government of the people and for the people does not mean a government for the SCs; equal opportunity for all does not include the SCs; equal rights for all cannot mean equal rights for the SCs. In every nook and corner of the country, the SCs not only face handicaps, but also suffer from various forms of discrimination. The extent to which this is true is known only to the SCs who labour under heavy disadvantages. This discrimination is the strongest barrier faced by the SCs. It has made their lives one of constant fear of one thing or the other – unemployment, assault, persecution, etc. It is a life of insecurity.

Atrocities on the SCs

If the SCs attempt to defy the social order, they are punished through social boycotts and acts of retaliatory violence. Over a period of time, the SCs have been increasingly asserting their basic right to gain a place of honour in terms of equality in the social and economic life of the nation. The assertion of their rights by the SCs, particularly their refusal to accept humiliation, is being retaliated against in many areas. The incidence of retaliation has become so frequent that the government has had to take note of it and put them into a different category of crimes. Terming crimes against SCs and STs as 'atrocities', the government started collecting data on such crimes in 1974. The atrocities have been classified into four categories – murder, grievous hurt, arson and rape. Despite the various measures adopted to check atrocities by the Centre and states, they continue to persist. A crime-wise analysis indicates that there are three main reasons for atrocities being committed against the SCs:

1. Unresolved land disputes relating to the allotment of government land or distribution of surplus land to the landless SCs;
2. Tension and bitterness arising from non-payment or underpayment of the minimum wages prescribed by the states; and

3. Resentment against the manifestation of awareness among the SCs about their rights and privileges as enshrined in the Constitution and various legislative and executive measures.[6]

A report issued by the National Commission for Scheduled Castes has underscored that 'untouchability' – the imposition of social disabilities on persons by reason of their birth in certain castes – is still practised in many forms throughout the country. Untouchability is present not only in its physical form, but also deep in the minds of the people. The main causes for the continuance of untouchability even 63 years after independence are:[7]

1. the deep-rooted caste system;
2. carrying on of unclean occupations by the SCs;
3. illiteracy;
4. lack of awareness among the SCs; and
5. rigidity and bias created by religious literature.

In many cases, instead of 'physical' untouchability, there are instances of mental and social distancing. There are a number of social manifestations of caste-based discrimination. SC bridegrooms are not permitted to ride a mare as per tradition in villages. SCs cannot sit on their charpoys (rope beds) when caste Hindus pass by. SCs are not permitted to draw water from common wells and handpumps. In many tea shops and food stalls, the SCs are served their food in crude crockery, which is not used for caste Hindu customers.[8] In September 2002, in Chakwar, a village in Rajasthan, a community of SCs was persecuted by caste Hindu Jats for using a temple tank which was prohibited to the SCs. By taking a dip in the tank, the use of which was restricted to the SCs of the village, Babulal Bairwa, a former security guard, unwittingly set off a chain reaction that led to the SCs deciding to convert to Buddhism. Babulal's dip in the pond led to the entire Bairwa community being fined ₹ 50,000 by the Jat-dominated village panchayat. When they refused to pay the fine, the entire community was excommunicated.

Whenever the SCs try to organize themselves against oppression or assert their rights, there is a backlash from the caste Hindus resulting in mass killings, gang-rapes, looting and arson in the SC colonies. The atrocity data compiled in the Fourth (1996–97 and 1997–98) and Sixth (1999–2000 and 2000–01) Reports of the National Commission for Scheduled Castes proves this point. The data showing crimes and atrocities perpetrated against the SCs are depicted in Table 7.1.

Table 7.1 Atrocities Committed against SCs between 1995 and 2000

Type of Case	*1995*	*1996*	*1997*	*1998*	*1999*	*2000*	*Total*
Murder	571	543	513	516	506	486	3,135
Hurt	4,544	4,585	3,860	3,809	3,241	3,298	23,337
Rape	873	949	1,037	923	1,000	1,034	5,816
Kidnapping and abduction	276	281	243	253	228	242	1,523
Dacoity	70	90	58	49	36	37	340
Robbery	218	213	162	150	109	93	945
Arson	500	464	389	346	337	260	2,296
Under PCR Act	1,528	1,417	1,216	724	678	666	6,229
Under POA Act, SCs and STs Act	13,925	9,620	8,070	7,443	7,301	6,617	52,976
Other offences	10,492	13,278	12,396	11,425	11,657	11,009	70,257
Total	32,997	31,440	27,944	25,638	25,093	23,742	1,66,854

Source: Reports of the National Commission for Scheduled Castes.

The table reveals that between 1995 and 2000, 1,66,854 cases of crimes and atrocities committed against the SCs have been registered. These include 3,135 cases of murder, 23,337 cases of hurt, 5,816 cases of rape, 1,523 cases of kidnapping and abduction, 340 cases of dacoity, 945 cases of robbery, 2,296 cases of arson, 6,229 cases under PCR Act(Protection of Civil Rights Act), 52,976 cases under SCS and STs Act (Prevention of Atrocities Act) and 70,257 cases of other offences. This means there are two cases of murder and three cases of rape and 13 cases of hurt committed against the SCs every day. And these are just the reported cases; a substantial number of atrocities against SCs go unreported.

We can point to some cases of inhuman behaviour by caste Hindus against SCs in 2002. 'On 5 September 2002, at Kaundampatti village of Dindigul district of Tamil Nadu, Sankan, a Dalit agricultural worker, was forced to drink urine for registering a police complaint of trespass against the caste Hindus, following a dispute between them over a piece of land. An equally horrifying incident occurred at Thinniyam village in Tiruchi district of the state on 22 May 2002. Two Dalits, Murugesan and Ramasami, were forced to feed each other their excreta. Their crime was that they stood by another Dalit, Karuppiah, who was engaged in a prolonged struggle against a former panchayat president and her husband to recover some money he said he had given them as a bribe to get a house allotted for his sister.'[9]

Both these incidents are related to the growing aspiration of the SCs to own land, either for cultivation or to build a house, and the continued opposition or indifference of the caste Hindus and the government.

On 8 November 2002, at Barishwan village in Ara district of Bihar, an upper caste Hindu landlord raped an SC's wife after accusing him of not repaying a loan of ₹ 100. This is one of the most horrendous rape incidents by an upper caste Hindu, who wanted to show his power over the SC couple.[10]

Role of Government Machinery

The government machinery is also playing its part in maintaining the Hindu social order and following the caste Hindu code. This can be seen in the National Police Commission's recommendations. The report includes a section on 'police and the weaker sections', which details police abuse specific to the SCs. The section notes that complaints against the police in their handling of cases of atrocities against the SCs often relate to refusal to register complaints, delayed arrival on the scene, half-hearted action while investigating specific cases, extreme brutality in dealing with accused persons belonging to the weaker sections and soft treatment of accused persons belonging to the more influential sections, making arrests or failing to make them on mala fide consideration, etc.[11]

Ironically, even after decades, none of the Commission's recommendations have been adopted and the police continue to detain, torture and extort money from the SCs without fear of punishment.

The Protection of Civil Right Act of 1955 and the SC/ST Prevention of Atrocities Act of 1989 are meant for the protection of the SCs. Under the provisions of these Acts, the police play a key role in helping the SCs and punishing the upper caste Hindus who are found to be guilty. Instead of helping the SCs, the police themselves perpetrate atrocities on them. The National Commission for Scheduled Castes and Scheduled Tribes[12] has received information about the involvement of police officials in crime and atrocities only from Orissa and Rajasthan. Such cases numbered eight in 1994, five in 1995 and four in 1996. During the past three years, 23 police officials were found to have been involved in such acts, of which 20 have already been convicted. Other states are yet to furnish details of crimes and atrocities committed against SCs and STs by police officials.

On 15 October 2002, at the Dulina police post in Jhajjar district of Haryana, five SCs were allegedly lynched to death by the police in connivance with the local activists of the ultra-Hindu outfit, the Vishwa Hindu Parishad. The very fact that the whole incident happened in the presence of the city magistrate, the deputy superintendent of police of Jhajjar and Bahadurgarh, the block development officer and at least 50 policemen, shows that it had their sanction. The very presence of so many government officials at the time the crime occurred points directly to their involvement. Instead of arresting the culprits, the police merely filed an FIR against unknown people and, ironically enough, registered a case against the victims under the Cow Slaughter (Prevention) Act. The police claim in the FIR that a lathi-charge was carried out on the mob, but the mob beat them back. But the police do not deem it necessary to explain why no tear gas or even firing in the air were resorted to in order to disperse the blood-thirsty upper caste mob, despite the fact that the police were brought from the Jhajjar police station and a host of police and civil officials were present at the Dulina police post at the time of the crime. This shows the partisan attitude of the government officials against the SCs.

In another incident, which occurred on 31 October 2002 at Burh Ganjoi village under the Fatehpur police station of Gaya district in Bihar, four members of an SC family were killed by caste Hindus. The incident put a question mark on the efficiency of the Gaya police, who, despite prior information, could not protect the unfortunate Dalit family. The villagers expressed their resentment over the partisan role of the police, who were allegedly pandering to the caste Hindus, instead of providing security to the victims.

Conclusion

We may conclude that discrimination/atrocities against the SCs are merely a reflection of the deep and strong Hindu sentiment, which is carried over in law and administration and which justifies the making of distinctions between Hindus and the SCs to the disadvantage of the latter. Such acts of discrimination have their roots in the fear of the caste Hindus that on a level playing field, the SCs may rise above their prescribed status in life and become a menace to the Hindu social order, the cardinal principle of which is the maintenance of Hindu superiority and domination over the untouchables. So long as the Hindu social order exists, discrimination against the SCs will continue in various forms and degrees.

Notes

1. B.R. Ambedkar, 1987.*Writings and Speeches, Vol. 3*. Bombay. Education Department, Maharashtra.
2. Rabindra Kumar, 2002. *Impact of Rural Development on Scheduled Castes.* New Delhi: Anmol Publications,
3. Rabindra Kumar, 1995. 'Changing Patterns of Caste Relationship in Bihar', Unpublished PhD Dissertation, JNU, New Delhi.
4. S. Radhakrishnan, 1949. *The Hindu View of Life*. New York: George Allen and Unwin.
5. Ambedkar, B.R. 1987. *Writings and Speeches, Vol. 5*. Bombay. Education Department, Government of Maharashtra.
6. 'The Report of the National Commission for Scheduled Castes and Scheduled Tribes, 1986–87', Government of India.
7. 'Fourth Report 1996–97 and 1997–98, Vol. 1', National Commission for Scheduled Castes and Scheduled Tribes, Government of India.
8. 'Highlights of the Report for 1994–95 and 1995–96', National Commission for Scheduled Castes and Scheduled Tribes, Government of India.
9. *Frontline,* 25 Oct. 2002, p. 39.
10. *The Telegraph,* 11 Nov. 2002, Kolkata.
11. 'Police and the Weaker Sections of Society', Chapter XIX, 'Third Report of the National Police Commission, 1980', Government of India, p. 4.
12. Op. cit., 'Fourth Report, Vol. I', p. 243.

8

Issues and Challenges Facing SC Women

In recent years, women's studies have appeared in many languages, both Indian as well as foreign, with the focal points ranging from aborting of female foetuses to bride burning and the practice of the *sati,* in which the wife is expected to immolate herself on her deceased husband's funeral pyre. But amazingly, there is little interest in SC women. Most of women's studies concentrate on middle class women, among whom very few are SCs because only an estimated 5–10 per cent of SC women belong to the middle class. In general SC literature, too, usually, no special attention is paid to women and their specific problems.

SC Women as Token Representatives

Since many of the vocal feminists of the 1970s were upper caste, middle class and university educated and rich women, it was their experience which came to be universalized as 'women's experience'. Thus, sweeping statements such as 'all women are equal to Dalits' were made in India. There was either complete invisibility of the experiences of SC women or, at best, only a token representation of their voices.

Class, Caste and Gender

The 1970s and early 1980s were times of the reinvention of the revolution in the country[1] and saw the emergence of several organizations and fronts: the Shramik Mukti Sanghatana, Satyashodhak

Communist Party, Shramik Mukti Dal, Yuvak Kranti Dal, to name a few, all of which did not limit SC women to a token inclusion. Their revolutionary agenda, in different ways, accorded a central role to SC women. This was, however, not the case with the two other movements of the period, the Dalit Panthers and the Women's Movement, which were constituted mainly of the Left parties based women's fronts and the newly emergent autonomous women's groups. The Dalit Panthers did make a significant contribution to the cultural revolution of the 1970s and, both in their writings as well as their programmes, SC women remained firmly encapsulated in the roles of the 'mother' and the 'victimised sexual being'.

The Leftist women's organizations highlighted economic and work related issues as also helped to develop a critique of the patriarchal capitalist state, while the autonomous women's groups politicized and made public the issue of violence against women. Though this led to serious debates on class versus patriarchy, these formations did not address the issue of Brahminism.

An analysis of the practices of the caste basis of violence against women reveals that while the incidence of dowry deaths and violent control and regulation of their mobility and sexuality by the family is frequent among the dominant upper castes, SC women are more likely to face the collective and public threats of rape, sexual assault and physical violence at the workplace and in public places.

Consider also the campaign against dowry. While the Leftist women's organizations viewed dowry in terms of the ways in which capitalism was developing in the country, the autonomous women's groups focused on patriarchal power and violence within the family. To get the real picture, the current practice of dowry needs to be viewed in the context of the processes of Brahminization and their impact on marriage practices. That the Brahminic ideals led to a preference for dowry in marriages is well documented. In fact, it was the colonial establishment that legitimized the Brahma form of marriage, which institutionalized and expanded the dowry system. The Brahminizing castes adopted the Brahma form of marriage over the other forms and thereby established dowry as an essential ritual.[2]

Moreover, the principle of endogamy and its coercive and violent perpetuation through collective violence against inter-caste alliances are crucial to the analysis of the menace called dowry.

Despite all these, the issues of sexuality and sexual politics, which are crucial for feminist politics, remains largely within an individualistic and lifestyle framework. Since issues of sexuality are intrinsically linked to caste, addressing sexual politics without challenging Brahminism results in lifestyle feminism. During the post-Mandal agitations and the caste violence at Chunduru and Pimpri Deshmukh in Maharashtra, women of the upper castes were invoked as feminist subjects, who were assertive, non-submissive and protesting the injustice done to them as women and as citizens. In the anti-Mandal protests, young middle class women declared that they were against all kinds of reservations (including those for women) and they mourned the death of merit and declared that they were out to save the nation.[3]

At Pimpri Deshmukh, following the brutal killing of an SC *kotwal*, who was also an active mobilizer of the local Buddha Vihar, by upper caste men, the upper caste women of the area complained publicly that he had harassed them and was a sexual pervert. They claimed to have incited their men to protect their honour, thereby invoking the agency of upper caste women. The issue was not merely one of molestation or violence against the SCs, but one that underlined the complex reformulations that the Brahminical patriarchies undergo in their bid to counter the collective SC resistance to them, which was becoming more vocal.

The increasing visibility of SC women in power structures as *sarpanch* and as members of the panchayat, in addition to their presence in the new knowledge making processes (Bhanwari Devi's intervention through the Saathin programme, for instance), has led to an increased backlash against them. This backlash was expressed through a range of humiliating practices and often culminated in rape or killing of their family members. Such incidents underline the need for a dialogue between SC and feminist activists since inter-caste relations at the local level might be mediated through a redefinition of gender spaces. The emancipatory agenda of the SC and women's movements would have to be sensitive to these issues and underline the complex interplay between caste and gender as structuring hierarchies in society.

Reformulation of Women's Issues

In the era of globalization and Hindutva, gender issues are being appropriated as cultural issues. This calls for a reformulation and reconceptualization of the feminist agenda. Feminist politics poses a challenge to the caste/class conceptualization of Brahminical Hindutva. Such a reconceptualization calls for a critique of the entire Brahminical hierarchy from a gender perspective. In the Brahminical social order, the caste-based and sexual divisions of labour are intermeshed in such a way that elevation in caste status is preceded by the withdrawal of the women of that caste from productive processes and their placing outside the private sphere. Such a linkage operates on presumptions about the accessibility of the sexuality of lower caste women because of their participation in social labour. Brahminism, in turn, locates this as a failure of lower caste men to control the sexuality of their women and underlines it as a justification of their notional impurity.

Many high caste Hindus have certain ideas about people belonging to the lower castes – that they are dirty, lazy, quarrelsome, unreliable, that the women enjoy much more freedom than rural high caste women and, above all, that the women have no morals and, therefore, deserve to be raped.[4] Thus, gender ideology legitimizes not only the structures of patriarchy, but also the very organization of caste.

Religious Texts and Indian Women

Drawing upon Ambedkar's analysis, it can be noted that caste ideology (endogamy) is the very basis of the regulation and organization of women's sexuality. Hence, caste determines the division of labour, both the sexual division of labour as well as the division of sexual labour. Ambedkar identifies the deep-rooted malaise of the Indian socioreligious milieu, wherein women are discriminated against mainly on the basis of the *Manusmriti*. Analysing women's exploitation and oppression in his book, *The Rise and Fall of Hindu Women*, Ambedkar points out that not only did the Hindu *Shastra* reduce women to non-entities in a male-dominated society, it also regarded the killing of women as an *upapataka* or a minor offence. Besides this, the conservative, tradition bound nature of our society forces women to always abide by its customs, despite the majority of them being unscientific, unhealthy and devoid of meaning. Women are denied the right to education, property and religion. They are just part and parcel of their husband's property and, on that account, no better than slaves or mere objects of pleasure. The *Manusmriti* places no value on women and says they can be subjected to corporal punishment at any time by their husbands. According to Ambedkar, the *Manusmriti* embodies the views of Brahminism in which women occupy a degraded position in society.

Nevertheless, women are divided along caste and class lines and by their consent also to patriarchies and compensatory structures. If the feminists are to challenge these divisions, their mode of organization and struggle should encompass all the social inequalities that are related to, embedded in and structured by patriarchies.[5] Does the recent assertion of the different voices of SC women challenge these divisions?

Autonomous SC Women's Organizations

There were several independent and autonomous assertions of SC women's identity in the 1990s, one of which was the National Federation of Dalit Women's Forum. Other such women's organizations include the Dalit Mahila Sanghatana, which is the women's wing of the Bharatiya Republican Party, and the Bahujan Mahila Sangh. The Vikas Vanchit Dalit Mahila Parishad made a proposal to commemorate 25 December, the day on which Ambedkar set fire to the *Manusmriti* in 1927, as Bharatiya Streemukti Divas. The Christi Mahila Sangharsh Sanghatana, an organization of Dalit Christian women, was established in 1997. Though these organizations are based on different non-Brahminical ideological positions, they come together and work together on several issues. For instance, they all jointly celebrate the Bharatiya Streemukti Divas.

The emergence of autonomous SC women's organizations has led to a major debate, sparked off by an essay, 'Dalit Women Talk Differently',[6] by Gopal Guru, in which he argues that to understand why SC women talk differently, it is necessary to delineate both the internal and external factors that have a bearing on this phenomenon.

SC women justify the case for talking differently on the basis of external factors (non-SC forces homogenizing the issue of SC women) and internal factors (the patriarchal domination within the SCs). SC women assert that the representation of their issues by non-SC women are less valid and less authentic. But focusing on certain external factors does not provide access to the complex reality of SC women. For example, the question of rape cannot be understood or explained merely in terms of class, criminality or as a psychological aberration or an illustration of male violence. The caste factor, which makes sexual violence against SC or tribal women much more severe in terms of intensity and magnitude, should also be taken into account. This differential experience has been expressed by SC women activists at various meets. However, the activists lament that the caste factor does not get adequate recognition in analyses by non-SC, middle-class, urbanized women activists.

The claim for women's solidarity at both the national and global levels subsumes the contradictions that exist between high caste and SC women. The latest manifestations of these contradictions involve the subtle forms of caste discrimination as practised by upper caste women against SC women in urban areas or the way in which SC women are slandered in rural areas. The contradictions also take a violent form, as, for instance, when the women followers of the Shiv Sena attacked SC women at Sawali, in Maharashtra's Chandrapur district, in 1988.[7] Thus, beneath the call for women's solidarity, the identity of SC woman as 'Dalit' gets whitewashed and allows a 'non-Dalit' woman to speak on her behalf. It is against this background that, of late, SC women have protested against their 'guest appearances' in a text or speech of a non-SC woman and demanded to organize such events on their own terms. They consider the feminist theory developed by non-SC women as unauthentic since it does not capture their reality. SC women define the concept of the 'Dalit' strictly in caste terms, refuting the claims of upper caste women to 'Dalithood'. SC women activists quote Phule and Ambedkar to invalidate the attempts of non-SC women to don an SC identity.

SC Patriarchy

Besides these factors, there are certain internal factors that have prompted SC women to organize themselves separately vis-à-vis their male counterparts. In the post-Ambedkar era, SC leaders have always subordinated and, at times, suppressed any independent political expression of SC women. This political marginalization has been openly condemned by SC women at various conferences.

SC women also criticize their male counterparts for dominating the literary scene. SC male writers do not take serious note of the literacy output of SC women and tend to be dismissive of it. SC women rightly question why they are not considered for the top positions at SC literary conferences and institutions. According to Gopal Guru, this dissent brings to the fore three things:

1. It is not only caste and class identity, but also one's gender positioning, that decides the validity of an event.
2. SC men are reproducing the same mechanisms against their women, which their high caste adversaries used to dominate them.
3. The experience of SC women shows that local resistance within the SCs is important.

Conclusion

We may conclude that Indian society is a caste-based society and it is characterized by immobility, marked by sharp divisions and structures of domination, inequality and power in the overall context of hierarchical value systems. Women have historically borne the brunt of the oppression generated by the Indian social structure and, in many ways, continue to carry it even today. Structurally and functionally, SC women suffer from triple – caste, class and gender – disabilities. They are deprived in society because of their caste status and in the family because of their gender status. Thus, elements of class, caste and gender operate in our domestic context. These structures in their correlating operations would multiply the oppression on SC women.

Notes

1. Judith Grant, 1993. *Fundamental Feminism*. New York: Routledge.
2. Sharad Patil, 1982. *Dasa-Shudra Slavery*. Mumbai: Allied Publishers.
3. Susie Tharu and Tejswani Niranjana. 1994. 'Problems for a Contemporary Theory of Gender in India'. *Social Scientist*, Vol. 22, March–April.
4. K. Pawade, 1995. 'The Position of Dalit Women in Indian Society'. In B. Das and J. Massey (eds) *Dalit Solidarity*. Delhi: ISPCK.
5. Kumkum Sangari, 1995. 'Politics of Diversity: Religious Communities and Multiple Patriarchies'. *Economic and Political Weekly*, 23 December.
6. Gopal Guru, 1995. 'Dalit Women Talk Differently'. *Economic and Political Weekly*, 14–21 October, pp. 2548–9.
7. Ibid.

9

Naxalism or Survival for Existence?

Naxalism has become the biggest internal threat to India today. Naxalites already operate in 223 of 600 districts in 20 states. On 11 November 2009, Operation Green Hunt was initiated with the blessings of the then Home Minister P. Chidambaram. Its objective was to cleanse the country of Naxalism. As many as 50,000 soldiers have been deployed for two years under this operation. State-specific resistance was already in place in the form of the Salwa Judum in Chhattisgarh, Grey Hounds in Andhra Pradesh and Cobra in Orissa. But, are these the right approaches to address the issue of the menace of Naxalism? The fact of the matter is that neither the government nor the elites of this country want to solve this problem. What is the root cause of Naxalism? Most Indian intellectuals and the government consider this problem to be related to economic and law and order issues.

This chapter tries to understand the issue of Naxalism using the specific example of Central Bihar to develop an understanding of the problem from the perspective of the people who make up its mass base, including its members, supporters and activists at the village level. This approach involves identifying who the Naxalites are, how they act and why they act the way they do. Is this a socio-economic problem or is it a structural problem or is it related to the Maoist ideology? This chapter seeks answers to these questions.

Naxalism is a serious problem in Bihar. A full 50 per cent or 19 of the 38 districts in Bihar are Naxal infested. Recent years have witnessed not only a consolidation of these extremists in their strongholds, but also their expansion into newer areas. Apart from their traditional strongholds of Patna, Gaya, Aurangabad, Arwal, Bhabhua, Rohtas and Jahanabad in south-western Bihar, there has been a spurt of activity in the northern parts of the state bordering Nepal, including West Champaran, East Champaran, Sheohar, Sitamarhi, Muzaffarpur, Darbhanga and Madhubani. The Naxals have also extended their influence into Saharsha, Begusarai, Munger, Bhagalpur and Vaishali as well as the areas along the state's border with Uttar Pradesh.

Socio-economic Conditions in Bihar

Agrarian Structure

The population of Bihar is primarily rural. As many as 86.85 per cent of its population lives in rural areas, while a whopping 90.97 per cent of the SCs live in villages. Nearly 80 per cent of the population is directly dependent on agriculture.[1]

The economic relationship is fundamentally represented in terms of *malik* (upper caste landlord) and *praja* (lower castes without any control over land). The *malik* consists of the Brahmins, Rajputs, Bhumihars and Kayasthas, who control the means of production. The power structure is also based on the capacity of the caste authority to control the land. In any part of India that is predominantly agrarian, land is a formidable instrument for controlling people and communities. The *praja* consider the *maliks* to be their *sarkaar* (law incarnate), *deobhagwan* (god incarnate) and *maibaap* (parents). The *praja* are subordinate to the *malik* for benefits from the land and their livelihood. The traditional position of the *praja* corresponds to the general underdog position of the peasantry. The Hindu principle of differentiated hierarchy, which still continues to differentiate the peasantry by setting them apart in numerous capsules of castes arranged neatly and vertically one upon the other in the social structure, still holds sway. This social hierarchy is clearly related to economic status as shown below.

The SCs, who are at the lowest occupational status level, are considered to live in the most wretched *bastis* of all in the real sense. Their villages are known as *tolas*.[2] The severity of the structural polarity that exists between the *maliks* and the SCs can be expressed in one sentence: They are *persona non grata* for the caste Hindus, especially the *malik,* for their mud dwellings are on the *malik's* land. Even the timber and straw used to roof their dwellings are supplied by the *malik*. Traditionally, they and their families are brought there to work as a domestic servant as well as field labourer from a distant village of another *malik* of a different class. The food that they consume is provided by the *malik*. The relation of super and subordination between an SC and a *malik* cannot be broken by anyone except the *malik*, who has the right to throw out the SC whenever he so wants from his *abadi* land.

Table 9.1 Social Hierarchy in Agrarian Bihar

Economic Status	*Social Status*	*Occupational Status*
Malik	Upper Castes	Zamindar/Landlords
Praja	(a) Upper Backward Castes	Tenants
	(b) Most Backward Castes	Landless Agricultural Labourers
	(c) Untouchables	Landless Agricultural Labourers

Table 9.2 shows that as a result of the redistribution of land and agrarian reforms, the number of landholdings has increased inversely.

Table 9.2 Landholding Patterns in Bihar

Size of Landholding in Acres	*Per cent of Holding*	*Per cent of Area*
0–2.54	72.6	23.2
2.5–10	21.4	36.9
10–25	5.2	26.9
25 and more	0.8	13.2

Source: Based on Agricultural Census of Bihar (1976–77), as calculated by the Directorate of Statistics and Evaluation, 1981, Patna Secretariat Press, p. 70.

As shown in Table 9.3, the big and middle landowners are mostly upper caste Hindus who continue their hold as *maliks*. Only a small number of SCs are big and middle landowners. There are many small landowners and those who own no land. Most of the SCs are predominantly landless labourers.

In all the groups, upper caste households show an overwhelming preference for leasing out or cultivating their lands with the help of hired workers over working their holdings themselves or with the help of family labour. The Bhumihars and the Rajputs have emulated the

Brahmins in hiring ploughmen to enhance their social status. The Brahminical style has provided the authoritative social model for the few landholders of Shudra rank, too.

Table 9.3 Patterns of Landownership by Caste in Bihar

Caste	*Landowner Groups*			
	Landless People	*Big Landowners (More Than 10 Acres)*	*Middle Landowners (More Than 2.5–10 Acres)*	*Small Landowners (More Than) 0–2.5 Acres)*
STs	32	80	231	217
OBCs	392	18	89	457
SCs	477	0	7	203

Source: Based on a survey of 2,531 households in Bihar conducted in the early 1980s under the auspices of the World Employment Programme.

Amongst the Hindu landowners in Bihar in the early 20th century, there were hardly any castes other than the Brahmins, Bhumihars and Rajputs. Even as late as in 1951, about 80 per cent of all landowners in the state were from these three castes. There were a few Muslims and Kayasthas, but only a negligible number from the lower and middle castes. The four richer castes of the Brahmins, Rajputs, Bhumihars and Kayasthas enjoyed better social status than the rest of the Hindu castes in the traditional Hindu social system. Thus, we observe that caste hierarchy is generally compatible with economic hierarchy.

The agrarian reforms and, more importantly, the various Tenancy Acts (1885, 1961), the Zamindari Abolition Act (1948) and other reform movements generated a lot of change in the economic and social domains of Bihar. Even as late as in 1951, two-thirds of the tenants in Bihar came from the backward castes, mostly from the Yadavs, Kurmis and Koeries. By the end of the 20th century, with the passage of the Tenancy Act by various states, which recognized the rights of tenants vis-à-vis the zamindars, the latter turned more hostile to the cause of the tenants. A large number of zamindars turned absentee landlords, interested only in the realization of rents.

The Zamindari Abolition Act (1948) was passed almost immediately after independence, following which some of the big zamindars lost their land and their tenants became the landowners. Post-independence, the government took several measures to improve agriculture, with the result that some of the hardworking intermediate caste – the backward castes – tenant landowners prospered and became rich peasants. The migration of Muslim zamindars from Central Bihar to Pakistan at the time of the partition made some backward caste tenants the *de facto* landowners. After independence, a land ceiling legislation was passed, which pressurized traditional landowners to sell their excess land to the new groups, which could afford to buy it, especially in Central Bihar. This new group belonged to the upward backward castes. They, especially the Yadavs, Kurmis and Koeries, grew as neo-landlords. Thus, the composition of landownership was drawn from various castes – the Brahmins, the Rajputs, the Bhumihars, the Yadavs and the Kurmis. Nonetheless, certain oppressive feudal practices, which were institutionalized by the caste system, continued to perpetuate the servility of the untouchables.

Despite all these measures, most of the landless poor from the SCs and other lower castes remain tied to the land and the landowning families of the higher castes in a complex web of social and non-commercial relationships. This has had a strong impact on the SCs, who faced harsh economic and social deprivation. However, a few years ago, some land was given to the backward castes on lease or *bataiya*[3] (sharing) basis or sold to them. This followed a large number of higher castes finding jobs outside their villages, which enabled them to leave their lands to the Backward Castes in arrangements such as *bataiya, nagadi* (cash), *manjay* or *rehan* (lease). This ensured they would continue to derive an income from their lands. Since there was scarcity of employment in the rural areas, it is easy for a landlord to obtain cheap labour to work on his land. SCs are usually employed on a landlord's farm as bonded agricultural labour. The landlord does not pay the SC the minimum wages as fixed by the government, but no one dares to protest for fear of bloodshed.

Table 9.4 Sector-wise Distribution of Main Workers in Total Population and SCs of Bihar in 1991

Sectors	*Total Population (%)*	*SCs (%)*
Primary Sector	82.36	89.79
Secondary Sector	4.64	3.52
Tertiary Sector	13	16.69

Source: Ashish Bose. 1996. *India's Basic Demographic Statistics.* New Delhi: B.R. Publishing Corporation, p. 121.

After the introduction of the Land Ceiling Act (1961) some lands were seized from the landlords and distributed among the landless labourers and SCs in Bihar. But a large number of the SC allottees have not been able to claim their land. The landlords continue to claim and occupy the land and the SCs, who now actually own the land, dare not take it from them.

Even decades after the legal abolition of bonded labour, the incidence of bonded labour is quite high in Bihar. The shockingly poor agricultural labourers survive with whatever little they get. Their proportion, as shown in Table 9.5, is about 72 per cent in the state. They are in a state of perpetual debt. They take loans from the landlord for their marriages and for fulfilling their social obligations. In lieu of small sums of money, the landlord actually purchases them in person or their whole family to work for him in his fields. Thus, debts usually manifest another form of bondage to the landlord. At times, debts appear to function as an indissoluble bond between the landlord and the SCs as the rate of interest charged is exorbitant. However, their situation is gradually changing from agriculture to other economic areas as shown in Tables 9.4 and 9.5.

As a whole, 82.86 per cent, 4.64 per cent and 13 per cent main workers in the state are engaged in the primary, secondary and tertiary sectors, respectively. Within the SCs, 89.79 per cent, 3.52 per cent and 16.69 per cent are engaged in the primary, secondary and tertiary sectors, respectively (see Table 9.4 for more details). Nearly half of the state's population (43.58%) are cultivators and 37.13 per cent are agricultural labourers;15.63 per cent SCs are engaged as cultivators and 72.24 per cent as agricultural labourers, as shown in Table 9.5.

Table 9.5 Category-wise Percentage Distribution of Main Workers in Bihar, 1991

Categories of Main Workers	*General Population*	*SCs*
Cultivators	43.58	15.63
Agricultural Labourers	37.13	72.24
Household Industries	1.75	1.74
Other Workers	17.54	10.15

Source: Ashish Bose, op. cit., p. 123.

Similarly, up to March 1999, surplus government land to the tune of 13,37,09,040 acres were distributed to the all categories in Bihar. Of these, some 5,47,571.82 acres were distributed to the SCs (see Table 9.6).

Table 9.6 Distribution of Land in Bihar up to March 1999

Social Group	*Area in Acre*	*% of Share*	*Number of Beneficearise*	*% of Beneficearise*	*Average Land per Beneficiary in Acre*
(1) Ceiling Land					
(a) Scheduled Castes	1,81,701	58.95	2,34,334	61.74	0.78
(b) Scheduled Tribe	39,937	12.95	43,004	11.33	0.92
(c) Other	84,8492	7.52	1,01,392	26.71	0.83
Total	3,08,223	100	3,79,518	100	0.81
(2) Government Land					
(a) Scheduled Castes	5,47,571.82	40.95	6,09,565	47.05	0.78
(b) Scheduled Tribes	4,00,523.99	29.95	2,58,731	19.97	1.54
(c) Ex-Army	7,759.57	0.58	9,669	0.74	0.80
(d) Backward Castes	2,44,266.19	18.26	2,81,746	21.75	0.86
(e) Others	50,425.70	3.7	49,755	3.84	1.01
(f) Net Categories	86,583.33	6.47	86,002	6.64	3.32
Total	13,37,09,040	100	12,95,468	100	

Source: Revenue and Land Reforms Department, Bihar 1998–99.

The SC beneficiaries accounted for about 47.05 per cent, while their share in area was around 40.95 per cent. The land distributed to the SCs per beneficiary comes to 0.89 acre.

Table 9.7 depicts the situation of the SCs with respect to ownership of agricultural land in rural areas during 1982 and 1992. It is observed that about 19.73 per cent of SC households in Bihar were landless in 1992. This is much higher than the national average of 8.58 per cent.

Despite the distribution of land under the ceiling of government land, the percentage of landless SC households has more than doubled from 7.92 per cent in 1982 to 19.73 per cent in 1992. Nearly 80.27 per cent of SC households owned some land in 1992. However, of these, nearly 77.08 per cent owned less than 2.49 acres. The average area owned by these small farmers was 0.89 acre, which is near to being landless. The landless and near-to-landless, put together, account for nearly 96.8 per cent of the total SC households. This indicates the pitiable condition of the SCs in Bihar.

Access to Housing and Basic Amenities

Housing and basic amenities are also an indicator of development and these include other amenities such as safe drinking water, toilet facilities

Table 9.7 Ownership of Agricultural Land by Size, Class of Holding SCs all Household in Bihar (1982–1992)

Size of Class	*SCs*					*All Households*		
	1982		*1992*			*1992*		
	% Holding	*Area*	*% Holding*	*Area*	*Average Area Owned hec/acre*	*% Holding*	*Area*	*Average Area Owned hec/acre*
Landless	7.92	0	19.73	0	0	8.58	0	0
Less than 1 hectare (2.49)	88.77	60.18	77.08	58.37	0.36(0.89)	71.98	28.58	0.37(0.91)
1.01–2.00 hectare (2.50–4.96 acre)	2.03	17.28	1.97	17.80	1.37(3.39)	11.10	23.84	1.38(3.41)
2.01–4.00 hectare (4.98–9.90 acre)	1.11	17.3	1.05	17.78	2.92(7.24)	6.00	24.46	2.87(7.11)
4.01–10.00 hectare (9.92–24.79 acre)	0.17	5.24	0.16	6.04	5.39	2.14	18.68	6.19(15.34)
10.01 and above	0	0	0	0	0	0.2	4.44	16.34(40.44)
	100	100	100	100		100	100	

Source: National Sample Surveys (1982,1992), Department of Statistics, New Delhi.

and electricity which is a priority of government developmental programmes in rural areas. It has to be seen how many people are availing of or possessing these basic amenities.

Information about the distribution of houses – *pucca*, semi-*pucca* and *kuchcha* – are available only generally and not category-wise. The data for this are taken from the 1981 and 1991 censuses and it is presented in Table 9.8. In 1991, about 24.07 per cent people had *pucca* houses, 38.38 per cent had semi-*pucca* houses and 37.56 per cent lived in *kuchcha* houses. While comparing 1981 and 1991, it is found that there was a marginal decline in the number of people living in *kuchcha* and semi-*pucca* houses.

Table 9.8 Distribution of Households Living in *Pucca,* Semi-*Pucca* and *Kuchcha* Houses in Rural Areas (%)

Households	*1981*	*1991*
Pucca	17.77	24.07
Semi-*pucca*	42.26	38.38
Kuchcha	39.97	37.56
Total	100	100

Source: Ashish Bose, *India's Basic Demographic Statistics,* B.R. Publishing Corporation, Delhi, 1996.

Table 9.9 Social Groups with Access to Safe Drinking Water, 1991 (%)

Social Groups	*Rural*	*Urban*	*Total*
Scheduled Castes	54.18	67.81	55.40
Scheduled Tribes	29.68	49.54	31.17
Others	60.20	75.44	62.17

Source: Ashish Bose, *India's Basic Demographic Statistics,* B.R. Publishing Corporation, Delhi, 1996.

Table 9.9 presents the percentage of social groups among the SCs, STs and others who had access to safe drinking water in 1991. It shows clearly that 55.40 per cent of the SCs and 62.17 per cent of the others had safe drinking water facilities in urban areas, while only 54.18 per cent of the SCs and 60.20 per cent of the others had access to safe drinking water facilities in rural areas.

From the hygienic point of view, toilet facilities are important for the masses. Table 9.10 presents the percentage of households in the different social groups that have access to proper toilet facilities. The table presents an alarming picture for all groups. Only a miniscule 2.19 per cent of rural SC households have toilets. Most of them use open land for this purpose.

Table 9.10 Households in Various Social Groups with Access to Proper Toilets, 1991 (%)

Social Groups	*Rural*	*Urban*	*Total*
Scheduled Castes	2.19	33.45	4.99
Scheduled Tribes	0.97	32.39	3.33
Others (non-SCs/STs)	6.08	61.00	14.16

Source: Ashish Bose, *India's Basic Demographic Statistics,* BR Publishing Corporation, Delhi, 1996.

Table 9.11 Households in Various Social Groups with Electricity Connections, 1991 (%)

Social Groups	*Rural*	*Urban*	*Total*
Scheduled Castes	4.08	41.53	7.44
Scheduled Tribes	2.91	43.22	5.64
Others (non-SCs/STs)	6.23	61.97	14.43

Source: Ashish Bose, *India's Basic Demographic Statistics,* BR Publishing Corporation, Delhi, 1996.

Table 9.11 presents the percentage of households with electricity connections and it shows that only 4.99 per cent of rural SC households had electricity, while the corresponding figure for the others was 14.16 per cent.

There is a general consensus that education is an important aspect of development. Recently, education has been accepted as one of the components and indicators of social and individual development. Education is an important social resource and a means of reducing social inequalities. It helps the individual to raise his social status in various ways. Knowledge, skills, values and attitudes acquired through education helps one obtain the desired quality of life. Beyond being a basic need, education, especially vocational, technical and professional education, is necessary for job placement and it thus acts as a catalyst in improving many other aspects of life. With this realization, after independence, the Centre and the states have been adopting various policies and programmes aimed at improving education, and with considerable progress. But when it comes to the SCs, not surprisingly, this effort seems to die out.

In the census enumeration, a person is counted as literate if he or she can read and write in any language with understanding. The literacy rate of the various social groups of Bihar is presented in Table 6.5, which shows the literacy rates for 1961, 1971, 1981 and 1991.

The general condition of education among the SCs is pitiable. It is a matter of public knowledge that the SCs have lagged behind in the field of education not only in Bihar, but all over the country. The literacy rate among SCs, according to the 1991 Census, was only 37.41 per cent as against the national average of 52.71 per cent among the general communities. It is alarming to note that literacy among the SCs in Bihar was the lowest at 15.1 per cent (Table 6.5). The rural and urban literacy rates are much lower among the SCs than among other groups. The increase in female literacy among the SCs has also been very slow.

Social Status of SCs

The SCs comprise 15.7 per cent of the total population of Bihar. The status of the SCs in the state is not distinct from their counterparts elsewhere in the country. They continue to be marginalized sections and subject to exploitation and humiliation. They form a large labour force for the landowning upper castes. They are confronted by a plethora of problems even today. They have been serving the higher castes for several centuries, but are not allowed to draw water from public wells or visit temples. They are called untouchables and forbidden to visit public places. Even in the 1970s, they could not sit with the others. They are still expected to serve caste Hindus, who fear that if the SCs are educated, they will lose their potential workforce. Educated SCs are also looked upon with contempt as *neech jati* by caste Hindus. Such castes prejudices on the part of the higher castes are considered legitimate or normal behaviour. Resistance by the SCs to such humiliating and exploitative practices results in frequent violence by the caste Hindus. The various forms of violent behaviour ranges from murder and massacres to atrocities on women. The SCs are paid very low wages for the services they offer to the upper castes and so continue to remain dependent for their livelihood on their exploiters, who own all the land and have monopoly over all other occupations and sources of income. Their inability to protest against these atrocities and continuous harassment is due to two reasons: one, they are socially backward and have served the caste Hindus for generations, and two, their economic condition is precarious even after the implementation of the reservation policy and various developmental schemes for many years.

Even in contemporary times, the higher castes expect the untouchables to serve them in all respects. It is pertinent to note that till a few decades ago, a custom in Barh block of Patna district demanded that after an SC wedding, the bride should spend her marriage night with the area's landlord. Though it does not seek to explain as to how on this occasion the untouchability principle does not function. However, this abominable custom came an end during the 1950s.

Central Bihar

The Central Bihar (now southern Bihar) region is mostly the Gangetic plain and comprises the eight districts of Patna, Nalanda, Bhojpur, Rohtas, Aurangabad, Jahanabad, Gaya and Nawada. It forms part of the area brought under the Green Revolution during the late 1960s. Significantly, it is this region that has been the centre of peasant movements and the Naxal movement. Both North Bihar and the central plains are mainly dependent on agriculture.

According to the 1991 Census, the tot·l SC population in Central Bihar was 36,01,625, or 28.56 per cent of the SCs in the state. The total population in the central region consists of the following categories:

Table 9.12 Category-wise Percentage Distribution of Workers in Central Bihar

Categories	*Percentage*
Main workers	36.65
Marginal worker	01.55
Non-workers	61.77

Source: Census of 1991.

Table 9.13 Category-wise Percentage Distribution of Main Workers in Central Bihar

Categories	*Percentage*
Cultivators	11.66
Agricultural Labourers	79.32
Workers in Household Industries	01.26
Other Workers	07.74

Source: Census of 1991.

This shows that a whopping 79.32 per cent of SCs are engaged as agricultural labourers in Central Bihar. In the absence of proper land records, it is difficult to know the exact details of land distribution in the region. However, according to estimates based on various studies, as much as 80 per cent of the land there is in the possession of the upper caste Bhumihars and Rajputs. The SCs, who constitute about 28.56 per cent of the population in these districts, are generally landless. Some of the Yadavs, Kurmies and Koeries have also become landowners due to land reforms measures. The main economic activity in the region is agriculture. A very large proportion of rural labour is employed as cultivators or as agricultural labourers. As we have seen, about 91 per cent SCs are engaged in agricultural activities. The consequence of such pressure on land resources for those who depend on the land for sustenance is that large sections of them either end up with holdings below subsistence level or they are pushed into the ranks of landless agricultural labourers. They are then forced to work at a wage that is generally below the legally stipulated minimum as unrecorded tenants on the land controlled or owned by the upper caste landlords.

In fact, the main reason for poor agricultural development in Central Bihar is the nature of the relationship that dominates agricultural production in general and the tenancy relationship in particular. Firstly, the tenancy relationships are varied with more than one type of tenancy prevailing in the same village. What is significant is that all these are unrecorded tenancies, the terms of which can change at the whim and fancy of the landlord. Under *bataidari* (sharecropping in which the produce is shared and the arrangement is entirely oral, not written or recorded), the labouring tenant puts in all the inputs such as fertilizer, manure, seeds, water and his own cattle and labour and then has to hand over half the produce to the landowner. Another type of tenant-landlord relationship is *mani*, in which the tenant leases the land for a year, uses his own inputs and implements and pledges a certain amount of the produce. The *mani* level varies at between 20 and 30 *man* per *bigha* (each *man* is equal to about 40 kilos). The third type of relationship is known as the *nagdi* system and this is qualitatively different from the first two types. In the *nagdi,* a total sum of money, ranging between ₹ 3,000 and ₹ 5,000 per *bigha* is paid in advance. The tenant keeps all the produce. It is evident that only the well-off with substantial savings can afford to enter into this kind of relationship. The fourth type of relationship is the *banihari*, in which the Banihars pledge their labour power, usually for a season or a year, against a loan or 10 *katha* of land for cultivating. They are thus attached or fixed labourers as opposed to casual labourers. They are forced to work on the landowner's land during the period.

Undoubtedly, the landless labourers and those on the lowest rungs of the agrarian hierarchy in Central Bihar are generally drawn from the lowest of the backward castes, such as the Lohars, Kumbhars, Mallahs, Telis, Nais, and from the SCs, such as the Chamars, Dusadhs, Musahars, Bhuiyas and Rajwars. A very high proportion of these lower backward castes and SCs are landless and work as agricultural labourers. According to a study by the A.N. Sinha Institute in Patna, in the 1980s, roughly 61 per cent of the lower backward castes and 69.5 per cent of the SCs in the central plains were landless. None among the SCs owned more than 10 acres of land and the proportion of those owning more than five acres was minimal. At the same time, more than 65 per cent of the upper castes own less than five acres of land in the region.

Social Organizations

A distinct feature of Bihar is the emergence of private caste armies, an offshoot of the continuing conflict of caste prejudices and class interests. This phenomenon needs to be perceived within a broader framework of the feudalistic structure prevailing in Bihar, which has witnessed the growth of middle castes, new centres of political power, caste consciousness and the disintegration of feudalistic ties. The landlords and rich peasants, particularly the neo-rich middle castes (the Yadavs, Kurmis and Koeris) are reported to suffer from a sense of insecurity. So, *senas* or private armies are constituted with support from the guardians of law and order. The *senas* or caste-based private armies organized by landlords to keep agricultural labourers and poor peasants under their heel are notorious. They indulge in violent activities such as butchering of the SCs, setting their hutments on fire and raping and molesting their women. Each such army or *sena* is generally identified with specific castes. For example, the Lorik Sena belongs to the Yadavs, the Bhumi Sena to the Kurmis, the Brahmrishi Sena to the Bhumihars, the Kuer Sena to the Rajputs, the Savarn Liberation Front to the upper castes and the Ranvir Sena to the Bhumihars. All such armies that were in place before the formation of the Ranvir Sena were wiped out in the war with the Naxalites. The Ranvir Sena, the private army of the upper caste Bhumihar landlords, was formed at Belaur in Bhojpur district. The Ranvir Sena is better organized than the other armies. It carried out major operations against the SCs at Bathanitola in 1996, Laxmanpur Bathe in 1997 and Shankarbigha-Narayanpur in 1999. Every attack by the Ranvir Sena was countered by the Naxal groups and, in most of these counterattacks, the victims belonged to the Bhumihar community.

There are several ultra-left organizations that operate in Central Bihar. The Bihar Pradesh Kisan Sabha (BPKS), which is affiliated to the CPI-ML (Communist Party of India (Marxist-Leninist)) and has been active since the 1970s, is one of these. It is locally referred to as Ma-Le. The Mazdoor Kisan Sangrami Parishad (MKSP), which is affiliated to the CPI-ML Party Unity, emerged from the Mazdoor Kisan Sangram Samiti. The Maoist Communist Centre (MCC) has also launched violent struggles against landlords.

Naxalite Activities

Naxalite activities in Bihar can be divided into two phases: the formative phase from 1967 to 1977 and the current phase, which began in 1977 (Bhatia, 2005). Prior to the Emergency in 1975, the movement had spread in some parts of two or three districts, but during the Emergency, it faced heavy state persecution and had to lie low. However, by the late 1970s, it was able to reorganize itself and was once again on an upswing. The phase after 1977, therefore, saw the revival of its activities, significant reformulations of its political manoeuvres and the emergence of new Naxalite groups.

During the formative phase of the Naxalite movement in Bihar, local struggles sprang up in the Mushahari region of Muzaffarpur district in North Bihar, in parts of Bhojpur and Patna districts in Central Bihar, and in Hazaribagh, Ranchi, Singhbhum and Dhanbad districts of South Bihar (now Jharkhand). These struggles were modelled after the Naxalbari uprising and were initiated by various members of the All-India Coordination Committee of Communist Revolutionaries (AICCCR), its successor, the CPI-ML, and by various Naxalite groups outside the AICCCR fold (mainly the Maoist Communist Centre).

Many of violent actions by these groups were sporadic and not part of a sustained movement. However, in Bhojpur, the Naxalite movement first took root in the village of Ekwari, where Jagadish Mahato, a local teacher who had clandestine links with the Naxal leaders of West Bengal, led a protracted struggle against exploitative landlords. The Naxalites who came to Bhojpur belonged to the Pro-lin Piao Group, which later developed into the present CPI-ML Liberation, also known as Liberation.

Like in the other states, the Naxalite movement in Bihar is heavily factionalized. There are 17 Naxalite factions functioning in different parts of the state. Except for the Maoist Communist Centre (MCC), all the others are CPI-ML groups. The most important groups are Liberation, Party Unity and MCC. Among these, MCC is considered to be extreme left, Liberation is drifting towards the parliamentary path and Party Unity lies somewhere in between. This section examines some important features of each of these groups.

Liberation

Central Bihar is the stronghold of the Liberation group. The group first found a firm footing in Bhojpur in the late 1960s and early 1970s. From Bhojpur, it spread to the adjoining areas of Central Bihar, to parts of South Bihar, which is now Jharkhand, and also to North Bihar. The Liberation group considers itself the true inheritor of the CPI-ML legacy, though its political line is almost completely different from the original CPI-ML. In 1978, a rectification campaign was launched by the party with the purpose of bringing about changes in its style of work. These changes were formalized in a special party conference held in July 1979. The most important outcome of this conference was the decision to begin open mass activities through the formation of appropriate mass organizations.

This ushered in a phase of mass politics. The Indian People's Front (IPF) and the Bihar Pradesh Kisan Sabha (BPKS) were formed in the early 1980s. The aim of the BPKS was to lead the peasant movement, while the IPF was to intervene in the national political scene. Both organizations flourished. The IPF was banned in 1994, but it was recognized by the Election Commission in 1995 and was able to contest the 1995 assembly polls and 1996 parliamentary elections as the CPI-ML.

Party Unity

Party Unity came into existence on 1 January 1982 following the merger of two CPI-ML groups, the CPI-ML Unity Organisation (UO) and Central Organizing Committee CPI-ML (COC). In the following years, three other CPI-ML groups joined it. Party Unity itself merged with the CPI-MC People's War Group (PWG) in August 1998. The united group is now called the CPI-ML People's War. Jehanabad is the stronghold of Party Unity. Besides, the Party Unity led peasant movements are also strong in parts of the adjoining Gaya and Patna regions and in Palamau. The most popular open front of Party Unity is the Mazdoor Kisan Sangram Samiti (MKSS), which was banned in 1986 and renamed Mazdoor Kisan Sangram Parishad (MKSP) in 1994.

Maoist Communist Centre

In its self-identity and political image, the Maoist Communist Centre (MCC) represents the hardline wing of the Naxalite movement. It was formed on 20 October 1969. Completely banned now, the MCC leads an entirely underground existence. The initial differences between the MCC and the CPI-ML were spelt out in a document circulated by it in June 1971. It considers the CPI-ML's political line and practice until 1971 as suffering from left deviationism and asserts that this trend would have to be opposed like its right counterpart, represented by the CPI-ML.

Even though the MCC's central critique of the CPI-ML line was its then extreme position, paradoxically, it is the MCC which is today accused of being the most extremist outfit among the various Naxalite groups. In its inner-party functioning in general and in the implementation of the principle of democratic centralism in particular, the MCC is known to be more centralized than democratic.

As it turns out, the MCC has achieved little success in building a mass people's army for guerrilla warfare; instead, it has become known for actions that have invited condemnation not only from bourgeois circles, but also from the Naxalite movement itself. For example, the MCC has retaliated against massacres by upper caste landlords by carrying out counter-massacres of upper caste men. In fact, MCC leaders have threatened to kill four upper class enemies for every victim of a massacre. Other examples of actions that have attracted wide criticism include brutal punishments in people's courts (justified as the will of the people) and severe threats against those who participate in elections.

The MCC is most active in the districts that are now part of Jharkhand. In Central Bihar, it is considered to be the strongest in Gaya, followed by parts of Jehanabad, Aurangabad and Patna.

Social Base of the Naxalites

The social base of these movements in Central Bihar consists overwhelmingly of small, landless peasants with marginal landholdings and, to a lesser extent, the medium peasants. In caste terms, the base of the movements consists of the SCs, the Most Backward Classes and the intermediate castes. However, these movements also have some supporters among the higher castes.

Their presence is particularly felt in the leadership of the movement. Even though the term, Naxal, is part of the vocabulary of the people of Central Bihar for all the wrong reasons, the fact of the matter is that they are only demanding their rights and wanting to lead a dignified and respectable life. When they ask for their rights, the upper castes, the police and the bureaucracy call them Naxalites.

Besides being dominated by Brahminism and the Brahminical culture, India is a semi-feudal society. In fact, the SCs and the Most backward castes want to end this culture and want to rise above the system. But this is easier said than done as the fundamental cause of Naxalism is the fact that these downtrodden sections of society are abjectly poor and illiterate. To lead a decent social life, people need food and education. But these sections of society have neither. Marx and Lenin called for the complete destruction of this rotten system and an end to the exploitation of one human being by another. Pithily put, mankind should be liberated from all clutches, be they social, economical, political or religious.

How do the people who join the Naxalite movement conceptualize the revolution? People do not have a textbook understanding of the revolution, but these people do have some notion of a radical change. They use the word, *badalaav* (change), more often than *kranti* (revolution). One can safely say that change represents their own understanding of the social and economic uplift they seek so desperately, while revolution or *nayi janwadi kranti* (new democratic revolution) is an addition to their political vocabulary. They understand change as a change in their existing situation or liberation from the tyranny of the Brahminical social order, while their newly learnt notion of revolution adds a vision of building a new society that is more equitable and just than the one in which they are living. They also understand revolution to be a struggle between them, i.e., their party or the organized SCs and the most backward classes, and their opponents, i.e., the agents of the tyrannical Brahminical social order such as the landlords, the police and the government.

Do the members and supporters of revolutionary movements such as the Naxalite movement perceive themselves to be revolutionaries? Within the Naxalite movement, the revolutions are understood to be a long process in which they have seen many of their comrades die. The self-perception of the people as revolutionaries can be felt more at the cadre level than at the level of the village people. Similarly, it can be felt more in the underground party organization than in the open fronts. Outside the former, people rarely call themselves revolutionaries or *krantikaaris*.

Ideological Motives behind Public Participation

An individual who chooses to join the Naxalite movement with full knowledge of its ideology and revolutionary agenda can be understood to be motivated by the formal ideology. Leaders at the district level and upwards tend to fall into this category. That apart, there are those who have got attracted to the movement because they have an instinctual urge to fight injustice and who get attracted to the revolutionary message of the movement. These revolutionaries may have witnessed the oppression perpetrated by the upper castes and police forces and rebel instinctively against these injustices. A large majority of the cadres, especially those at the village level, and the people who comprise the backbone of the movement fall into this category.

Thus, individuals who have been victimized by the tyrannical Brahminical social order want to free themselves from it. Most Naxalites belong to this category. Some high caste landlords and rich peasants join the movement out of fear of becoming the Naxalites' next targets. Similarly, in situations where the upper castes (Rajputs and Bhumihars) are in conflict with each other, one side may align with a Naxalite group for protection. The upper castes usually participate in these groups to cleverly maintain the tyrannical Brahminical social order and divert the issues of the transformation of the same social order.

Naxalite Issues

Naxalism is best understood through its actions on the ground. The Naxalites are raising issues such as land rights, minimum wages and the tyranny of the Brahminical social order and challenging the age-old patterns of social order and common property resources.

Land Rights

The big, middle and small land owners, among them the Bhumihars, Rajputs, Brahmins and Kayasthas, are mostly upper caste Hindus who continue their hold as *maliks*. Some of the Yadavs, Kurmies and Koeries have also become land owners through land reform measures or by capturing surplus land (those falling in excess of the land ceiling) or misappropriated common land.

Many of the landless poor from the SCs and other lower castes remain tied to the land and the landowning families of the higher castes in a complex web of social and pre-commercial relationships. This has had strong impacts on the SCs who have faced economic and social deprivation because of it. Though successive governments have allotted land to landless people, even decades later, these people are yet to get possession of the land.

The organized landless poor have staked their claim over the surplus land. They have also attempted to change the tenancy relationships, for example, by demanding implementation of tenancy regulations and better sharecropping terms.

Minimum Wages

In many villages, prior to a wage struggle, the labourers were given around 1.75 kilos of coarse rice with some lunch and sometimes breakfast. Today, in these areas, even though the wages are not uniform, they tend to be 3 kilos of grain per day. In monetary terms, this comes to ₹ 30–35, whereas the official minimum wage is ₹ 51.10. (Kumar, 2002). Thus, the struggle for equitable wages is one of the most important issues taken up by the Naxalite movement.

Other Economic Issues

The Naxalite movement has also fought for the rights of the poor to common property resources. In doing so, the members of a village struggle for *gairmajarua* land as well as full access to the village ponds. Used for washing clothes, bathing cattle, etc., these ponds are also an important source of fish. The upper caste landlords get the fish for a low price since their bids go unchallenged. This system is considered unfair by the poorer villagers for whom the fish is a much-needed food supplement. The Naxalite movement has challenged the landlords' monopoly, established control over the ponds on behalf of the poor and devised a fairer system of distribution of the fish.

Another issue often taken up by the Naxalite movement is housing. Owning a residential plot is very important for the poor. Living on homestead land belonging to the upper caste landlord increases the dependence of the labourers on their employers.

Basic Social Rights

The Naxalite movement has fought against exploitative relations, both social as well as economic. Dignity or honour is one of the crucial elements of social freedom that it has attempted to restore. The SCs want to be considered as human beings and individuals entitled to equal rights. They are fighting against atrocities on lower caste women and arbitrary harassment. They want to be able to sell their labour to whomsoever they want. They want to be able to send their children to school. They want to be able to wear clean clothes, sit in front of their homes on string cots, and welcome their guests without interference from the upper castes. All this has come about because the landed are no longer in a position to exercise illegitimate power with impunity. Another important social right is protection from violence and harassment. Insecurity and fear have always been part of the daily lives of the SCs. To some extent, this continues even today; the Naxalite movement itself, and the repression it has unleashed, have contributed to the general atmosphere of fear, mistrust and suspicion that prevails in Central Bihar.

Basic Political Rights

The above mentioned struggles for economic and social rights, by their very nature, involve an assertion of basic political rights. For example, when the SCs and the Most Backward Castes struggle for minimum wages and for land reforms, they are asserting their constitutional right to justice. Similarly, women who used to be constantly exposed to arbitrary sexual harassment and rape and who now have the power to resist and even punish their aggressors can be seen to defend their constitutional right to personal liberty and dignity.

Another important political right that has been denied to many in Central Bihar is the right to vote. The SCs are often kept away from the polling booths by the henchmen of the upper castes and even the police so that they can be forced to cast their votes for the upper caste candidates.

Brahminical Attitudes of Bureaucrats and Police

The government and its machinery are also responsible for the rising Naxalite violence in Central Bihar. They play their parts in maintaining the Brahminical social order. This can be seen in the National Police Commission's recommendations, which we have discussed earlier.

The PCR Act, 1955 (Protection of Civil Rights Act), and the Scheduled Caste/Scheduled Tribe (PoA) Act(Prevention of Atrocities), 1989, are meant for protecting the SCs and STs. Under these Acts, the police play a key role in helping the SCs and punishing the guilty. But instead of helping the SCs, the police perpetrate further atrocities on them. The face of the police is not humane. They are acting as legalized goondas. Such kinds of police activities also motivate the SCs to join the Naxalite bandwagon.

The administration, run and manned by Brahminical and caste conscious bureaucrats along Brahminical principles, normally ignores the legitimate and genuine grievances of the SCs. The whole milieu of the official world seems to be surcharged with a feeling of animosity towards the interests of the SCs.

In fact, during the chief ministerships of Lalu Prasad Yadav and Nitish Kumar, both of whom belonged to the backward castes, the harassments and cruelties on the SCs and the most backward classes increased. Even the administration and the police were found indifferent towards the genuine grievances of these people. The fact that backward caste men were in power made no difference to the woes and worries of the downtrodden. These leaders were also guided by the Brahminical principles because of which they could not improve the lot of the downtrodden sections of their society.

Government Initiatives

A government of the people and for the people cannot mean a government for the SCs. Equal opportunities for all do not mean equal opportunities for the SCs; equal rights for all cannot mean equal rights for the SCs. The government of our day, when it comes to the SCs, is not guided by the principles of equality, liberty and fraternity. Rather, it is guided by the Brahminical principles of graded inequality, fixity of occupation, and the notions of purity and pollution and superiority and inferiority. It is also guided and regulated through the religious scriptures. Government officials behave like the masters of the public and not their servants. They are also working as the agents of the upper castes and the police are working as the henchmen of these oppressors. The money meant for the uplift of the SCs is misused, misappropriated and diverted by government officials. Naxalism has emerged because of the insensitiveness and Brahminical attitude of the government and its machinery.

According to the 2004–05 annual report of the Union Home Ministry, 'as many as 76 districts in nine states – Andhra Pradesh, Bihar, Chhattisgarh, Jharkhand, Madhya Pradesh, Maharashtra, Orissa, Uttar Pradesh and West Bengal – are afflicted with Naxalism'. The CPML-PW and Maoist Communist Centre India (MCCI) have been trying to increase their influence and operations in some parts of three other states, namely, Tamil Nadu, Karnataka, and Kerala, and also in certain new areas in some of the already affected states. 'Now the Naxals have a strong influence in about 170 districts out of the 602 in the country. Wherever they are perpetrated, particularly in remote and most underdeveloped rural belts, development has stopped because they have been resisting them both by violence and mass mobilization'. In some areas, the Naxals are taking some commission (*rangadari* taxes) from the contractors and government officials. Otherwise, they will not allow the contractors and officials to start work.

There is another difficulty. The Naxalites have been actively campaigning among the rural poor in underdeveloped areas and the tribal areas, saying that the government wants development by taking away their forest wealth and mineral resources such as iron ore and coal. It is true that the government is signing memoranda of understanding (MoUs) with multinational corporations (MNCs) without taking the tribals into confidence and by displacing them from their age-old habitats. In some parts, this has created an anti-development mentality among the people. Besides, even after 63 years of independence, the fruits of development have not been tasted by the tribals. It has been observed that the tribal sub-plan budget has not been allotted properly and also that some of the allotted money has been misused by government functionaries. Government officials actively seek postings in tribal areas so that they can make money. Because of that, the tribals have anti-government feelings. The non-tribals are also exploiting the tribals. This creates anti-feelings towards the non-tribals. All of this, put together, leads to Naxalism.

The Naxalites have established parallel governments in parts of Andhra Pradesh, Madhya Pradesh, Jharkhand and Bihar. The best known things about these parallel governments are the *jan adalats* and their summary, brutal punishments. These parallel governments give the Naxalites a territory to train on and plan their revolutionary forays, but they also simultaneously trigger alienation. In fact, the Naxalite movement has become computational and violent by relying on the terror struck by its guerrilla squads rather than on peasant mobilization.

These days, they are targeting the police because the police and government officials have not addressed the people's problems. As we discussed earlier, the police force is guided by the Brahminical forces and reduced to acting as the henchmen of the upper castes.

Prime Minister Dr Manmohan Singh, while addressing the chief ministers of the Naxalite infested states on 13 April 2006, had called for a two-pronged strategy to tackle the menace – effective police response and socio-economic development in the affected areas. The government considers Naxalism a law and order problem. That is why it wants an effective police response and to declare the Naxalites terrorists. The Centre and the states have once again taken a militaristic approach to address the problem of Naxalism.

The total annual outlay committed from the Centre and states for police modernization, which basically means buying more arms or raising more forces for anti-Naxalite operations, is about ₹ 2,000 crore. In comparison, the Centre allocates a meagre ₹ 2 crore annually to each Naxalite affected district for development activities.

Conclusion

Naxalism – a symptom of entrenched discrimination and failure of the state to enable the fruits of development to reach those who need it the most – cannot be resolved by military means. Had the Centre and the states decided to spend ₹ 2,000 crore per annum for undertaking development programmes, including land reforms, attitudinal changes among the upper castes and bureaucrats, and humanizing the police in the Naxalite affected areas, this problem would have vanished long ago. The fact of the matter is that Naxalism is not just related to economic issues and law and order problems. It is related to the sociocultural divide and oppression created by the Brahminical social order, which is supported and regulated by bureaucrats, who also have a deep Brahminical or high caste attitude and background.

Notes

1. Most of the data have been collected during my fieldwork during 1998 and 1999 in undivided Bihar.
2. *Tola* is a residential place meant only for the untouchables. It is separated from other places so that they do not pollute the whole village. The inhabitant of a *tola* are mostly Chamars (in the Chamar *tola*), the Musahars (in the Musahar *tola*) and the Dusadhs (in the Dusadh *tola*).

3. The word, *bataiya*, comes from the Hindi word, *batwara*. After the harvest, the grain is distributed in equal proportions between the cultivator and the landowner. The cultivator will use the land and cultivate it and will remain a tenant at will.

References

Annual Report of the Union Home Ministry, 2004–05.

Bhatia, Bela. 2005. 'The Naxal Movement in Central Bihar'. In *Economic and Political Weekly*, 9 April.

Bhojpur has been bifurcated into Arrah and Buxar in Bihar.

'Police and the Weaker Sections of Society'. 1980. 3rd Report of the National Police Commission, Government of India, Chapter XIX, p. 4.

Rao, M.S. 1974. *Social Movements and Social Transformation: A Study of Two Backward Classes Movements in India*. New Delhi: Macmillan, p. 110.

Rohtas has been bifurcated into Rohtas and Bhabua in Bihar.

Roy, Ramashray. 1970. 'Caste and Political Recruitment in Bihar'. In Rajni Kothari (ed.) *Caste in Indian Politics*. New Delhi: Orient Longman, pp. 228–255.

10

Resistance Movements in Orissa and Bihar

The Scheduled Castes (SCs) have been subjected to various forms of social discrimination and economic deprivation through the ages across the country. They are one of the most disadvantaged groups in Indian society. They are a stigmatized people and, on this account, suffer from numerous disabilities, which are regulated through religious beliefs and practices. Some of these disabilities are untouchability, low economic status, segregation, lack of political power, low levels of literacy and the resultant limitations on their social mobility. All these together reinforce the wretched condition of the SCs.

Theoretical Perspective

There is a dominant ideological current among social scientists now for the study of SC movement. There is a liberal trend among a group of scholars who believe that it is the ancient Hindu reactionary traditions and the deep-rooted prejudice of the upper castes against the SCs that have led them to protest and resist the injustices they face on a daily basis. This liberal group also has a strong tendency to assume that the SC movement is limited to achieving a partial advance in the socio-economic, civic and political fields within the existing social order. Thus, hardly any thought is expended on a radical transformation in other respects. It is due to this ideological position that concepts such as social mobility, reference groups and relative deprivation figure so prominently in their writings on the SC movement, which, over time, has become a major frame of reference in studying this movement.

One of the notable scholars in the liberal category is M.S.A. Rao (1982), who uses the above concepts to understand the emergence of the protest movements among the backward classes and the SCs.

Taking a cue from Morton and Runciman, Rao argues that social mobility forms the major basis of the theory of relative deprivation (1982). Social conflict as a basis of relative deprivation finds mention in Rao's study, who has also taken cues from Marx and Engel. Rao further argues that relative deprivation is connected with the evolution of a positive reference group (1982). Other scholars, too, try to link the emergence of the SC movement with relative deprivation, reference groups and social mobility (Joshi, 1987; Issac, 1964; Lynch, 1974; Silverberg, 1968; Singer and Cohen, 1968; Sachchidananda, 1978; Bhat, 1971; Ram, 1988; Patwardhan, 1973).

It is obvious from the works of these scholars that terms such as social mobility and relative deprivation form the major frames of reference in discussions on the emergence of resistance, protests and movements among the SCs.

Socio-economic Status of SCs in Bihar and Orissa

India is a semi-feudal country and it is dominated by Brahminism and Brahminical culture. Bihar and Orissa represent two ideal and extreme cases of multi-standard dominance by the upper castes. While the Brahmins, Bhumihars, Rajputs and Kayasthas dominate Bihar, the Brahmins, Karans and Khandayats do so in Orissa. Although these groups are small in number, their dominance is complete when it comes to their ritual status, concentration of land rights, position in the legitimate social hierarchy and concentration of resources. They have been controlling the society around them for at least a thousand years.

The economic relationship in Bihar and Orissa is fundamentally represented in terms of the *malik* (upper castes with full control over means of production) and the *praja*. The *maliks* are the Brahmins, Rajputs, Bhumihars and Kayasthas in Bihar and the Brahmins, Karans and Khandayats in Orissa and these castes control the means of production, while the *prajas* consist of the upper backward castes, the most backward castes and the SCs. The power structure is also based on the capacity of the castes to control the land and the means of production. Land and means of production are a formidable instrument for controlling people and communities. The *maliks* are considered by the *prajas* as their *sarkar* (law incarnate), *deobhagwan* (god incarnate) and *mai-baap* (parents). The *prajas* are subordinate to their *maliks* for all benefits of land and livelihood. The traditional position of the *prajas* corresponds to the general underdog position of the peasantry. The Hindu principle of differentiated hierarchy still continues to differentiate the peasantry in rural areas by setting them apart in numerous capsules of castes that are arranged neatly and vertically one upon the other like high and low and superior and inferior in terms of purity and pollution and ritual status. This social hierarchy is clearly related with economic status as shown below:

Table 10.1 Social Hierarchy

Economic Status	*Social Status*	*Occupational Status*
Maliks (ruling classes)	Upper castes: Brahmins, Bhumihars, Rajputs and Kayasthas (in Bihar), Brahmins, Karans and Khandayats in Orissa	Zamindars and landlords (rural areas), rulers and bureaucrats (urban areas)
Prajas (ruled classes)	Upper Backward Castes	Tenants (rural areas), petty business classes (urban areas)
	Most Backward Castes	Landless agricultural labourers (rural areas), labourers (urban areas)
	Untouchables	Landless agricultural labourers (rural areas), labourers (urban areas)

Radhakrishnan (1949) says that over the years, the Hindu social order has degenerated into an instrument of exploitation, tyranny and oppression. It tends to perpetuate inequality and inhumanity and has developed the spirit of separatism, hatred and enmity, low and high.

The central tendency in Hindu society was and still is that the *jatis* in the twice-born varna are the value givers, norm setters and institution builders and the rest are just followers. The caste Hindus also have a code that the SCs are required to follow. This code lays down the acts of commission, which the caste Hindus treat as offences (see chapter V).

The caste Hindus have internalized this code through a process of socialization. These codes are visible in rural areas and invisible in urban areas. It has become a state of mind in each and every caste Hindu. Due to this code, the caste Hindus have never shown any fellow-feeling towards the SCs. Although the caste Hindus are dependent on the SCs for many a crucial job in their everyday lives, they continually ill treat them, humiliate them and deprive them of their basic right to lead a life of dignity and freedom.

It is clear that the sources of deprivation and exclusion of the SCs were and still are their low social status, appalling poverty, powerlessness, and cultural and educational backwardness. Understandably, the responses of the victims are organically linked to the sources of deprivation. But to understand this linkage, one should be clear about the identity of the population under reference. This is presented in the following table:

Table 10.2 Types of Identities and Modes of Resistance

Sources of Deprivation Exclusion	*Types of Identities*	*Nature of Oppression*	*Patterns of Resistance/Mobilization*
Degrading social status	Untouchables	Social repression	Social reform movements for social equality
Powerlessness	Subject	Political disenfranchisement	Mobilization for political participation
Poverty	Slave	Economic exploitation	Bargaining for the better economic conditions
Cultural	Not a human being/sub-human	Cultural repression	Cultural revolution and negation of Brahminism
Educational	Ignorant/illiterate	Repression at various levels	Equal educational facilities

Resistance Movements in Orissa

In Orissa, caste and religion have played a vital role in establishing an unequal society. The operation of the religious factor is more predominant due to the presence of large temples, priestly castes and other religious symbols. Whenever the SCs try to lead a life of dignity and self-respect, it hurts the upper castes because they want the lower castes to continue doing their traditional menial jobs. The other castes recall legends of when people were more religious than today. They oppose the assimilation and integration of the lower castes with the so-called mainstream as they consider this to be societal adulteration. They also fear that if this happens, the lower castes may occupy a higher position, violating age old customs, which will lead to social disturbances. By virtue of constitutional guarantees, the lower castes have been given protective measures, but the caste Hindus do not accept these measures. They do not hesitate to attack the downtrodden.

Pre-independence Era

Resistance was visible in the development of popular cults such as the Mahima Dharma as a counter to Hinduization and upper caste domination. The Mahima cult not only resisted the varna order, but also posed a serious challenge to it. It attracted the Kandhas as well. In fact, one of its leading exponents was Bhima Bhoi, a blind Kandha, who was associated with a host of fascinating compositions. People who became associated with this plebeian cult were expected to begin a new chapter in their lives, without any reference to their past (Pati, 2003).

During the British period, the SC resistance movements were led by the upper caste leaders. The Orissa branch of the Harijan Sevak Sangh was started in 1933 with Balukeswar Acharya as president and Rama Devi, Laxminarayan Mishra and Satyanarayan Sengupta as secretaries. Its other leading members were Acharya Harihar Dash, Harekrushna Mahatab, Bichitrananda Dash, Radhanath Rath and Gunanidhi Mohanty. The main demands of the organization were temple entry and access to public wells.

The anti-untouchability campaign was opposed by the Utkal Sanatan Dharma Rakhini Sabha led by Parilhita Dasasharma and it was supported by the then king of Puri, Emara Matha Mahant, and the owner of the Goenka Dharmasala, Hariram Goenka. Nilkanth Dash, Loknath Mishra and Raghunath Mishra, along with some Brahmin priests, mobilized support for the Harijan movement in Puri.

The kings of Puri and Sonepur, the Matha *mahantas* and some conservative people formed a council to oppose any law for the eradication of untouchability and to counter the movement against untouchability.

Mahatma Gandhi came to Orissa as part of his *padyatra* in 1934 to make the people aware of the issue of untouchability and to mobilize funds for Harijan development programmes. The then Congress leaders from the upper castes took the initiative to organize meetings at different places, but the meetings were attended mostly by the SCs. The leadership of the SCs was almost absent with every passing year. Besides, some SC leaders like Uchaba Mallik, Padamshree Mohan Naik, Purnananda Samal, Matia Mallik, Santanu Kumar Das and Bika Naik resisted the prevailing system of untouchability and exploitation.

Uchaba Mallik raised his voice against the oppressive and exploitative tax system of the then zamindars and Matha *mahantas*, who were the agents of the British.

Mohan Naik stood firm against the untouchability practices of the Hindus. Once, in 1937, he was prevented from entering the Kali temple in Berhampur, and from that day onwards, he took a vow to not visit any Hindu temple and resolved to fight against the unjust practices of the caste Hindus. He declared that temple entry was the right of the SCs and he fought for their temple entry rights.

In 1920, Naik was introduced to Thakarbapa who was working with the Hind Sevak Sangh founded by Gopal Krishna Gokhale. The Harijan Sevak Sangh unit was set up in Ganjam district with Naik as its secretary.

On 18 December 1938, Naik formed the Berhampur Harijan Sangh and involved the youth to fight against untouchability. He started conducting awareness meetings and mobilized the Dalits to enter eateries and hotels, but the hotel owners resisted him. The court fined the owners of the Barajksar Malabar Hotel and Brundaban Bilas Hotel, but the local SCs collected the money needed to bail them out.

Santanu Kumar Das was the founder president of the Dalit Jati Sangh. Purnanand Samal and Kanduri Malik were also associated with this organization. They were influenced by Babu Jagjivan Ram. Das was instrumental in the distribution of homestead lands to the landless SC families in the state and initiated a number of education development programmes for the SCs. He wrote a number of books calling for the eradication of caste-based discrimination. Among his popular books were *Bhai Bhai*, *Bhitamati* and *Ahwan*.

Thus, the SCs resisted the oppressive and exploitative system under the banner of the Congress. But both untouchability and the exploitative social order are still in existence 63 years after independence. The SC leaders and the upper caste leaders were both fighting for space within the fold of Hinduism. An SC leader called Matia Malik said, 'We fought against the local king with the support of the Congress, but the Congress accommodated the princes and the zamindars. Moreover, we had to accept the sons and daughters of those people who became Congress members as the new Congress leaders.' (Jena, 2006).

Post-independence Period

Let's look at some specific cases of resistance movements in the post-independence era.

The Gadarodanga Incident

Gadarodanga village is situated 3 kilometres away from the block headquarters of Brahmagiri in Puri district. It is a gram panchayat and has a multicaste composition, but is dominated by the Khandayats. There are only 13 SC families in the village and most of them are landless. Others include the Dhobas, who are washermen, and the Doms and Hadis, who are agricultural labourers. The caste system is so strong that the lower castes do not dare to violate the caste traditions for fear of vicious retaliation.

On 10 March 2002, in Gadarodanga, the Dhobas, who are traditionally washermen belonging to the SCs, were prevented from erecting a tent for a marriage ceremony. The Khandayats entered the venue, pulled down the decorated tent, broke the tube lights, took away the generator and mike set and misbehaved with the women present there. This was despite the fact that the bridegroom, Ashok Sethy, the son of Suratha Sethy, had got police permission to put up a tent for his marriage after personally going and informing the police on the eve of the incident. Ashok's parents had informed the village head, too. The question of informing the police and the village head about the erection of the tent arose because there had been problems about such incidents in the past.

Earlier, in 1999, when the Dhobas had put up a *chhamundia* (leaf tent) for the marriage of Nidhi Sethu's daughter in the village, the Khandayats opposed it, saying that it was against the established social custom. The lower castes had not done any extravaganza in the past because of their economic situation. But now they could afford it. When the Khandayats did not allow the erecting of the leaf tent, the Dhobas agreed, but after the marriage ceremony, a meeting was called, which was attended by both the Dhobas and the Khandayats. In the presence of the police, it was decided at the meeting that the Dhobas and other lower castes could also put up tents on festive occasions. The resolution of the meeting was circulated among the police, the Dhobas and the Khandayats.

Shortly after the incident, a five member fact finding team comprising human rights activists and lawyers, formed under the aegis of the Ambedkar-Lohia Vichar Manch, visited Gadarodanga to obtain a firsthand account of the incident. The fact finding team visited the village and released the report to the press in Bhubaneswar on 10 April. The report said the Khandayats had scant regard for the rights of the

SCs and blamed the police and officials for supporting the Khandayats and decried the fact that no political leaders had come to the rescue of the affected families. 'The police were also apathetic to the plight of the washermen's families. Even though four complaints had been lodged with the police, only one FIR had been filed,' said the report.

The Kodala Incident

The SCs know that they are not treated at par with others. They are barred from getting simple services such as haircuts and shaves at local barbershops. And this issue exploded into communal tension at Kodala village on 8 September 2004. The issue that led to the clash was whether SCs could be allowed to have haircuts and shaves at barbershops that were frequented by the upper castes.

The Bhandari community, who are upper caste barbers, of Kodala village in Ganjam district, decided not to offer their services to the SCs. Over the past many years, the SCs of the village had been having caste related issues with the upper castes.

Some SCs of the area reached a barbershop asking for haircuts. The shop owner refused to cut their hair fearing the wrath of his upper caste customers. The SCs then sought police intervention. The Kodala police called a meeting of the SC leaders, barbers and upper castes to settle the issue. But the SC representatives did not attend the meeting. The meeting was called off, forcing the barber community and the upper castes to hold a meeting of their own at Jatra Padia field on 8 September 2004. While they were holding the meeting, an SC youth allegedly manhandled a person at the meeting. It agitated the upper castes and the barbers present there. Following this, around a thousand of them reached the Bauri Sahi, a locality inhabited by the SCs and attacked their houses. In retaliation, the SCs of the Bauri Sahi, Marathi Sahi, Hadi Sahi localities got together and pelted stones at the upper caste attackers.

Keredagada Temple Entry

On 15 December 2005, the day of the auspicious Kartik Purnima, Shakuntala and six other village girls went to the 300 year old Keredagada Jagannath temple, which is prohibited territory for lower caste Hindus.

The team broke the barrier to enter the circumference of the temple. But before they could make their way to the citadel, the priest stopped the 'intruders'. A year later, on 14 December 2006, the SCs, backed by a High Court verdict, entered the temple, which had hitherto been the exclusive preserve of the upper castes.

There was a sharp divide along caste lines in this part of the state after the SCs broke the age-old social barriers and entered the three centuries old Jagannath temple on 14 December. It is pertinent to note here that *puja* was stopped and the doors of the sanctum sanctorum housing Lord Jagannath shut for a few minutes after the four SC girls walked quietly into the temple. The fuming upper castes resorted to a hunger strike in front of the temple's main gate.

After hours of suspense, the SCs and the upper caste Hindus sat together at the Keredagada revenue circle office in close proximity to the temple. Some 50 local residents from both sections were allowed to take part in the meeting. After much persuasion, the upper caste representatives agreed to allow the SCs into the temple. Since then the SCs can move up to the first step leading to the sanctum sanctorum. Significantly, it was agreed to demolish the wall with nine holes through which the SCs were earlier allowed to peep through and offer *puja* to the deity – a new entrance would replace it.

Prior to this, the more than 3,000 SCs of Keredagada village had threatened to convert to Buddhism, SC leader Ashok Mallick of the Orissa Mukti Morcha and the Ambedkar Mission told this author. To protect the SCs' right to enter the temple, the police filed a case under Section 3 of the Scheduled Castes and Scheduled Tribes (Prevention of Atrocities) Act, 1989 against three upper caste leaders on charges of making gullible upper caste people oppose the entry of SCs into the temple by violating the court order.

The police action followed the revelation that the district administration had illegally replaced the nine holed wall with an iron grill in violation of the court's order. Following this, the Ambedkar-Lohia Vichar Manch, a pro-SC outfit, urged the SCs to not embrace Buddhism.

Resistance Movements in Bihar

Bihar has always exhibited a rigid and unequal socio-economic structure in which there is a concentration of land rights and a strong legitimization of the social hierarchy by Brahminical ideology. The Brahmins, Bhumihars and Rajputs have dominated this socio-economic structure for many centuries. These groups have been identified as the zamindar castes of Bihar in the past. The Ahirs, Kurmis and Koeries are categorized as the tenant and small cultivating castes, while the other untouchables castes were seen as providers of menial and agricultural labour.

Pre-independence Phase

Dr Rajendra Prasad initiated Babu Jagjivan Ram into his own organization, the Anti-Untouchability Society, which worked for the uplift of SCs in Bihar. Later on, he introduced him to Gandhi, who entrusted him with the responsibility of the Harijan Sevak Sangh in Bihar. In 1934, it was decided at the annual conference of the Ravi Das Mahasabha in Kolkata to establish the Depressed Classes League, following which a conference was organized in 1935 in Kanpur.

The conference formally declared the official establishment of the Depressed Classes League with Rastik Lal Biswas as its president and Jagjivan Ram and P.N. Rajbhoj as its secretaries. During 1935, Jagjivan Ram also participated in the Hindu Mahasabha Conference held in Lucknow. The main aim of the conference was to plan a policy to stop the SCs from converting to other religions. In fact, Jagjivan Ram moved a resolution to throw open public places such as temples, watering places and schools to the SCs, a move that was opposed by the Shankarcharya of Puri. Nevertheless, the resolution was passed later on. Madan Mohan Malviya praised Jagjivan Ram in his presidential address for his services to Hinduism and keeping the SCs within the Hindu fold.

As Jagjivan Ram wanted to uplift the SCs within the Hindu fold, he opposed their conversion to other religions. When Ambedkar solemnly proclaimed that he would not die a Hindu, it was Jagjivan Ram who persuaded the SCs to postpone their mass conversion plan at the Lucknow conference in 1936. It can be said that Jagjivan Ram aligned with the dominant sociopolitical forces of his time to achieve some rights and privileges for the SCs.

Post-independence Phase

In 1983, the Dalit Sena was formed by Ram Vilas Paswan to work towards the emancipation and welfare of the SCs. Initially, he developed a sense of consciousness among them regarding the socio-economic structure and cultural reality that kept them in subjugation. He used the ideologies of Ambedkar, Phule and Periyar to attack the Brahminical social order. He also used other icons such as Ravi Das, Kabir, Ram Manohar Lohia and Jai Prakash Narayan to mobilize the SCs. He raised SC issues both inside and outside Parliament and sensitized the upper castes towards these issues. He actively promoted other backward caste movements, strongly raised the issues of their development and challenged the domination of the upper castes in Bihar. Because of the united efforts of the SCs and backward castes, the political dominance of the upper castes has changed radically in the 1990s. But the SCs still feel betrayed by the upper backward caste leaders.

In the post-independence period, with the implementation of legal provisions such as universal suffrage and land reforms, there have been drastic changes in the dominance of the upper castes. Thereafter, there emerged a group of neo-twice-born castes consisting of the Yadavs, the Kurmis and the Koeries.

Despite all these efforts, the SCs continue to be marginalized and subjected to exploitation and humiliation throughout the state. They form a large labour force for the landowning upper castes. They are confronted by a plethora of problems even today. Even during the 1970s, they were not allowed to sit with other non-SCs. Till today, they are meant to serve the upper castes, who are apprehensive that if the SCs obtain education, they will lose their potential workforce. Resistance by the SCs against such humiliating and exploitative practices results in frequent violent attacks from the upper castes.

There have been caste rivalries and caste tensions in the state. Earlier, the contradiction was mainly within the upper caste Hindus, but now a tension exists between the upper caste Hindus and the backward castes and between the backward castes and the SCs as well. The primary victims of these tensions are the members of the poorer SCs who have dared to challenge the age-old pattern of domination. Often, there are killings between these mutually contradictory groups in addition to the killings by the private caste armies. Such armies or *senas* are generally identified with specific castes (see Table 10.3 for a better view).

At the village level, a more violent repression has been perpetrated by the upper castes and upper backward castes to suppress the discontent and grievances of the SCs. Table 10.4 indicates the aggressors and the victims by caste.

At present, the Ranvir Sena is the most active private army in Central Bihar. The Ranvir Sena was founded by upper caste Bhumihars in 1994 at Belaur village in Bhojpur district. Since its inception, the Ranvir Sena has been implicated in mass killings, rapes and looting in villages such as Belaur, Ekwari, Chandi, Nanaur, Narhi, Sarathau, Habiaspur, Laxmanpur-Bathe, Shankarbigha and Narayanpur. Its victims are mostly the SCs.

Table 10.3 Major Caste *Senas* in Bihar

Name of Private Army	*Caste Affiliation*	*Year of Formation*	*Operational Districts*	*Remarks*
Kuer Sena	Rajputs	1979	Bhojpur Rohtas	In 1985, the organizer was killed. Fight for supremacy led to disintegration.
Kisan Suraksha Samiti	Kurmis	1979	Patna, Jehanabad, Gaya	This is for the Kurmi caste.
Bhomi Sena	Kurmis	1983	Patna, Nawada, Nalanda, Jehanabad	The ML squads killed the leaders, the others were put in jail.
Lorik Sena	Yadavs	1983	Patna, Jehanabad, Nalanda	In 1986, one of the leaders, Ramanand Yadav, was killed; the others were also eliminated.
Brahmarshi Sena	Bhumihars	1984	Bhojpur, Patna, Jehanabad, Aurangabad	ML squads eliminated the main leaders.
Kisan Sangh	Rajputs, Brahmins	1984	Palamu	ML squads eliminated the main leaders.
Kisan Sevak Samaj	Rajputs	1985	Palamu, Aurangabad	The main commander, Yogeshwar Tyagi, was killed.
Sunlight Sena	Pathanas, Rajputs	1989	Palamu, Gaya, Garwah, Aurangabad	Many of its leaders were eliminated, but it is still active in some areas.
Sawarna Liberation Front	Bhumihars	1990	Gaya, Jehanabad	The ML squads eliminated the leaders and the others were arrested.
Kisan Sangh	Bhumihars	1990	Patna, Bhojpur	Ram Lakhan Singh Yadav supported this sena.
Kisan Morcha	Rajputs	1989–90	Bhojpur	The chief, Jwala Singh, was killed and the group disintegrated.
Ganga Sena	Rajputs	1990	Bhojpur	This operates mainly in the Diara belt of the Ganges.
Ranvir Sena	Bhumihars	1994	Bhojpur, Patna, Jehanabad Rohtas, Gaya, Aurangabad	It has committed more than two dozen massacres. It is the most dreaded sena at present.

Source: Fernando Franco (ed.). 2002. Pain and Awakening. New Delhi: Indian Social Institute.

Table 10.4 Caste Violence in Bihar

Aggressors			*Victims*		
Place	*Caste*	*Economic Status*	*Caste*	*Economic Status*	*Issues*
Bajitpur	Bhumihars	Landlord	SCs	Agricultural labourers	Wages, sharecroppers' land rights
Belchi	Kurmis	Landlord	All castes	Poor peasants, agricultural labourers, sharecroppers	Social oppression
Belapur	Kurmis	Landlord	Dalits	Agricultural labourers	Wages
Bishrampur	Kurmis	Landlord	Dalits	Agricultural labourers, sharecroppers	Wages, sharecroppers' rights
Chandadano	Kurmis	Landlord	Dalits	Agricultural labourers	Wages
Dharampuri	Brahmins	Landlord	Dalits	Agricultural labourers, sharecroppers	Wages, sharecroppers' rights
Gopalpur	Kurmis	Landlord	Dalits	Agricultural labourers	Wages
Kalia	Kurmis	Landlord	Dalits	Sharecroppers	Sharecroppers' rights
Khijuria	Brahmins	Landlord	Dalits	Agricultural labourers	Wages
Pipra	Kurmis	Landlord	Dalits	Agricultural labourers	Wages
Pathada	Yadavs	Landlord	Dalits	Agricultural labourers	Wages
Pupri	Kurmis	Landlord	Dalits	Agricultural labourers	Wages, land possession

Source: Dipankar Gupta (ed.). 1991. Social Stratification. Oxford University Press.

Reasons for Resistance

The SCs have resisted both social and economic exploitative relations. Dignity or honour is one crucial social freedom they have attempted to restore unto themselves. The SCs want to be considered as human beings entitled to equal rights. They are fighting against the rape of their women and arbitrary attacks on their community; the SC labourers want freedom to sell their labour to whomsoever they please. The SC children want to attend school. The SCs want to wear clean clothes, sit openly in front of their homes, and welcome their guests without interference from the upper castes. All this has come about because the landed are no longer in a position to exercise illegitimate power with impunity. Besides, they are also raising issues such as land rights, minimum wages, common property resources and housing, and changing the age-old patterns of the Brahminical social order.

Conclusion

The SC resistance movement in Orissa and Bihar is challenging Brahminical values through a process of emulation and sanskritization. This attempts to imitate the twice-born caste values, which contributed to the development of a negative consciousness, which, according to Gramsci, may not constitute a mature and fully evolved class consciousness, but is certainly the first glimmer of such consciousness constituting the basic negative, polemical attitudes. Gramsci further argues that the lower classes have historically been on the defensive, and they can only achieve self-awareness through the identity and class limits of their energy (Guha, 1983).

The SCs' resistance movement in Orissa focused on entry into upper caste Hindu temples and tried to improve the status of the SCs, who had been made into slaves, by the process of Sanskritization, which is imitating the Hindu lifestyle by adopting the gods and rituals of the upper castes. The process of Sanskritization has created a negative class consciousness among the SCs, which, in turn, made them the slaves of the upper castes. This movement, in terms of relative deprivation and social mobility, helped reveal the role of the castes and inherited status that have for long influenced the monopolizing of the jobs market by the upper castes, who viewed caste mobility as dangerous and disruptive to the social fabric.

But, the present scenario of the SCs reveals the total marginalization and annihilation of the rural SCs, the Hinduization of the poor SCs and the growing crisis in the Indian welfare state. It seems to be questioning the theoretical validity of relative deprivation both as a concept and as a form of consciousness. However, the concepts of relative deprivation and social mobility are quite inadequate to explain this reality at the theoretical level. Given the happenings in rural areas, where the upper castes or class forces are committing brutal atrocities on the SCs, and where the state response to these inhuman acts is either callous or repressive, the SCs not only feel a sense of relative deprivation, but total alienation and exclusion and threat of their physical elimination.

What one observes in rural Orissa and Bihar is the complete alienation of the SCs from resources such as land and water and agricultural implements. The SCs do not find sufficient access to either natural or human resources and, therefore, feel totally marginalized in relation to the so-called decentralization of political power in rural India. Moreover, it is this perception of total exclusion from the developmental processes that forces the SCs to resist in the most militant ways, ranging from radical reaction to physical retaliation in self-defence. Thus, militancy is evident among the SCs in Bihar.

We may conclude that the Oriya SCs have tried to reform the caste system in their bid to resolve the problem of untouchability by remaining within the fold of Hinduism. In contrast, in Bihar, the SCs are trying to create an alternative sociocultural structure through radical movements. Besides, various SC organizations and their leaders have developed consciousness among the oppressed regarding the socio-economic structure and cultural reality that are keeping them subjugated.

References

Ambedkar, B.R. 1987. Vol. 5. Writings and Speeches. Bombay Maharashtra: Education Department, Maharashtra.

'Atrocities on Dalits: Structural Dysfunction'. 2002. In *Fourth World*, Vol. 16 (Oct.). NISWASS.

Bose, Pradip K. 1991. 'Mobility and Conflicts: Social Roots of Caste Violence in Bihar'. In Dipankar Gupta (ed.) *Social Stratification*. New Delhi: Oxford University Press.

Broken People: Caste Violence against India's Untouchables. 1999. New York: Human Rights Watch.

'Changing Patterns of Caste Relationship in Bihar'. 1995. Unpublished Dissertation. New Delhi: Jawaharlal Nehru University.

Fernando, Franco (ed.). 2002. *Pain and Awakening*. New Delhi: Indian Social Institute.

Guha, Ranajit. 1983. *Elementary Aspects of Peasant Insurance in Colonial India*. Delhi. Oxford University Press.

Guru, Gopal. 1999. 'The Dalit Movement in Mainstream Sociology'. In S.M. Michael (ed.) *Dalits in Modern India: Vision and Values*. New Delhi: Vistaar Publications.

Issac, R. Harold. 1965 *India's Ex-Untouchables*. Mumbai: Asia Publishing.

Jena, Manas. 2006. *Dalit Freedom Fighters of Orissa*. Bhubaneswar: Development Initiative.

Joshi, Barbara. 1987 'Recent Developments in Inter-Regional Mobilisation of Dalit Protest in India'. In *South Asian Bulletin,* 7, 112–135.

Kumar, Rabindra. 2002. *Impact of Rural Development on Scheduled Castes*. New Delhi: Anmol Publications.

Kumar, Vivek. 2002. *Dalit Leadership in India*. Delhi: Kalpaz Publications.

'*Laxmanpur Bathe Narsanhar*' (in Hindi). 1998. In *Bharat Ashvagosh,* Jan.–Feb., Nagpur.

Lynch, Owen. 1974. *The Politics of Untouchability*. New Delhi: National Publications.

Oommen, T.K. 1990. *Protest and Change: Studies in Social Movements*. New Delhi: Sage Publications.

Pati, Biswamay. 2003. *Identity, Hegemony, Resistance: Three Essays*. New Delhi: Collective.

Patwardhan, Sunanda. 1973. *Change among India's Harijan*. New Delhi: Orient Longman.

Radhakrishnan, S. 1949. *The Hindu View of Life*. op. cite.

Ram, Nandu. 1988. *The Mobile Scheduled Castes: Rise of a New Middle Class*. Delhi Hindustan Publishing Corp.

Rao, M.S.A. 1982. *Social Movements in India*,Vol. 1. Delhi: Manohar Publications.

Runciman, W. 1966. *Relative Deprivation*. London: Routledge and Kegan Paul.

Sachchidanand, S. 1978. *Harijan Elite*. Faridabad: Thomson Press.

Silverberg, James (ed.). 1968 *Social Mobility in the Caste System in India*. The Hague, Paris: Mouton.

Singer, M., and Cohen, Bernard (eds). 1968. *Structure and Change in Indian Society*. Chicago.

The Statesman. 18 and 19 Dec. 2006. Bhubaneswar.

The Statesman. 9 Sep., 2004. Bhubaneswar.

The Times of India. 22 Dec. 2006. Bhubaneswar.

11

The Relevance of Ambedkar in Social Reconstruction

Most people remember Babasaheb Dr B.R. Ambedkar as the principal architect of the Constitution and as a crusader for the rights of the oppressed. Indeed, he was all this and much more. Whether an erudite scholar, ardent champion of human rights, eloquent and well-informed parliamentarian or eminent educationist and economist, Ambedkar left his mark on everything he involved himself in. Most importantly, he became the messiah of hundreds of millions of untouchables.

Ambedkar's thoughts, as reflected in his extensive writings and speeches, have played a significant role in tracing the history and growth of social thought in India. With the passing of time, many of his observations on social, economic and political matters are coming true. Social tensions and caste conflicts are continuously on the increase, making his thoughts even more relevant today. If his solutions and remedies for various socio-economic problems are understood and followed, they may help us steer through the present turmoil and guide us to a better future.

Reconstruction of the Ideal Society

Ambedkar was a social liberal, the towering enlightenment figure of modern India, who applied committed reason to social reconstruction. His concept of an ideal society was most suited to the needs of a modern society. To him, society was an integrated whole, and each individual was related to the other through a web of social ties. His views on society fully endure – an individual is mainly responsible for his own welfare, but, at the same time, he shares collective responsibility for the good of the larger society. Ambedkar's cherished goal of an ideal society was one that guaranteed to all its members political, social and economic justice, and according to him, the attainment of this human ideal should be through the democratic process.

The Hindu social order is a ladder of castes placed one above the other, together representing an ascending scale of respect and descending scale of contempt. As opposed to the principles of liberty, equality and fraternity, according to Ambedkar, the Hindus social order is based on the principles of graded inequality, in terms of occupation, lifestyle and social interaction.[1]

According to Ambedkar, 'The caste system is not merely a division of labour. It is also a division of labourers – it is a hierarchy in which the divisions of labourers are graded one above the other. This division of labour is not spontaneous, it is not based on natural aptitudes. Nor is the division of labour brought about by the caste system a division based on choice. Individual sentiment, individual preference, has no place in it. It is based on the dogma of predestination.' He asserted, 'Caste does not result in economic efficiency. Caste cannot and has not improved the race. Caste has, however, done one thing. It has completely disorganized and demoralized the Hindus.' Not only that, 'the effect of caste on the ethics of the Hindus is simply deplorable. Caste has killed public spirit. Caste has destroyed the sense of public charity. Caste has made public opinion impossible. A Hindu's public face is his caste. His loyalty is restricted only to his caste. Virtue has become caste-ridden and morality has become caste-bound. There is no sympathy to the deserving. There is no appreciation of the meritorious.' Finally, he says there cannot be a more deadened paralysis that cripples people from helpful activity. What is the way out? How can the dreaded caste system be destroyed? According to Ambedkar, caste is a notion. It is a state of mind. The destruction of caste does not, therefore, mean the destruction of a physical barrier. It means a notional change. 'All the same, it must be recognized that the Hindus observe caste not because they are inhuman or wrong-headed. They observe caste because they are deeply religious. Hence, the enemy that one must grapple with is not the people who observe caste, but the *Shastras* which teach them this religion of caste. Therefore, the real remedy is to destroy the belief in the sanctity of the *Shastras*. Make every man and woman free from the thraldom of the *Shastras*',[2] he says.

Thus, Ambedkar called upon the Hindus to annihilate caste, which was a great hindrance to social solidarity and to set up a new social order based on the ideals of liberty, equality, justice and fraternity in consonance with the principle of democracy. He advocated inter-caste marriage as one of the solutions for the problem of casteism. But he stressed that belief in the *Shastras* is the root cause of the existence of multitudinous castes. Therefore, he suggested that every man and woman who was free from the thraldom of the *Shastras* must cleanse their minds of the pernicious notions founded on the *Shastras* and he or she should interdine and intermarry. According to him, society must be based on reason and not on the atrocious traditions of the caste system.[3]

Model of State Socialism

In the India of today, debates rage about the role of the state and markets and about the effects of liberalization, globalization and privatization. It is crucially important to examine these issues from the perspective of the most deprived communities. Guiding this will be the framework that Ambedkar formulated, which, drawing inspiration from Buddhism, seeks to lay out principles for economic development that assigns appropriate roles to the state (welfare and protection), the markets (the wealth increasing activities of private households) and the community (the voluntary sharing and equality of the Bhikku Sangh). The spirit of the efforts to achieve 'liberty, equality and fraternity', which Ambedkar took as his basis for social action and by which he evaluated the socialist and other economic systems of his day, will also guide us in our effort to analyse the burning economic issue of contemporary India.

In his book, *States and Minority*, Ambedkar presents the blueprint of his model of development. His model of economic development represents a modified form of state socialism.

The state socialism model proposed by Ambedkar has the following salient features:

1. Key industries, or those that are declared to be key, shall be owned and run by the state;
2. The agricultural industry shall be a state industry;
3. It shall be the state's obligation to finance the cultivation on the collective farms by supplying water, draught animals, implements, manure, seeds, etc.;
4. Farms should be cultivated as collective farms; and

5. Thus, he proposed state ownership of agriculture with a collectivized method of cultivation and a modified form of state socialism in the field of industry.

Ambedkar said that the above scheme of state socialism should not be left to the will of the legislature alone. It should be established by the Constitution so that it will be beyond the reach of a parliamentary majority to suspend, amend or abrogate. This guarantees state socialism while retaining parliamentary democracy. 'It is only by this that one can achieve the triple object of establishing socialism, retaining parliamentary democracy and avoiding dictatorship.[4]' Ambedkar believed that his plan of state socialism was essential for increasing productivity without closing every avenue to the private sector and also for distributing wealth equitably. The main purpose behind this clause was to put an obligation on the state to plan the economic life of the people so that it would lead to the highest point of productivity without closing all the avenues to private enterprise and also provide for the equitable distribution of wealth.[5] Ambedkar further argued that if democracy were to live up to its principle of 'one man, one value', it was essential to define both the economic as well as political structures of society in the Constitution. But due to strong opposition in the Constituent Assembly, he could not incorporate his scheme of state socialism in the Fundamental Rights. However, the Constitution clearly lays down in the Directive Principles that the state should secure a social order in which justice, social, economic and political, shall form all institutions of life. Accordingly, after independence, the government adopted a national economic policy under which was incorporated various special development measures for the socio-economic development of deprived sections such as the Scheduled Castes (SCs) and the Scheduled Tribes (STs), in addition to the several general developmental measures already under implementation.

It has to be noted that untouchability, a by-product of the caste system, is not only a form of social discrimination, but also a source of economic exploitation. The SCs are discriminated against both at the product market as well as at the factor market on the ground of untouchability.[6] The SCs are denied the right to education. They are denied the right to own land and wear jewellery. They are denied the right to bargain for better wages and expected to accept whatever is paid to them. They are assigned unclean occupations and they are forced to remain in those occupations all their lives because the caste system does not permit vertical mobility. They have to perform a number of duties in the village without any remuneration. According to Ambedkar, untouchability is not merely a religious system, but an economic system that is worse than slavery. Untouchability, as an economic system, permits exploitation without obligation. 'Untouchability is not only a system of unmitigated economic exploitation, but also a system of uncontrolled economic exploitation'.[7]

Equal opportunity in the process of development has been provided through the policy of reservation in the legislatures, educational institutions and employment for these underprivileged groups. The policy of reservation is not only viewed as an important instrument for breaking the caste system and promoting occupational mobility, but also seen as a measure for strengthening the integrity and unity of the country by enabling the underprivileged sections to participate on equal terms in the process of national development. It promotes confidence among the marginalized groups as the people from these sections also hold important positions in the governance process and represent the interests of these underprivileged groups. Thus, state intervention in the form of positive discrimination is viewed as a necessary measure for promoting competition and growth with justice, given the imperfections of a caste-based society.

The economic policy has been oriented towards growth with justice and the public sector has been assigned a crucial role in the process of economic development since the First Five-Year Plan. It is believed that given the degree of underdevelopment, industrial take-off must be actively steered by the state. The importance of the public sector is spelled out in the Industrial Policy Resolution of 1956, which spells out that the public sector should strategically control the key sectors of the economy. And one of the important objectives of planning is self-reliance.

Reconstruction through Buddhism

According to Ambedkar, the ideal to be realized is 'one man one value' in all walks of life – whether political, economic or social. The ideal of 'one man one value' is achieved by stopping religious, economic and social exploitation of man by man. The absence of exploitation in any form is the essence of socialism. To Ambedkar, socialism not only embraced economic equality, but also political and social equality. Being an untouchable, Ambedkar had to undergo a litany of sufferings and humiliations. Untouchability is the neglected child of Hinduism.

Due to the caste system, untouchability is despised by the Hindus as the caste system is more anti-social than non-social in its attitude towards one another. As Ambedkar had himself suffered the most horrible agonies created by the Hindu caste system, he realized that the caste Hindus are more antisocial towards the SCs. Explaining the disabilities imposed upon the SCs by the caste Hindus with the support of religion and social customs, he writes:

> 'The Hindus will not allow the Untouchables to take water from a well, the Hindus will not allow the Untouchables entry into schools; the Hindus will not allow the Untouchables to travel in buses; the Hindus will not allow the Untouchables to travel in the same railway compartment; the Hindus will not allow the Untouchables to wear jewellery; the Hindus will not allow the Untouchables to put tiles on the roofs of the houses; the Hindus will not tolerate the Untouchables to own land; the Hindus will not allow the Untouchables to keep cattle; the Hindus will not allow the Untouchables to sit when a Hindu is standing. These are not isolated acts of a few bad men among the Hindus, they are the emanations of the permanent anti-social attitude of the Hindu community against the Untouchables'.[8]

Therefore, Ambedkar set himself the great task of creating radical change by putting an end to the exploitation of the SCs by creating in them a sense of self-respect, dignity of the individual and consciousness of equality of status. Ambedkar organized social reform movements under the banner of the Bahiskrita Hitakarini Sabha (1924) to bring about socioreligious and political consciousness among the Mahars of Maharashtra. The year, 1927, was a landmark in the history of the SC movement as it was in this year that Ambedkar organized many temple entry movements, held the Mahad Satyagraha to fetch water from the public tank at Chowdwar village, burnt the *Manusmriti* stating that it was responsible for the plight of the SCs and submitted a memorandum to the Simon Commission demanding political rights for the SCs.

Ambedkar believed that social reform was a precursor of political reform and that the common masses had to be made politically conscious before they joined the freedom struggle. He and his followers had to face strong resistance from the orthodox Hindus for their social reform programmes and they had to endure a lot of criticism and humiliation. That there was no change among the Hindus in the direction of accepting the SCs led Ambedkar to characterize the SCs as a separate element distinct from the Hindus and advise them to seek equal status in any other religion by renouncing Hinduism.

Ambedkar did not adopt Marxian methods to end the exploitation of the SCs as he was against Marx's irreligious and anti-religious outlook on life. He regarded the Marxist way of life to be inferior to the Buddhist way, saying that man was a factor in the making of history and that environmental forces, whether impersonal or social, were the first and not the last thing in this process. In his view, historical change was also the result of the biography of great men. He insisted that economic forces were important in so far as they are moulded intelligently by man. He admitted that economic factors played an important role in human relations, but not to the extent to which Marx said they did. Marx stood for the abolition of private property and sided with those who were stricken by poverty, disease and illiteracy.

Regarding private property, Ambedkar said, 'The Buddha enjoined that no monk should have private property, the rules of the Buddhist Sangha regarding private property are far more severe than any rule that the Marxists have made in Russia. The means used by Marx to bring prosperity to the poor is violence, while the Buddha's method is based on life, persuasion and moral teaching. The Buddhists in any case will not allow violence for effecting changes in social conditions.'

Ambedkar felt that dictatorship was not a good method by which to rule over people because it robbed people of their individual liberty and deprived them of the freedom to act in accordance with their conscience. He was not content with the Marxist way of life because he felt that it was less satisfactory than the Buddhist way of life.

The philosophy of Ambedkar was deeply influenced by his socioreligious ideas. His attitude towards religion was not spiritual like that of Gandhi. His approach to religion was intellectual, social and political. To him, the foundations of religion were essential to life and social practices and religion was not merely a concept of faith and a means of worship, but a science for social reconstruction.

Ambedkar struggled throughout his life for the emancipation of the SCs from the stigma of caste and untouchability. His struggle was directed against the oppression and exploitation of man against man and man against woman. He held Hinduism responsible for the disorganization and demoralization of society and particularly for the pathetic condition of the SCs. He observed:

> 'The religion, which discriminates between its followers, is partial and the religion which treats crores of its adherents worse than dogs and criminal and inflicts upon them insufferable disabilities is no religion at all. Religion is not the appellation for such an unjust order.'[9]

Therefore, Ambedkar was busy spreading the message of Lord Buddha by writing books and delivering speeches. He addressed people across the world through the British Broadcasting Corporation in May 1956 and told them that he preferred Buddhism because it offered three principles in combination, which no other religion did. According to him, Buddhism could bring peace and happiness to the world. At a press conference on 13 October 1956, he said he chose only the least harmful way for the country and the greatest benefit he conferred on the country was embracing Buddhism, as it was part and parcel of Indian culture.

In the 6th century BC, Gautam Buddha started a social protest movement against oppression and exploitation in the name of religion. Although he propounded an enlightened and egalitarian philosophy for mankind, it was no revelation.[10] The Buddha did not promise salvation: He said he was the *Margadaata* (pathfinder) and not the *Mokshadaata* (giver of salvation). Salvation must be sought by each for himself by his own effort.[11] Buddhism is based on reason, experience, morality and humanism and, hence, the Buddha's followers should not accept these blindly. It is a dynamic religion and its followers are free to modify the Buddha's teachings according to time and circumstances.

In fact, it may be stated that the Buddha was the first teacher in the world who made morality the essence and foundation of religion.[12] He wanted to take concrete steps to destroy the gospel of inequality. In his opposition to casteism, the Buddha practised what he preached. He not only preached against casteism, but also admitted the Shudhras, women and the low castes to the rank of Bhikkus, who held the same status in Buddhism as the Brahmins in Brahminism. This shows the humanitarian and egalitarian tenets of Buddhism. Through this equality of all, the Buddha wanted to mould the character of one and all and he desired that even ordinary men and women should lead a life of purity. His mission was to construct anew a social order on the principles of the Panchshila and the Noble Eightfold Path.

Ambedkar wanted to make the Buddhist philosophy a political philosophy to achieve equality. Preferring Buddhism over communism, he underlined the fact that the Buddha had said the same thing 2,400 years ago that Karl Marx said in the later part of the 19th century. There is indeed a deep similarity between the Dhamma Chakra Pravartan Sutta and the philosophy of Marx. The only difference between them is related to the dictatorship of the proletariat. The Buddha established communism as far as the Sangha was concerned, but without dictatorship. It was communism on a very small scale, but it was communism without dictatorship. Marxian communism prescribes a bloody revolution for establishing equality. Buddhist communism prescribes a bloodless revolution and offers all the three tenets of communism – liberty, equality and fraternity. The Buddha was a political reformer and a social revolutionary who longed for the welfare and happiness of all people.

Cultural Reconstruction

Most of those who talk of Indian culture identify it with the upper caste Brahminical tradition. Marxists, who criticize the unitary notion of culture and often argue for the existence of a 'people's culture', usually think of this simply in economic or class terms. In fact, within any complex civilization, there are contending cultures and sub-cultures and within the caste-based civilization of India, these have in fact a caste linkage. The SCs and tribals have their own unique cultural features, which are not simply the absence of either Brahminical or Western cultural elements. To varying degrees, these are shared by the other low castes or the Bahujan groups. Ambedkar's fervent conviction was that it was this culture, and not the culture of the '3.5 per cent' (what is assumed to be the dominant culture), that could provide the foundation for achieving the goals of liberty, equality and fraternity. From his examination of 'riddles' to his essays on 'revolution and counter-revolutions' in society to his efforts to analyse the foundations of caste and untouchability to his conversion to Buddhism, in all of these, Ambedkar was attempting to lay the basis for the cultural reconstruction of India.

The Hindu Code Bill for the Emancipation of Women

Ambedkar is remembered within the most conscious sections of the women's movement as the enactor of the Hindu Code Bill, which proposed to erase the subordinate status of women under the traditional Hindu laws and which eventually resulted in legal reforms. Unfortunately, the right to property given to women remained mostly a dead letter, especially in rural areas. Similarly, though the entire anti-caste movement fought for women's education on par with men, 'universal compulsory primary education' remains a distant dream and illiteracy rates among the tribals and SC women are still shamefully high.

Being the country's first law minister and chairman of the Drafting Committee of the Constituent Assembly, Ambedkar thought it his duty to free women from the age old thraldom by reforming the Hindu social laws created by Manu. He, therefore, took the initiative to draft and introduce the Hindu Code Bill in the Constituent Assembly. The Hindu Code Bill, the most formidable legislative measure of modern India, sought, among other reforms, to put an end to a variety of marriage systems prevailing in the country and to legalize only monogamous marriages. The code also sought to confer on women the rights of property and adoption, which were denied by Manu. It put men and women on an equal footing in all legal matters.

Social reactionaries raised a hue and cry in the name of religion both inside and outside parliament. The Congress, too, was divided over this issue. Prime minister Nehru declared vehemently on his arrival from the United States that his government would resign if the Hindu Code Bill was not passed by parliament, while his deputy and Home Minister, Sardar Vallabhbhai Patel, declared his all-out opposition to the Bill and said it would not be taken into consideration at all. But Nehru walked his talk and threw his weight in favour of the bill even though Patel and Rajendra Prasad continued to oppose it. It was in such an atmosphere that Ambedkar introduced the bill on 5 February 1951.[13]

The bill introduced four new things in the then existing law: abolition of the doctrine of the rights by birth (to son); investing the right to property on women; entitling daughters to a share of parental property; and giving women the right to seek divorce. That apart, the bill also insisted on the consent of the wife for the adopting of a son by the husband. The provisions dealing with property in a joint family included abolition of the rule of pious obligation and the liability to pay primary debt, which belongs to the family.[14] These provisions were new as far as the then existing Hindu law was concerned. But there was nothing either anti-social or anti-religious in them.

Therefore, we can conclusively conclude that it was because of the steadfast efforts of Ambedkar that women could get legal rights to judicial separation, divorce, alimony, succession, adoption, guardianship of minor children and parental property, among others. It was because of Ambedkar that the Special Marriage Act providing for inter-caste and inter-community marriage was enacted, as a result of which a revolutionary change was brought about in Indian society. He was strongly opposed to child marriage because, in his opinion, it stifled the proper development of a person. He vehemently condemned the provision made in the *Manusmriti*, which made it obligatory for a father to arrange a daughter's marriage before she went into puberty.

Ambedkar wanted women to enter all spheres of life, educational, economic and political, and wanted them to organize themselves to fight effectively for all those rights that are necessary for leading a decent, dignified and emancipated life. In short, he laid a solid foundation for the emancipation of women.

Conclusion

We may conclude that Ambedkar's thoughts are more relevant to present times than ever before. The recent developments in the socio-economic and political arenas of our country pose serious threats to social, economic and political justice to some sections of the society, especially the SCs, STs and other marginalized groups. The writings and speeches of Ambedkar offer solutions to these problems confronted by the marginalized groups as a whole. His concept of an ideal society is most suited to the needs of modern society. He considered the spirit of efforts to achieve 'liberty, equality and fraternity' to be the basis for social action, by which he evaluated the socialist and other bases for social action, and by which he evaluated the socialist and other economic systems of his day. This can help us analyse today's burning contemporary economic issues. From his examination of riddles in his essays on social revolutions and counter-revolutions, to his efforts at analysing the foundations of caste and untouchability, to his conversion to Buddhism, he was attempting to lay the foundation for a cultural reconstruction of India. In brief, he played an unparalleled role in the history of mankind in this part of the globe in improving not only the conditions of the marginalized sections of society, but also in bringing about the concept of social justice, especially through various constitutional and legal provisions and mass movements. He fought to establish an egalitarian society based on the principles of liberty, equality and fraternity in India.

Notes

1. B.R. Ambedkar, 1987. *Writings and Speeches,* Vol. 3. Bombay: Education Department, Government of Maharashtra.
2. B.R. Ambedkar, 1987. *Writings and Speeches,* Vol. 1. Bombay: Education Department, Government of Maharashtra.
3. Ibid.

4. B.R. Ambedkar, 1987. *Writings and Speeches,* Vol. 1. Bombay: Education Department, Government of Maharashtra, pp. 396–397.
5. Ibid.
6. G. Nancharaiah, 1988. *Land and Caste*. Mumbai: Himalaya Publishing House.
7. B.R. Ambedkar, 1987. *Writings and Speeches,* Vol. 5. Bombay: Government of Maharashtra, pp. 61–87.
8. B.R. Ambedkar, 1987 *Writing and Speeches,* Vol. 9: *What Congress and Gandhi have done to the Untouchables*, Bombay, Education Department, Government of Maharashtra.
9. Dhananjay Keer, Reprinted 1981. *Dr Ambedkar: Life and Mission*. Mumbai: Popular Prakashan, p. 72.
10. B.R. Ambedkar, 1980, *Buddha and the Future of His Religion*. Jullunder: Bheem Patrika Publication, pp. 3–4.
11. B.R. Ambedkar, 1984. *Buddha and His Dhamma*. Mumbai: Siddharth Publication, p. 153.
12. Ibid., pp. 160–171.
13. Ibid., p. 396.
14. G.S. Lokhande, 1982. *B.R. Ambedkar: A Study in Social Democracy*. New Delhi: Intellectual Publishing House.

Appendices

Appendix A
The Scheduled Castes and Scheduled Tribes (Prevention of Atrocities) Act, 1989

CHAPTER I

Preliminary

A. Short title, extent and commencement

1. This Act may be called the Scheduled Castes and the Scheduled Tribes (Prevention of Atrocities) Act, 1989.
2. It extends to the whole of India except the State of Jammu and Kashmir.

B. Definitions

1. In this Act, unless the context otherwise requires
   a. "atrocity" means an offence punishable under Section 3;
   b. "code" means the Code of Criminal Procedures, 1973 (2 of 1974);
   c. "Scheduled Castes and Scheduled Tribes" shall have the meanings assigned to them respectively under clause (24) and clause (25) of Article 366 of the Constitution;
   d. "special court" means a court of session specified as a Special Public Prosecutor or an advocate referred to in Section 15;
   e. Words and expression used but not defined in this Act defined in the code or the Indian Penal Code (45 of 1860) shall have

the meanings assigned to them respectively in the code, or as the case may be, in the Indian Penal Code.

2. Any reference in this Act to any enactment or any provision thereof shall, in relation to an area in which such enactment or such provision is, not in force, be construed as a reference to the corresponding law; if any in force in that area.

CHAPTER II

Offences of atrocities

C. Punishments for offence of atrocities

1. Whoever, not being a member of a Scheduled Caste or a Scheduled Tribe,
   a. forces a member of a Scheduled Caste or Scheduled Tribe to drink or eat any inedible or obnoxious substance;
   b. acts with intent to cause injury, insult or annoyance to any member of a Scheduled Caste or a Scheduled Tribe by dumping excreta, waste matter, carcasses or any other obnoxious in his premises or neighbourhood;
   c. forcibly removes clothes from the person of a member of a Scheduled Caste or a Scheduled Tribe or parades him naked or with painted face or body or commits any similar act which is derogatory to human dignity;
   d. wrongfully occupies or cultivates any land owned by or allotted to, or notified by any competent authority to be allotted to, a member of a Scheduled Caste or a Scheduled Tribe or get the land allotted to him transferred;
   e. wrongfully dispossesses a member of a Scheduled Caste or a Scheduled Tribe from his land or premises or interferes with the enjoyment of his rights over any land, premises or water;
   f. compels or entices a member of a Scheduled Caste or Scheduled Tribe to do 'begar' or other similar forms of forced or bonded labour other than any compulsory service for public purposes imposed by Government;
   g. forces or intimidates a member of a Scheduled Caste or a Scheduled Tribe not to vote or to vote for a particular candidate or to vote in a manner other than provided by law;
   h. institutes false, malicious or vexatious suit or criminal or other legal proceedings against a member of a Schedules Caste or a Scheduled Tribe;

i. gives any false or frivolous information to any public servant and thereby causes such public servant to use his lawful power to the injury or annoyance of a member of a Scheduled Caste or Scheduled Tribe;

j. intentionally insults or intimidates with intent to humiliate a member of a Scheduled Caste or Scheduled Tribe in any place within public view;

k. assaults or uses force to any woman belonging to a Scheduled Caste or Scheduled Tribe with intent to dishonour or outrage her modesty;

l. being in a position to dominate the will of a woman belonging to a Scheduled Caste or a Scheduled Tribe and uses that position to exploit her sexually to which she would have not otherwise agreed;

m. corrupts or fouls the water of any spring, reservoir or any other source ordinarily used by members of a Scheduled Caste or Scheduled Tribe so as to render it less fit for the purpose for which it is ordinarily used;

n. denies a member of a Scheduled Caste or Scheduled Tribe any customary right of passage to a place of public resort or obstructs such member so as to prevent him from using or having access to a place of public resort to which other members of the public or any section thereof have a right to use or access;

o. Forces or causes a member of a Scheduled Caste or Scheduled Tribe to leave his house, village or other place of residence, shall be punishable with imprisonment for a term which shall not be less than six months, but which may extend to five years and with fine.

2. Whoever, not being of a Scheduled Caste or a Scheduled Tribe, –

   a. gives or fabricates false evidence intending thereby to cause, or knowing it to be likely that he will thereby cause, any member of a Scheduled Caste or Scheduled Tribe to be convicted of an offence which is capital by the law for the time being in force shall be punished with imprisonment for life and with fine, and if an innocent member of a Scheduled Caste or Scheduled Tribe be convicted and executed in consequence of such false or fabricated evidence, shall be punished with death;

b. Gives or fabricates false evidence intending thereby to cause, or knowing it to be likely that he will thereby cause, any member of a Scheduled Caste or Scheduled Tribe to be convicted of an offence which is not capital but punishable with imprisonment for a term of seven years or upwards, shall be punishable with imprisonment for a term that shall not be less than six months but which may extend to seven or upwards and with fine;
c. Commits mischief by fire or any explosive substance intending to cause or knowing it to be likely that he will thereby cause damage to any property belonging to a member of a Scheduled Caste or Scheduled Tribe shall be punishable with imprisonment for a term which shall not be less than six months but which may extend to seven years and with fine;
d. Commits mischief by fire or any explosive substance intending to cause or knowing it to be likely that he will thereby cause destruction of any building which is ordinarily used as a place of worship or as a place of human dwelling or as a place for custody of the property by a member of a Scheduled Caste or Scheduled Tribe, shall be punishable with imprisonment for life and with fine;
e. Commits any offence under the Indian Penal Code (45 of 1860) punishable with imprisonment for a term of ten years or more against a person or property on the ground that such person is a member of a Scheduled Caste or Scheduled Tribe or such property belongs to such members, shall be punishable with imprisonment for life and with fine;
f. Knowingly or having reason to believe that an offence has been committed under this chapter, causes any evidence of the commission of that offence to disappear with the intention of screening the offender from legal punishment, or with that intention gives any information respecting the offence which he knows or believes to be false, shall be punishable with the punishment provided for that offence; or
g. Being public servant, commits any offence under this section, shall be punishable with imprisonment for a term which shall not be less than one year but which may extend to the punishment provided for that offence.

D. Punishment for neglect of duties

Whoever, being a public servant but not being a member of a Scheduled Caste or a Scheduled Tribe, wilfully neglects his duties required to be performed by him under this Act, shall be punishable with imprisonment for a term which shall not be less than six months but which may extend to one year.

E. Enhanced punishment for subsequent conviction

Whoever, having already been convicted of an offence under this chapter is convicted for the second offence or any offence subsequent to the second offence, shall be punishable with imprisonment for a term which shall not be less than one year but which may extend to the punishment provided for that offence.

F. Application of certain provisions of the Indian Penal Code

Subject to the provisions of this Act, the provisions of Section 34, Chapter III, Chapter IV, Chapter V, Chapter V-A, Section 149 and Chapter XXIII of the Indian Penal Code (45 of 1860), shall, so far as may be, apply for the purpose of this Act as they apply for the purposes of this Act as they apply for the purposes of the Indian Penal Code.

G. Forfeiture of property of certain persons

a. Where a person has been convicted of any offence punishable under this chapter, the special court may, in addition to awarding any punishment, by order in writing, declare that any property, movable or immovable or both, belonging to the person which has been used for the commission of that offence, shall stand forfeited to Government.

b. Where any person is accused of any offence under this chapter, it shall be open to the special court trying him to pass an order that all or any of the properties, movable or immovable or both, belonging to him, shall, during the period of such trial, be attached, and where such trial ends in conviction, the property so attached shall be liable to forfeiture to the extent it is required for the purpose or realization of any fine imposed under this chapter.

H. Presumption as to offences

In a prosecution for an offence under this chapter, if it is proved that–

1. The accused rendered any financial assistance to a person accused of, or reasonably suspected of committing, an offence under this chapter, the Special Court shall presume, unless the contrary is proved, that such person had abetted the offence;

2. A group of persons committed an offence under this chapter and if it is proved that the offence committed was a sequel to any existing dispute regarding land or any other matter, it shall be presumed that the offence was committed in furtherance of the common intention or in prosecution of the common object.

I. Conferment of powers

1. Notwithstanding anything contained in the Code or in any other provision of the Act, the State Government may, if it considers it necessary or expedient so to do, –
   a. for the prevention of and for coping with any offence under this Act, or
   b. for any case or class or group of cases under this Act, in any district or part thereof, by notification in the Official Gazette, on any officer of the State Government, the powers exercisable by a police officer under the Code in such district or part thereof or, as the case may be, for such case or class or group of cases, and in particular, the powers of arrest, investigation and prosecution of persons before any Special Court.
2. All officers of police and all other officers of Government shall assist the officer referred to in Sub-section (i) in the execution of the provisions of this Act or any rule, scheme or order made thereunder.
3. The provisions of the Code shall, so far as may be, apply to the exercise of the powers by an officer under Sub-section (1).

CHAPTER III

Externment

J. Removal of person likely to commit offence

1. Where the Special Court is satisfied, upon a complaint or a police report, that a person is likely to commit an offence under Chapter II of this Act in any area included in 'Schedule Areas' or 'Tribal Areas' as referred to in Article 244 of the Constitution, it may, by order in writing, direct such person to remove himself beyond the limits of such area, by such route and within such times as may be specified in the order, and not to return to that area from which he was directed to remove himself for such period, not exceeding two years, as may be specified in the order.
2. The Special Court shall, along with the order under Sub-section (1), communicate to the person directed under that Sub-section the grounds on which such order has been made.

3. The Special Court shall revoke or modify the order made under Sub-section (1), for the reasons to be recorded in writing, on the representation made by the person against whom such order has been made or by any other person on his behalf within 30 days from the date of the order.

K. Procedure of failure of person to remove himself from area and enter thereon after removal

1. If a person to whom a direction has been issued under Section 10 to remove himself from any area
   a. fails to remove himself as directed; or
   b. having so removed enters such area within the period specified in the order, otherwise than with the permission in writing of the Special Court under Sub-section (2), the Special Court may cause him to be arrested and removed in police custody to such place outside such area the Special Court may specify.
2. The Special Court may, by order in writing, permit any person in respect of whom an order under Section 10 has been made, to return to the area from which he was directed to remove himself for such temporary period and subject to such conditions as may be specified in such order and may require him to execute a bond with or without surety for due observation of the conditions imposed.
3. The Special Court may at any time revoke any such permission.
4. Any person who, with such permission, returns to the area from which he was directed to remove himself, observes the conditions imposed and at the expiry of the temporary period for which he was permitted to return or on the revocation of such permission before the expiry of such temporary period shall remove himself outside such area and shall not return thereto within the unexpired portion specified under Section 10 without a fresh permission.
5. If a person fails to observe any of the conditions imposed or to remove himself accordingly or having so removed himself enters or returns to such area without fresh permission, the Special Court shall cause him to be arrested and removed in police custody to such place outside such area as the Special Court may specify.

L. Taking measurements and photographs, etc., of persons against whom order under Section 10 is made

1. Every person against whom an order has been made under Section 10 shall, if so required by the Special Court, allow his measurements and photographs to be taken by a police officer.

2. If any person referred to in Sub-section (1) when required to allow his measurements or photographs to be taken, resists or refuses to allow the taking of such measurements or photographs, it shall be lawful to use all necessary means to secure the taking thereof.
3. Resistance to or refusal to allow the taking of measurements or photographs under Sub-section (2) shall be deemed to be an offence under Section 186 of the India Penal Code (45 of 1860).
4. Where an order under Section 10 is revoked, all measurements and photographs (including negatives) taken under Sub-section (2) shall be destroyed or made over to the person against whom such order is made.

M. Penalty for non-compliance of order under Section 10

Any person contravening an order of the Special Court made under Section 10 shall be punishable with imprisonment for a term which may extend to one year and with fine.

CHAPTER IV

N. SPECIAL COURTS

For the purpose of providing for speedy trial, the State Government shall, with the concurrence of the Chief Justice of the High Court, by notification in the Official Gazette, specify for each district a Court of Session to be a Special Court to try offences under this Act.

O. Special Public Persecutor

For every Special Court, the State Government shall, by notification in the Official Gazette, specify a Public Prosecutor or appoint an advocate who has been in practice as an advocate for not less than seven years, as a Special Public Prosecutor for the purpose of conducting cases in that Court.

CHAPTER V

MISCELLANEOUS

P. Power of State Government to impose collective fine

The provisions of Section 10–A of the Protection of Civil Rights Act, 1955 (22 of 1955), shall, so far as may be, apply for the purposes of imposition and realization of collective fine and for all other matters connected therewith under this Act.

Q. Preventive action to be taken by the law and order machinery

a. A District Magistrate or a Sub-Divisional Magistrate or any other Executive Magistrate or any police officer not below the rank of a

Deputy Superintendent of Police may, on receiving information and after such enquiry as he may think necessary, has reason to believe that a person or a group of persons not belonging to the Scheduled Castes or Scheduled Tribes, residing in or frequenting any place within the local limits of his jurisdiction is likely to commit an offence or has threatened to commit any offence under this Act and is of the opinion that there is sufficient ground for proceeding, declare such an area to be an area prone to atrocities and take necessary action for keeping the peace and good behaviour and maintenance of public order and tranquillity and may take preventive action.

b. The provisions of Chapters VII, X and XI of the Code shall, so far as may be, apply for the purpose of Sub-section (1)

c. The State Government may, by notification in the Official Gazette, make one or more schemes specifying the manner in which the officers referred to in Sub-section (1) shall take appropriate action specified in such schemes or schemes to prevent and to restore the feeling of security amongst the members of the Scheduled Castes and Scheduled Tribes.

R. **Section 438 of the Code not to apply to persons committing an offence under the Act**

Nothing in Section 438 of the Code shall apply in relation to any case involving the arrest of any person on an accusation of having committed an offence under this Act.

S. **Section 360 of the Code and the provisions of the Probation of Offenders Act not to apply under this Act.**

The provisions of Section 360 of the Code and the provisions of the Probation of Offenders Act, 1958 (20 of 1958), shall not apply to any person above the age of 18 years who is found guilty of having committed an offence under this Act.

T. **Act to override other laws**

Save as otherwise provided in this Act, the provisions of this Act shall have effect notwithstanding anything inconsistent therewith contained in any other law for the time being in force or any custom or usage or any instrument having effect by virtue of any such law.

U. **Duty of Government to ensure effective implementation of the Act**

1. Subject to such rules as the Government may make in this behalf, the State Government shall take such measures as may be necessary for the effective implementation of this Act.

2. In particular, and without prejudice to the generality of foregoing provisions, such measures may include,–
   a. the provisions for adequate facilities, including legal aid, to the persons subject to atrocities to enable them to avail themselves of justice;
   b. the provisions for travelling and maintenance expenses to witnesses, including the victims of atrocities, during investigation and trial of offence under this Act;
   c. the provisions of the economic and social rehabilitation of the victims of the atrocities;
   d. the appointment of officers for initiating or exercising supervision over prosecution for the contravention of the provisions of this Act;
   e. the setting up committees at such appropriate levels as the State Government may think fit to assist the Government in formulation or implementation of such measures;
   f. provisions for a periodic survey of the working of the provisions of this Act with a view to suggesting measures for the better implementation of the provisions of this Act;
   g. the identification of the areas where the members of the Scheduled Castes and Scheduled Tribes are likely to be subjected to atrocities and adoption of such measures so as to ensure safety for members.

11. The Central Government shall take such steps as may be necessary to coordinate the measures taken by the State Government under Sub-section (1).
12. The Central Government shall, every year, place on the table of each House of Parliament a report on the measures taken by itself and by the State Government in pursuance of the provisions of this Section.

V. Protection of action taken in good faith

No suit, prosecution or other legal proceedings shall lie against the Central Government or against the State Government or any officer or authority or any other person for anything which is in good faith done or intended to be done under this Act.

W. Power to make rules

1. The Central Government may, by notification in the Official Gazette, make rules for carrying out the purpose of this Act.
2. Every rule made under this Act shall be laid, as soon as may be after it is made, before each house of Parliament, while it is in session for a total period of 30 days, which may be comprised in

one session or in two or more successive sessions, and if before the expiry of the session immediately following the session or the successive sessions aforesaid, both Houses agree in making any modification in the rule or both Houses agree that the rule should not be made, the rule shall thereafter have effect only in such modified form or be of no effect, as the case may be; so, however, that any such modification or annulment shall be without prejudice to the validity of anything previously done under that rule.

Appendix B
The Scheduled Castes and the Scheduled Tribes (Prevention of Atrocities) Rules, 1995

In exercise of the powers conferred by Sub-section (1) of Section 23 of the Scheduled Castes and the Scheduled Tribes (Prevention of Atrocities) Act, 1989 (33 of 1989), the Central Government hereby makes the following rules, namely:

A. Short title and commencement

a. These rules may be called the Scheduled Castes and the Scheduled Tribes (Prevention of Atrocities) Rules, 1995

b. They shall come into force on the date of their publication in the Official Gazette.

B. Definitions

In these rules, unless the context otherwise requires,–

1. "Act" means the Scheduled Castes and the Scheduled Tribes (Prevention of Atrocities) Act, 1989 (33 of 1989);
2. "dependent", with its grammatical variations and cognate expressions, includes wife, children, whether married or unmarried, dependent parents, widowed sister, widow and children of predeceased son of a victim of atrocity;
3. "identified area" means such area where the State Government has reason to believe that an atrocity may take place or there is an apprehension of re-occurrence of an offence under the Act or an area prone to victim of atrocity;
4. "Non-Government Organization" means a voluntary organization engaged in the welfare activities relating to the Scheduled Castes and Scheduled Tribes and registered under the Societies Registration Act, 1860 (21 of 1860) or under any law for the registration of documents of such Organization for the time being in force;

5. “Schedule” means the Schedule annexed to these rules;
6. “Section” means Section of the Act;
7. “State Government”, in relation to a union territory, means the Administration of that union territory appointed by the President under Article 293 of the Constitution;
8. Words and expressions used herein and not defined but defined in the Act shall have the meanings respectively assigned to them in the Act.

C. Precautionary and preventive measures,

With view to prevent atrocities on the Scheduled Castes and the Scheduled Tribes, the State Government shall,

1. identify the area where it has reason to believe that atrocity may take place or there is an apprehension of recurrence of an offence under the Act;
2. order the District Magistrate and Superintendent of Police or any other officer to visit the identified area and review the law and order situation;
3. if deemed necessary, in the identified area, cancel the arm licences of the persons, not being members of the Scheduled Castes or Scheduled Tribes, their near relations, servants or employees and family friends and get such arms deposited in the Government Armoury;
4. seize all illegal fire-arms and prohibit any illegal manufacture of fire-arms;
5. with a view to ensure the safety of person and property, if deemed necessary, provide arms licences to members of the Scheduled Castes and the Scheduled Tribes;
6. constitute a high power state-level committee, district and divisional level committees or such number of other committees as deemed proper and necessary for assisting the Government in implementation of the provisions of the Act.
7. set up a vigilance and monitoring committee to suggest effective measures to implement the provisions of the Act;
8. set up awareness centres and organize workshops in the identified area or at some other place to educate the persons belonging to the Scheduled Castes and Scheduled Tribes about their rights and the protection available to them under the provisions of various Central and State enactments or rules, regulations and schemes framed thereunder;

9. encourage non-governmental organizations in establishing and maintaining awareness centres and organizing workshops and provide them necessary financial and other sort of assistance;
10. deploy a special police force in the identified area;
11. by the end of every quarter, review the law and order situation, functioning of different committees, performance of Special Public Prosecutors, Investigating Officers responsible for implementing the provisions of the Act and the cases registered under the Act.

D. Supervision of prosecution and submission of report

1. The State Government on the recommendation of the District Magistrate shall prepare for each District a panel of such number of eminent senior advocates who have been in practice for not less than seven years, as it may deem necessary for conducting cases in the Special Courts. Similarly, in consultation with the Director-Prosecutors in charge of the prosecution, a panel of such number Public Prosecution as it may deem necessary for conducting cases in the Special Court, shall also be specified. Both these panels shall be notified in the Official Gazette of the State and shall remain in force for a period of three years.
2. The District Magistrate and the Director of Prosecution in charge of the prosecution shall review at least twice in a calendar year, in the month of January and July, the performance of Special Public Prosecutors so specified or appointed and submit a report to the State Government.
3. If the State Government is satisfied or has reason to believe that a Special Public Prosecutor so appointed or specified has not conducted the case to the best of his ability and with due care and caution, his name may be, for reasons to be recorded in writing, denotified.
4. The District Magistrate and the other Officer-in-Charge of the prosecution at the district level, shall review the positions of cases registered under the Act and submit a monthly report on or before the 20th day of each subsequent month to the Director of Prosecution and the State Government. This report shall specify the actions taken/proposed to be taken in respect of the investigation and prosecution of each case.
5. Notwithstanding anything contained in sub-rule (1), the District Magistrate or the Sub-Divisional Magistrate may, if deemed necessary or if so desired by the Victim of atrocity, engage an

eminent Senior Advocate for conducting cases in the Special Courts on such payments of fees as he may consider appropriate.

6. Payment of fee to Special Public Prosecutor shall be fixed by the State Government on a scale higher than the other panel advocates in the State.

E. Information to police officer in-charge of a police station

1. Every information relating to the commissioner of an offence under the Act, if given orally to an officer in-charge of a police station shall be reduced to writing by him or under his direction, and be read over to the informant, and every such information, whether given in writing or reduced to writing as aforesaid, shall be signed by the persons giving it, and the substance thereof shall be entered in a book to be maintained by that police station.
2. A copy of the information as so recorded under sub-rule (1) above shall be given forthwith, free of cost, to the informant.
3. Any person aggrieved by a refusal on the part of an officer in charge of a police station to record the information referred to in sub-rule (1) may send the substance of such information, in writing and by post, to the Superintendent of Police concerned who after investigation either by himself or by a police officer not below the rank of Deputy Superintendent of Police, shall make an order in writing to the officer in-charge of the concerned police station to enter the substance of that information to be entered in the book to be maintained by the police station.

F. Spot inspection by officers

1. Whenever the District Magistrate or the Sub-Divisional Magistrate or any other Executive Magistrate or any police officer not below the rank of Deputy Superintendent of Police receives information from any person or upon his own knowledge that an atrocity has been committed on a member of the Scheduled Castes or the Scheduled Tribes within his jurisdiction, he shall immediately himself visit the place of occurrence to assess the extent of the atrocity, loss of life, loss and damage to the property and submit a report forthwith to the State Government.
2. The District Magistrate or the Sub-Divisional Magistrate or any other Executive Magistrate and the Superintendent of Police, Deputy Superintendent of Police, after inspecting the place or area on the spot, shall
   a. Draw up a list of victims, their family members and dependents entitled for relief;

b. Prepare a detailed report of extent of atrocity, loss and damage to the property of the victims;
c. Order for intensive police patrolling in the area;
d. Take effective and necessary steps to provide protection to the witnesses and other sympathizers of the victims;
e. Provide immediate relief to the victims.

G. Investigating Officer

1. An offence committed under the Act shall be investigated by a police officer not below the rank of a Deputy Superintendent of Police. The investigating officer shall be appointed by the State Government, Director-General of Police, Superintendent of Police after taking into account his past experience, sense of ability and justice to perceive the implications of the case and investigate it within the shortest possible time.
2. The investigating officer so appointed under sub-rule (1) shall complete the investigation on top priority within 30 days and submit the report to the Superintendent of Police who in turn will immediately forward the report to the Director-General of Police of the State Government.
3. The Home Secretary and the Social Welfare Secretary to the State Government, Director of Prosecution, the Officer-in-Charge of Prosecution and the Director-General of Police shall review by the end of every quarter the position of all investigations done by the investigating officer.

H. Setting up of the Scheduled Castes and Scheduled Tribes Protection Cell

The State Government shall set up a Scheduled Castes and Schedule Tribes Protection Cell under the charge of the Director of Police or Inspector-General of Police. This cell shall be responsible for–

a. Conducting survey of the identified area;
b. Maintaining public order and tranquillity in the identified area;
c. Recommending to the State Government for the deployment of a special police force or establishment of a special police post in the identified area;
d. Making investigations about the probable causes leading to an offence under the Act;
e. Restoring a feeling of security amongst the members of the Scheduled Castes and Scheduled Tribes;
f. Informing the nodal officer and special officer about the law and order situation in the identified area;

g. Making enquiries about the investigation and spot inspections conducted by various officers;
h. Making enquiries about the action taken by the Superintendent of Police in the cases where an officer in-charge of the police station has refused to enter information in a book to be maintained by that police station under sub-rule (3) of rules 5;
i. Making enquiries about wilful negligence by a public servant;
j. Reviewing the position of cases registered under the Act; and
k. Submitting a monthly report on or before the 20th day of each subsequent month to the State Government and nodal officer about the action taken and proposed to be taken, in respect of the above.

I. Nomination of Nodal Officer

The State Government shall nominate a nodal officer of the level of a Secretary to the Government, preferably belonging to the Scheduled Castes or Scheduled Tribes, for coordinating the functioning of the District Magistrate and Superintendent of Police or other officers authorized by them, investigating officers and other officers responsible for implementing the provisions of the Act. By the end of every quarter, the nodal officer shall review –

i. The reports received by the State Government under sub-rules (2) and (4) of rule 6, CI. (xi) or rule 8.
ii. The position of cases registered under the Act;
iii. Law and order situation in the identified area;
iv. Various kinds of measures adopted for providing immediate relief in cash or kind or both to the victims of atrocity or his/her dependents;
v. Performance of non-government organizations, the Scheduled Castes and Scheduled Tribes Protection Cell, various committees and the public servants responsible for implementing the provisions of the Act.

J. Appointment of Special Officer

In the identified area, a Special Officer not below the rank of an Additional District Magistrate shall be appointed to coordinate with the District Magistrate, Superintendent of Police or other officer responsible for implementing the provisions of the Act, various committees and the Scheduled Castes and Scheduled Tribes Protection Cell–

1. Providing immediate relief and other facilities to the victims of atrocities and initiating necessary measures to prevent or avoid the recurrence of atrocities;

2. Setting up an awareness centre and organizing workshops in the identified area or at the district headquarters to educate people belonging to the Scheduled Castes and Scheduled Tribes about their rights and the protection available to them under the provisions of various central and state enactments or rules and schemes, etc., framed therein;
3. Coordinating with non-governmental organizations and providing necessary facilities and financial and other type of assistance to non-governmental organizations for maintaining centres or organizing workshops.

K. Travelling allowance, daily allowance, maintenance expenses and transport facilities to the victims of atrocities, their dependent and witnesses:

i. Every victim of an atrocity or his/her dependent and witnesses shall be paid for rail by second class in express/mail/passenger train or actual bus or taxi fare from his/her place of residence or place of stay to the place of investigation or hearing of trial of an offence under the Act.

ii. The District Magistrate or Sub-Divisional Magistrate or any other Executive Magistrate shall make the necessary arrangements for providing transport facilities or reimbursement of full payment thereof to the victims of an atrocity and witnesses for visiting the investigating officer, Superintendent of Police/Deputy Superintendent of Police, District Magistrate or any other Executive Magistrate.

iii. Every woman witness, victim of atrocity or her dependent being a woman or a minor, a person more than 60 years of age and a person having 40 per cent or more disability shall be entitled to be accompanied by an attendant of her/his choice. The attendant shall also be paid travelling and maintenance expenses as applicable to the witness or the victim or atrocity when called upon during hearing, investigation and trial of an offence under the Act.

iv. The witness, the victim of atrocity or his/her dependent and the attendant shall be paid daily maintenance expenses for the days he/she is away from the place of his/her residence or stay during investigation, hearing and trial of an offence, at such rates but not less than the minimum wages, as may be fixed by the State Government for agricultural labourers.

v. In addition to daily maintenance expenses, the witness, the victim of atrocity (or his/her dependent) and the attendant shall also be paid diet expenses at such rates as may be fixed by the State Government from time to time.

vi. The payment for travelling allowance, daily allowance, maintenance expenses and reimbursement of transport facilities shall be made immediately or not later than three days by the District Magistrate or the Sub-Divisional Magistrate or any other Executives Magistrate to the victims, their dependent/attendant and witnesses for the days they visit the investigating officer or in-charge of the police station or hospital authorities or Superintendent of Police, Deputy Superintendent of Police, Deputy Superintendent of Police or District Magistrate or any other officer concerned or the Special Court.

vii. When an offence has been committed under Section 3 of the Act, the District Magistrate or the Sub-Divisional Magistrate or any other Executive Magistrate shall reimburse the payment of medicines, special medical consultation, blood transfusion, replacement of essential clothing, meals and fruits provided to the victim(s) of an atrocity.

L. Measures to be taken by the District Administration

1. The District Magistrate and the Superintendent of Police shall visit the place or area where the atrocity has been committed to assess the loss of life and damage to the property and draw up a list of victims, their family members and dependents entitled for relief.
2. The Superintendent of Police shall ensure that the First Information Report is registered in the book of the concerned police station and effective measures for apprehending the accused are taken.
3. The Superintendent of Police, after spot inspection, shall immediately appoint an investigation officer and deploy such police force in the area and take such other preventive measures as he may deem proper and necessary.
4. The District Magistrate or the Sub-Divisional Magistrate or any other Executive Magistrate shall make arrangements for providing immediate relief in cash or in kind or both to the victims of atrocity, their family members and dependents according to the scale as in the schedule annexed to these Rules. (Annexure I). Such immediate relief shall also include food, water, clothing, shelter, medical aid, transport facilities and other essential items necessary for human beings.

5. The relief provided to the victim of the atrocity or his/her dependent under sub-rule (4) in respect of death, or injury to, or damage to property shall be in addition to any other right to claim compensation in respect thereof under any other law for the time being in force.
6. The relief and rehabilitation facilities mentioned in sub-rule (4) above shall be provided by the District Magistrate or the Sub-Divisional Magistrate or any other Executive Magistrate in accordance with the scales provided in the Schedule annexed to these rules.
7. A report of the relief and rehabilitation facilities provided to the victims shall also be forwarded to the Special Court by the District Magistrate or the Sub-Divisional Magistrate or the Executive Magistrate or Superintendent of Police. In case the Special Court is satisfied that the payment of relief was not made to the victim or his/her dependent in time or the amount of relief or compensation was not sufficient or only a part of payment of relief or compensation was made, it may order for making in full or part the payment of relief or any other kind of assistance.

M. Selection of officers and other state members for completing the work relating to the atrocity

1. The State Government shall ensure that the administrative officers and other staff members to be appointed in an area prone to atrocity shall have the right attitude and understanding of the problems of the Scheduled Castes and Scheduled Tribes.
2. It shall also be ensured by the State Government that persons from the Scheduled Castes and Scheduled Tribes are adequately represented in the administration and in the police force at all levels, particularly at the level of police posts and police stations.

N. Specific responsibility of the State Government

The State Government shall make necessary provisions in its annual budget for providing relief and rehabilitation facilities to the victims of atrocities. It shall review at least twice in a calendar year, in the months of January and July, the performance of the Special Public Prosecutor specified or appointed under Section 15 of the Act, various reports received, investigations made and preventive steps taken by the District Magistrate, Sub-Divisional Magistrate and Superintendent of Police, relief and rehabilitation facilities provided to the victims and the reports in respect of lapses on behalf of the concerned officers.

O. Contingency plan by the State Government

1. The State Government shall prepare a model contingency plan for implementing the provisions of the Act and notify the same in the Official Gazette of the State Government. It should specify the role and responsibility of various departments and their officers at different levels, the role and responsibility of rural urban bodies and non-government organizations. *Inter alia*, this plan shall contain a package of relief measures including the following:
    a. A scheme to provide immediate relief in cash or in kind or both;
    b. Allotment of agricultural land and house sites;
    c. Rehabilitation packages;
    d. Scheme for employment in Government or Government undertaking to the dependent or one of the family members of the victims;
    e. Pension scheme for widows, dependent children of the deceased, handicapped or aged victims of atrocity;
    f. Mandatory compensation for the victims;
    g. Scheme for strengthening the socio-economic condition of the victims;
    h. Provisions for providing brick/stone masonry house to the victims; and
    i. Such other elements as health care, supply of essential commodities, electricity, adequate drinking water facility, burial/cremation ground and link roads to the Scheduled Castes and Scheduled Tribes.
2. The State Government shall forward a copy of the contingency plan or a summary thereof and a copy of the scheme, as soon as may be, to the Central Government in the Ministry of Welfare and to all the District Magistrates, Sub-Divisional Magistrates, Inspectors-General of Police and Superintendents of Police.

P. Constitution of State-Level Vigilance and Monitoring Committees

1. The State Government shall constitute high power vigilance and monitoring committees of not more than 25 members consisting of the following:
    a. Chief Minister/Administration-Chairman (in case of a State under President's Rule, Governor-Chairman);
    b. Home Minister, Finance Minister and Welfare Minister (in case of a State under President's Rule, Advisory Members);

c. All elected Members of Parliament and Members of the State Legislative Assembly and Legislative Council from the State belonging to the Scheduled Caste and Schedule Tribe members;
d. Chief Secretary, Home Secretary, Director-General of Police, Director/Deputy Director, National Commission for the Scheduled Castes and the Schedule Tribes members; and
e. The Secretary in-charge of the welfare and development of the Scheduled Castes and the Schedule Tribes Convener.

2. The high power vigilance and monitoring committee shall meet at least twice in a calendar year, in the months of January and July, to review the implementation of the provisions of the Act, relief and rehabilitation facilities provided to the victims and other matters connected therewith, prosecution of cases under the Act, rule of different officers/agencies responsible for implementing the provisions of the Act and various reports received by the State Government.

Q. Constitution of District Level Vigilance and Monitoring Committees

i. In each district within the State, the District Magistrate shall set up a vigilance and monitoring committee to review the implementation of the provisions of the Act, relief and rehabilitation facilities provided to the victims and other matters connected therewith, prosecution of cases under the Act, role of different officers/agencies responsible for implementing the provisions of the Act and various reports received by the District Administration.

ii. The district level vigilance and monitoring committee shall consist of the elected Members of Parliament and the State Legislative Assembly and Legislative Council, Superintendent of Police, three Group 'A' Officers, Gazetted Officers of the State Government belonging to the Scheduled Castes and the Scheduled Tribes, not more than five non-official members belonging to the Scheduled Castes and Scheduled Tribes and not more than three members from categories other than the Scheduled Castes and Scheduled Tribes having association with non-governmental organizations. The District Magistrate and District Social Welfare Officer shall be Chairman and Member-Secretary, respectively.

iii. The district level committee shall meet at least once in three months.

R. Material for annual report

The State Government shall every year, before 31 March, forward the report to the Central Government about the measures taken for implementing the provisions of the Act and the various schemes/plans framed by it during the previous calendar year.

Appendix C

The Employment of Manual Scavengers and Construction of Dry Latrines (Prohibition) Act, 1993

An Act to provide for the prohibition of employment of manual scavengers as well as construction or continuance of dry latrines and for the regulation of construction and maintenance of water-seal latrines and for matters connected therewith or incidental thereto.

Whereas fraternity assuring the dignity of the individual has been enriched in the Preamble to the Constitution;

And whereas Article 47 of the Constitution, *inter alia*, provides that the State shall regard raising the standard of living of its people and the improvement of public health as among its primary duties;

And whereas the dehumanizing practices of manual scavenging of human excreta still continues in many parts of the country;

And whereas the municipal laws by themselves as a measure for conversion of dry latrines into water-seal latrines and prevention of construction of dry latrines are not stringent enough to eliminate this practice;

And whereas it is necessary to enact a uniform legislation for the whole of India for abolishing manual scavenging by declaring employment of manual scavengers for removal of human excreta an offence and thereby ban the further proliferation of dry latrines in the country;

And whereas it is desirable for eliminating the dehumanizing practice of employment of manual scavengers And for protecting and improving the human environment to make it obligatory to convert dry latrines into water-seal latrines or to construct water-seal latrines in new construction;

And whereas Parliament has no power to make laws for the states with respect to the matters aforesaid, except as provided in Articles 249 and 25 of the Constitution.

And whereas in pursuance of clause (1) of Article 250 of the Constitution, resolutions have been passed by all the Houses of the

Legislature of the states of Andhra Pradesh, Goa, Karnataka, Maharashtra, Tripura and West Bengal that the matters, aforesaid should be regulated in those states by Parliament by law;

Be it enacted by Parliament in the Forty-Fourth Year of the Republic of India as follows:

CHAPTER I

PRELIMINARY

1. Short title, application and commencement

1. This Act may be called the Employment Manual Scavengers and Construction of Dry Latrines (Prohibition) Act, 1993
2. It applies in the first instance to the whole of the states of Andhra Pradesh, Goa, Karnataka, Maharashtra, Tripura and West Bengal and to all the union territories and it shall also apply to such other states which adopt this Act by resolution passed in that behalf under clause (1) of Article 252 of the Constitution.
3. It shall come into force in the states of Andhra Pradesh, Goa, Karnataka, Maharashtra, Tripura and West Bengal and in the union territories on such date as the Central Government may, by notification, appoint and in any other state which adopts this Act under clause (1) of Article 252 of the Constitution, on the date of such adoption.

2. Definitions

In this Act, unless the context otherwise requires,

1. "area", in relation to any provisions of this Act, means such area as the State Government may, having regard to the requirements of that provision, specify by notification;
2. "building" means a house, outhouse stable, latrine, urinal, sheet house, hut, wall (other than a boundary wall) or any other structure whether made of masonry, bricks, wood, mud, metal or other material;
3. "dry latrines" means a latrine other than a water-seal latrine;
4. "environment" includes water, air and land and the interrelationship which exists among and between water, air and land and human beings, other living creatures, plants, re-organism and property;
5. "environment pollutant" means any solid, liquid or gaseous substance present in such concentrations as may be, or tend to be, injurious to environment;

6. “environmental pollution” means the presence in the environment of any environmental pollutant;
7. “Executive Authority” means an Executive Authority appointed under Sub-section (1) of Section 5;
8. “HUDCO” means the Housing and Urban Development Corporation Limited, a Government company registered by that name under the Companies Act, 1956;
9. “latrine” means a place set apart for defection together with the structure comprising such place, the receptacle therein for collection of human excreta and the fitting and apparatus, if any, connected therewith;
10. “manual scavenger” means a person engaged in or employed for manually carrying human excreta and for expression “manual scavenging” shall be construed accordingly;
11. “notification” means a notification published in the Official Gazette;
12. “prescribed” means prescribed by rules made under this Act;
13. “State Government”, in relation to a union territory, means the Administrator thereof appointed under Article 239 of the Constitution;
14. “water-seal latrine” means a pour-flush latrine, water flush latrine or a sanitary latrine with a minimum water-seal of 20 millimetres diameter in which human excreta is pushed in or flushed with water.

CHAPTER II

PROHIBITION OF EMPLOYMENT OF MANUAL SCAVENGERS, ETC.

3. **Prohibition of employment of manual scavengers, etc.**
1. Subject to Sub-section (2) and the other provisions of this Act, with effect from such date and in such area as the State Government may, by notification, specify in this behalf, no person shall–
    a. engage in or employ for or permit to be engaged in or employed for any other person for manually carrying human excreta; or
    b. construct or maintain a dry latrine.
2. The State Government shall not issue a notification under Sub-section (1) unless–
    i. It has, by notification, given not less than 90 days’ notice of its intention to do so;

ii. Adequate facilities for the use of water-seal latrines in that area exist, and
iii. It is necessary or expedient to do so for the protection and improvement of the environment or public health in that area.

4. Power to exempt

The State Government, by a general or special order published in the Official Gazette, and upon such conditions, if any, as it may think fit to impose, exempt any area, category of buildings or class of persons from any provisions of this Act or from any specified requirement contained in this Act or any rule, order, notification or schemes made thereunder or dispense with the observance of any such requirements in a class or classes of cases, if it is satisfied that compliance with such provisions or such requirements is or ought to be exempted or dispensed with in the circumstances of the case.

CHAPTER III

IMPLEMENTING AUTHORITIES AND SCHEMES

5. Appointment of executive authorities and their powers and functions

1. The State Government may, by order published in the Official Gazette, appoint a District Magistrate or a Sub-Divisional Magistrate, as an Executive Authority to exercise jurisdiction within such area as may be specified in the order and confer such powers and impose such area as may be specified in the order and confer such powers and impose such duties on him, as may be necessary to ensure that the provisions of this Act are properly carried out and the Executive Authority may specify the officer or officers, subordinate to him, who shall exercise all or any of the powers, and perform all or any of the duties, so conferred or imposed and the local limits within which such powers of duties shall be carried out by the officer or officers so specified.
2. The Executive Authority appointed under Sub-section (1) and the officer or officers specified under that Sub-section shall, as far as practicable, try to rehabilitate and promote the welfare of the persons who were engaged in or employed for as manual scavengers in any area in respect of which a notification under Sub-section (1) of Section 3 has been issued by securing and projecting their economic interests.

6. **Power of State Government to make schemes**
1. The State Government may, by notification, make one or more schemes for regulating the conversion of dry latrines into, or construction and maintenance of, water-seal latrines, rehabilitation of the persons who were engaged in or employed as manual scavengers in any area in respect of which a notification under Sub-section (1) of Section 3 has been issued in gainful employment and administration of such schemes and different schemes may be made in relation to different areas and for different purposes of this Act:

   Provided that no such schemes as involving financial assistance from the HUDCO shall be made without consulting it.
2. In particular, and without prejudice to the generality of the foregoing power, such schemes may provide for all or any of the following matters, namely:
   a. Time-bound phased programme for the conversion of dry latrines into water-seal latrines;
   b. Provisions of technical or financial assistance for new or alternate low cost sanitation to local bodies or other agencies;
   c. Construction and maintenance of community latrines and regulation of their use on a pay and use basis;
   d. Construction and maintenance of shared latrines in slum areas or for the benefit of socially and economically backward classes of citizens;
   e. Registration of manual scavengers and their rehabilitation;
   f. Specification and standards of water-seal latrines;
   g. Procedure for conversion of dry latrines into water-seal latrines;
   h. Licensing for collection of fees in respect of community latrines or shared latrines.

7. **Power of State Government to issue directions**

Notwithstanding anything contained in any other law but subject to the other provisions of this Act, the State Government may, in the exercise of its powers and performance of its function under this Act, issue directions in writing to any person, officer or local or other authority and such person, officer or a local or other authority shall be bound to comply with such directions.

8. **Executive authorities, inspectors, officers and other employees of such authorities to be public servants**

All executives authorities, all officers and other employees of such authorities, including the officers authorized under Sub-section

(1) of Section 9 and all officers and other employees authorized to execute schemes or orders made under this Act, when acting or purporting to act in pursuance of any provisions of this Act or the rules of schemes made or orders or directions issued thereunder, shall be deemed to be public servants within the meaning of Section 21 of the Indian Penal Code (45 to 1860).

9. Appointment of inspectors and their powers of entry and inspection:

1. The State Government may, by notification, appoint such persons as it may think fit to be inspectors for the purpose of this Act, and define the local limits within which they shall exercise their powers under this Act.
2. Every inspector within the local limits of jurisdiction of an Executive Authority shall be subordinate to such authority.
3. Subject to any rules made in this behalf by the State Government, an inspector may, within the local limits of his jurisdiction, enter, at all reasonable times, with such assistance as he considers necessary, any place for the purpose of
    a. Performing any of the functions of the Executive Authority entrusted to him;
    b. Determining whether and if so, in what manner, any such functions are to be performed or whether any provisions of this Act or the rules, orders or schemes made thereunder or any notice, directions or authorization served, made, given or granted under this Act is being or has been complied with;
    c. Examining and testing any latrine or for conducting an inspection of any building in which he has reason to believe that an offence under this Act or the rules, orders or schemes made thereunder has been or is being or is about to be committed and to prevent or mitigate environment pollution.

10. Power of the Executive Authority to prevent environment pollution in certain cases

1. On receipt of information with respect to the fact or apprehension of any occurrence of contravention of the provisions of Section 3, whether through intimation by some person or on a report of the inspector or otherwise, the Executive Authority shall as early as

practicable, besides taking any other action under this Act, direct the owner or occupier of the promises to take such remedial measures, as may be necessary, within such reasonable time may be specified therein and in case the owner or occupier, as the case may be, fails to comply with such directions, cause such remedial measures to be taken as are necessary to prevent or mitigate the environmental pollution at the cost of such owner or occupier of the premises.

2. The expenses, if any, incurred by the Executive Authority with respect to the remedial measures referred to in Sub-section (1), together with interest at such rate as the State Government may specify from the date when deemed for the expenses is made until it is paid, may be recovered by such authority or agency from the person concerned as arrears of land revenue or of public demand.

11. Duty of HUDCO to extend financial assistance in certain cases

1. Notwithstanding anything contained in its Memorandum of Association or Articles of Association or schemes for the grant of loans for housing and urban development, it shall be the duty of HUDCO to extend, in suitable cases, financial assistance for the implementation of such schemes for the construction of water-seal latrines as may be made under Section 6.
2. The financial assistance referred to in Sub-section (1) may be extended by HUDCO on such terms and conditions (including on easy and concessional rates of interest) and in such manner as it may think fit in each case or class or cases.

12. Power to levy fee

Any order or scheme which the State Government is empowered to make under this Act may notwithstanding the absence of any express provisions to that effect, provide for levy of fees in respect of–

a. Community latrines constructed under a scheme on pay and use basis; or
b. Shared latrines constructed under a scheme; or
c. Supply of copies or documents of orders or extracts thereof; or
d. Licensing of contractors for construction of water-seal latrines; or
e. Any other purpose or matter it involving rendering of service by any officer, committee, or authority under this Act or any rule, direction, order or scheme made thereunder:

Provided that the state may, if it considers necessary so to do, in the public interest, by general or special order published in the Official Gazette, grant exemption on such grounds as it deems fit from the payment of any such fee either in part or in full.

13. Constitution of committees

1. The Central Government may, by notification, constitute–
   a. One or more Project Committees for appraising of the schemes for the construction of water-seal latrines in the country;
   b. One or more Monitoring Committees to monitor the progress of such schemes;
   c. Such other committees for such purposes of the Act and with such names as the Central Government may deem fit.
2. The composition of the committees constituted by the Central Government, the powers and functions thereof, the terms and conditions of appointment of the members of such committees and other members connected therewith shall be such as the Central Government may prescribe.
3. The members of the committee under Sub-section (1) shall be paid such fees and allowance for attending the meetings as may be prescribed.
4. The State Government may, by notification, constitute–
   a. One or more State Coordination Committees for coordinating and monitoring of the programmes for the construction of water-seal latrines in the state and rehabilitation of the persons who were engaged in or employed as manual scavengers in any area in respect of which a notification under Sub-section (1) of Section 3 has been issued.
   b. Such other committees for such purpose of the Act and with such names as the State Government may deem fit.
5. The composition of the committees constituted by the State Government, the powers and function thereof, the terms and conditions of the members of such committees and other matters connected therewith shall be such as the State Government may prescribe.
6. The members of the committees under Sub-section (4) shall be paid such fees and allowance for attending the meetings as may be prescribed.

CHAPTER IV

PENALTIES AND PROCEDURES

14. Penalty for contravention of the provisions of the Act and rules, orders, directions and schemes–

Whoever fails to comply with or contravenes any of the provisions of this Act, or the rules or schemes made or orders or directions issued thereunder, shall, in respect of each such failure or contravention, be punishable with imprisonment for a term which may extend to one year or with a fine, which may extend to ₹ 2,000, or with both; and in case the failure or contravention continues, with an additional fine, which may extend to ₹ 100 for every day during which such failure or contravention continues after the conviction for the first such failure or contravention.

15. Offences by companies

1. If the person committing an offence under this Act is a company, the company as well as every person in charge of, and responsible to, the company for the conduct of its business at the time of the commission of the offence, shall be deemed to be guilty of the offence and shall be liable to be proceeded against and punished accordingly:

   Provided that nothing contained in this Sub-section shall render any such person liable to any punishment, if he proves that the offence was committed without his knowledge or that he had exercised all due diligence to prevent the commission of such offence.
2. Notwithstanding anything contained in Sub-section (1), where an offence under this Act has been committed by a company and it is proved that the offence has been committed with the consent or contrivance of, or that the commission of the offence is attributable to any neglect on the part of any director, manager, managing agent or such other officer of the company, such director, manager, managing agent or such other officer shall also be deemed to be guilty of that offence and shall be liable to be proceeded against and punished accordingly.

   Explanation-For the purpose of this Section–

   a. "company" means any body corporate and includes a firm or other association of individuals; and
   b. "director", in relation to a firm, means a partner in a firm.

16. Offences to be cognizable

Notwithstanding anything contained in the Code of Criminal Procedure, 1973, every offence under this Act shall be cognizable.

17. Provision in relation to jurisdiction

1. No Court inferior to that of a Metropolitan Magistrate or a Judicial Magistrate of the first class can try any offence under this Act.
2. No prosecution for any offence under this Act shall be instituted except by or with the previous sanction of the Executive Authority.
3. No Court shall take cognizance of any offence under this Act, except upon a complaint made by a person generally or specially authorized in this behalf by the Executive Authority.

18. Limitation of prosecution

No Court shall take cognizance of offences punishable under this Act unless the complaint thereof is made within three months from the date on which the alleged commission of the offence came to the knowledge of the complainant.

CHAPTER V

MISCELLANEOUS

19. Information, reports or returns

The Central Government may, in relation to its function under this Act, from time to time, require any person, officer, State Government or other authority to furnish to it, any prescribed authority or officer, any reports, returns, statistics, accounts and other information as may be deemed necessary and such person, officer, State Government or other authority, as the case may be, shall be bound to do so.

20. Protection of action taken in good faith

No suit, prosecution or other legal proceedings shall lie against the Government or any officer or other employee of the Government or any authority constituted under this Act or executing any scheme made under this Act or any member, officer or other employee of such authority or authorities in respect of anything which is done or intended to be done in good faith is pursuance of this Act or the rules or schemes made, or the orders or directions issued, thereunder.

21. Effect of other laws and agreements inconsistent with the Act

1. Subject to the provisions of Sub-section (2), the provisions of this Act, the rules, schemes or orders made thereunder shall have effect

notwithstanding anything inconsistent therewith contained in any enactment other than this Act, customs, tradition, contract, agreement or other instrument.

2. If any act or commission constitutes an offence punishable under this Act and also under any other Act, then the offender found guilty of such offence shall be liable to be punished under the Act and not under this Act.

22. Power of Central Government to make rules

1. The Central Government may, by notification, make rules to carry out the provisions of this Act.
2. Without prejudice to the generality of the foregoing power, such rules may provide for all or any of the following matters, namely–
   i. The composition of the Project Committees, Monitoring Committees and other committees constituted by the Central Government under Sub-section (1) of Section 13, the powers and functions thereof, the number of members and their terms and conditions of appointment and other matters connected therewith;
   ii. In fees and allowance to be paid to the members of the committees constituted under Sub-section (1) of Section 13.
3. Every rule made by the Central Government under this Act shall be laid, as soon as may be after it is made, before each House of Parliament, while it is in session, for a total period of 30 days, which may be comprised in one session or in two or more successive sessions, and if, before the expiry of the session immediately following the session or the successive sessions, aforesaid, both Houses agree in making any modification in the rule or both Houses agree that the rule should not be made, the rule shall thereafter have effect only in such modified form or be of no effect, as the case may be; so however than any such modification shall be without prejudice to the validity of anything previously done under that rule.

23. Power of State Government to make rules

1. The State Government may, by notification, make rules, not being a matter for which the rules are required to be made by the Central Government, for carrying out the provisions of this Act.
2. Without prejudice to the generality of the foregoing power, such rules may provide for all or any of the following matters, namely–
   i. The composition of the State Coordination Committees and other committees constituted by the State Government under

Sub-section (4) of Section 13, the powers and functions thereof, the number of members and their terms and conditions of appointment and other matters connected therewith;

ii. The fees and allowance to be paid to the members of the committees constituted under Sub-section (4) of Section 13;

iii. Any other matter which is required to be, or may be prescribed.

3. Every rule and every scheme made by the State Government under this Act shall be laid as soon as may be after it is made, before the State Legislature.

24. Power to remove difficulties

1. If any difficulty arises in giving to the provisions of this Act, the Central Government may, by order published in the Official Gazette, make such provisions, not inconsistent with the provisions of this Act, as may appear to it to be necessary or expedient for the removal of the difficulty:

   Provided that no such provision shall be made in relation to a state after the expiration of three years from the commencement of this Act in that state.

2. Every order made under this section shall, as soon as may be after it is made, be laid before each House of Parliament.

ANNEXURE 1

Schedule
[See rule 12 (4)]
Norms for Relief Amount

Sl. No.	*Name and Section Number of Offence*	*Minimum Amount of Relief*
1.	Drink or eat inedible or obnoxious substance [Sec. 3 (1) (i)]	₹ 25,000 or more, depending upon the nature and gravity of the offence to each victim and also commensurate with the indignity, insult and defamation suffered by the victim. Payment to be made as follows: 25% when the charge-sheet is sent to the Court; 75% when the accused are convicted by the lower Court.
2.	Causing injury, insult or annoyance [Sec. 3 (1) (ii)]	
3.	Derogatory Act [Sec. 3 (1) (iii)]	
4.	Wrongfully occupation or cultivation of land, etc. [Sec. 3 (1) (iv)]	At least ₹ 25,000 or more depending upon the nature and gravity of the offence. The land/premises/water supply shall be restored where necessary at Government cost. Full payment to be made when charge-sheet is sent to the Court.
5.	Relating to land, premises and water [Sec. 3 (1) (v)]	
6.	Begar or forced bonded labour [Sec. 3 (1) (vi)]	At least ₹ 25,000 to each victim. Payment of 25% at First Information Report stage and 75% on conviction in the lower court.
7.	Relating to right to franchise [Sec. 3 (1) (vii)]	Up to ₹ 20,000 to each victim depending upon the nature and gravity of the offence.
8.	False, malicious or vexatious legal proceedings [Sec. 3 (1) (viii)]	₹ 25,000 or reimbursement of actual legal expenses and damages, whichever is less, after conclusion of the trial of the accused.
9.	False and frivolous information [Sec. 3 (1) (xi)]	
10.	Insult, intimidation and humiliation [Sec. 3 (1) (x)]	Up to ₹ 25,000 to each victim depending upon the nature of the offence. Payment of 25% when charge-sheet is sent to the court and the rest on conviction.
11.	Outraging the modesty of a woman [Sec. 3 (1) (xi)]	₹ 50,000 to each victim of the offence. 50% of the amount may be paid after medical examination and remaining 50% at the conclusion of the trial.
12.	Sexual exploitation of a woman [Sec. 3 (1) (xii)]	
13.	Fouling of water [Sec. 3 (1) (xiii)]	Up to ₹ 1,00,000 or full cost of restoration of normal facility, including cleaning when the water is fouled. Payment may be made at the stage as deemed fit by District Administration.

Cont'd...

...Cont'd

14.	Denial of customary rights of passage [Sec. 3 (1) (xiv)]	Up to ₹ 1,00,000 or full cost of restoration of rights of passage and full compensation of the loss suffered, if any. Payment of 50% when charge-sheet is sent to the court and 50% on conviction in lower court.
15.	Deserting one from their place or residence	Restoration of the site/right to stay and compensation of ₹ 25,000 to each victim and reconstruction of the house at Government cost, if destroyed. To be paid in full when charge-sheet is sent to the lower court.
16.	Giving false evidence [Sec. 3 (2) (i)]	At least ₹ 1,00,000 or full compensation of the loss or harm sustained. 50% to be paid when charge-sheet is sent to the Court and 50% on conviction by the lower court.
17.	Committing offences under the Indian Penal Code, punishable with imprisonment for a term of 10 years or more [Sec. 3 (2)]	At least ₹ 50,000, depending upon the nature and gravity of the offence to each victim and/or his dependents. The amount would vary if specifically provided for otherwise in the Schedule.
18.	Victimization at the hands of a public servant [Sec. 3 (2)]	Full compensation on account of damages or loss or harm sustained. 50% to be paid when charge-sheet is sent to the Court and 50% on conviction by the lower court.
19.	Disability (a) 100% incapacitation	At least ₹ 1,00,000 for each victim of offence. 50% on FIR and 25% at charge-sheet and 25% on conviction by the lower court.
(i)	Non-earning member of a family.	
(ii)	Earning member of a family	At least ₹ 2,00,000 to each victim of offence. 50% to be paid on FIR/medical examination stage, 25% when charge-sheet sent to court and 25% at conviction in the lower court.
(b)	Where incapacitation is less than 100%	The rates laid down in (i) and (ii) above shall be reduced in the same proportion, the stages of payment also being the same. However, not less than ₹ 15,000 to a non-earning member and not less than ₹ 30,000 to an earning member of the family.
20.	Murder/death	At least ₹ 1,00,000 to each case. Payment of 75% after post-mortem and 25% on conviction by the lower court.
(a)	Non-earning member of a family	
(b)	Earning member of a family	At least ₹ 2,00,000 to each case, Payment of 75% after post-mortem and 25% on conviction by the lower court.

Cont'd...

...Cont'd

21.	Victim of murder, death, massacre, rape and gang rape, permanent incapacitation and dacoity	In addition to the relief amount paid under the above items, relief may be arranged within three months of date of atrocity as follows: (i) Pension to each widow and/or other dependent of deceased SC/ST at ₹ 1,000 per month, or employment to one member of the family of the deceased, or provision of agriculture land, a house, if necessary by outright purchase. (ii) Full cost of the education and maintenance of the children of the victims. Children may be admitted to the Ashram Schools/residential schools. (iii) Provision of utensils, rice, wheat, dal, pulses, etc., for a period of three months.
22.	Complete destruction/burnt houses	Brick/stone masonry house to be constructed or provided at Government cost where it has been burnt or destroyed.

Index